TWAYNE'S WORLD AUTHORS SERIES
A Survey of the World's Literature

FRANCE

Maxwell A. Smith, University of Chattanooga, Emeritus

EDITOR

Nathalie Sarraute

TWAS 534

Nathalie Sarraute

NATHALIE SARRAUTE

By GRETCHEN ROUS BESSER

TWAYNE PUBLISHERS
A DIVISION OF G. K. HALL & CO., BOSTON

Published in 1979 by Twayne Publishers,
A Division of G. K. Hall & Co.
All Rights Reserved

Printed on permanent/durable acid-free paper and bound
in the United States of America

First Printing

To
Jim, Neal, and Brian
with deepest affection

Library of Congress Cataloging in Publication Data

Besser, Gretchen R.
Nathalie Sarraute.

(Twayne's world authors series ; TWAS 534 : France)
Bibliography: p.
Includes index.
1.   Sarraute, Nathalie — Criticism and interpretation.
PQ2637.A783Z58   848'.9'1409   78-27319
ISBN 0-8057-6376-7

Contents

About the Author

A graduate of Wellesley College and a member of Phi Beta Kappa, Gretchen Rous Besser holds advanced degrees from Middlebury College and Columbia University. She was an early recipient of a Fulbright Grant for study at the Sorbonne, Paris. Dr. Besser has taught French language and literature at Fairleigh Dickinson University, Columbia, Lehman College, and Rutgers University. She is the author of *Balzac's Concept of Genius* (1969) and a contributor to the *Columbia Dictionary of Modern European Literature*. Among the books she has translated are Jean Filloux, *The Crossing of the "Copula"*; Gabriel Cousin, *Journey to the Mountain Beyond*; Georges Michel, *Aggression*; as well as a short story by Andrée Chedid. Her articles and book reviews have appeared in *Orbis Litterarum, Année Balzacienne, Hebrew Studies in Literature, French Review, World Literature Today, Modern Language Journal, L'Esprit Créateur, Nineteenth-Century French Studies,* and *Romanic Review*. Dr. Besser's forthcoming book will be in an entirely unrelated field; she is writing a history of the National Ski Patrol, of which she is an active member.

Preface

The first time I saw Nathalie Sarraute was in a crowded lecture hall at Columbia University, where she had come to explain "tropisms" to an enraptured group of students (myself among them) in the early spring of 1964. Ten years later, I heard her again, at the French Institute in New York. She had scarcely changed in the intervening period. Perhaps there was a touch more gray in the strand of hair she kept brushing impatiently from her forehead. But her eyes — a mellow, chocolate brown — were as piercing and magnetic as ever. They seem to notice and record everything. Her voice is low-pitched, urgent, erupting now and then in an infectious laugh. Diminutive in stature, modest and unassuming in appearance, Sarraute's energy and dynamism belie both her age and the initial impression she gives of fragility. She strides down the street at a pace so brisk that it is difficult to keep up with her. She crackles with an electrical charge of vitality from some secret and seemingly inexhaustible source.

In her work, Nathalie Sarraute is equally persistent and indefatigable. Her relentless schedule would make younger people blanch. She writes every day, seven days a week, winter and summer alike. She never allows an interruption to break the continuity of her "rhythm," except when she travels. Like anyone with a job and a daily commitment, she feels she has her work to do, no matter what.

Despite the heavy demands of her writing schedule, Sarraute has granted dozens, maybe scores, of interviews over the years — especially as her books have gained a wider public. Innumerable critics have made the pilgrimage to her large, airy apartment near the Place de l'Etoile and have been ushered into her small, comfortable, book-lined study. Glancing at the large, paper-strewn table in front of the window, which looks out on a leafy garden and a nearby view of the Eiffel Tower, the visitor assumes that this must be where Nathalie Sarraute writes her books. But no, not at all. She explains to her interlocutor that she cannot work at home. There are too many distractions. The telephone rings, the doorbell sounds, her husband receives clients, the cleaning woman putters around. Instead, she sets out from home each morning — like a businessman commuting to his office — and sits down at a table in a neighborhood café. Here she is left at peace and undisturbed — as if, she says, she were on a trip, or far away. She remains here from nine A.M. till noon, surrounded by her papers, thinking and writing. (Sarraute is surely one of the few remaining writers who still compose by hand.)

She claims to be a slow, methodical writer. Ideas take a long time to mature in her mind. She has said it took her three months to write the single essay, "The Age of Suspicion." In *The Planetarium,* she stumbled for days and days over what is today a paragraph of fifteen lines. She is meticulous in her search for suitable means of expression. There are passages in *The Planetarium* and *Between Life and Death* that have been reworked at least fifty times. Sarraute is never satisfied until she feels she cannot go any further. Only then is she ready to have her manuscript typed, and even so she sometimes rewrites it again. No detail escapes her critical eye. After the first edition of *The Planetarium,* she changed the spelling of a character's name from "Guimiez" to "Guimier" because she feared the final "z" might be pronounced and this would sound ugly and harsh. She had a long discussion with her New York publisher over the question of capitalizing the title of her novel, *"fools say."* Nonetheless, once a book is finished, she dislikes rereading it. In fact, she would rather repeat what she has already said than read over what she has written in the past.

In the light of what Sarraute has herself accomplished, it is understandable that she should have slight patience with her many compatriots who conform, so easily and unthinkingly, to the stereotypes that have been offered to them for emulation. No wonder she satirizes the women who remain enshrouded in the cocoons of their "women's lives" — running to their couturier, spending their afternoons sipping tea and gossiping like parakeets, parading on their backs the plumage of their husbands' wealth and position. In the 1930s, she would often address women's groups and exhort them to demand the right to vote, only to find a handful showing up at each meeting, the rest kept at home by father or husband or by an unwillingness to change their accepted role in life.

Sarraute herself is a pioneer, a pathfinder, an adventurer into the unknown — the unknown realms of the mind (her explorations in literature have always been in the nature of an excursion into uncharted regions) and the untracked paths of feminine equality. A remarkable person....

Chronology

1900 A daughter, Nathalie, is born on July 18 to Ilya and Pauline Tcherniak, in Ivanovo-Voznessensk, Russia.

1902- Her parents are divorced. Nathalie leaves Russia and lives
1905 with her mother in Paris. Visits her father for two months every year. Attends kindergarten on the rue des Feuillantines.

1906 Moves to Saint Petersburg with her mother. Spends summers with her father in France and Switzerland.

1907 Writes a "novel," set in the Caucasus. A family friend discourages this early literary effort.

1908 Moves definitively to Paris to live with her father, who has remarried.

1914 Attends the lycée Fénelon, from which she receives a baccalaureate degree.

1920 Obtains a *licence* in English from the Sorbonne.

1920- Begins work toward a B.A. in history at Oxford.
1921

1921- Studies sociology under Sombart at the Faculty of Letters,
1922 Berlin.

1922 Enrolls at the University of Paris Law School.

1923 Meets Raymond Sarraute, a fellow law student.

1925 Is admitted to Paris bar. Marries Raymond Sarraute. They share similar tastes in literature. His critical judgment and encouragement are invaluable assets in her future career.

1932- Composes two brief sketches, which she later incorporates
1933 into her first book, *Tropismes* (*Tropisms*).

1937 Rejected by Gallimard and Grasset, *Tropismes* is accepted by Robert Denoël.

1939 *Tropismes* appears, in February. A single review, by Victor Moremans, in the *Gazette de Liège.*

1941 Begins *Portrait d'un inconnu* (*Portrait of a Man Unknown*).

1946 Finishes *Portrait,* a chapter of which is published in *Les Temps Modernes.*

1947 Two essays, "Paul Valéry or the Baby Elephant" and

"From Dostoevsky to Kafka," appear in *Temps Modernes.*

1948 Robert Marin publishes *Portrait d'un inconnu.*

1950 Purchases a country home in Chérence, where she works two days a week. An essay, "The Age of Suspicion," appears in *Temps Modernes.*

1953 With the publication of *Martereau,* Gallimard becomes her regular publisher.

1956 "Conversation and Sub-Conversation" appears in the *Nouvelle N.R.F.* and is published with three other essays in *L'Ere du soupçon (The Age of Suspicion).*

1959 *Le Planétarium (The Planetarium)* appears and is hailed as an example of the New Novel.

1963 Publication of *Les Fruits d'or (The Golden Fruits).* With Alain Robbe-Grillet and Bernard Pingaud, serves as a member of the French delegation to the Leningrad conference of writers.

1964 *Les Fruits d'or* is awarded the International Prize for Literature. A radio play, *Le Silence,* is broadcast in Germany, Switzerland, and Scandinavia.

1965 An essay on "Flaubert, the Precursor" appears in *Preuves.*

1966 A second radio play, *Le Mensonge,* is broadcast simultaneously in German and French.

1967 Jean-Louis Barrault chooses *Le Silence* and *Le Mensonge* to inaugurate his new theater, the Petit Odéon, on January 14.

1968 *Entre la vie et la mort (Between Life and Death),* a novel.

1970 *Isma* is broadcast in German and French. Published together with *Le Silence* and *Le Mensonge.*

1971 Participates in a colloquium on the New Novel held at Cerisy-la-Salle.

1972 *Vous les entendez? (Do You Hear Them?),* a novel.

1973 Publication of a play, *C'est beau.* Claude Régy stages a production of *Isma* at the Espace Cardin.

1975 Claude Régy produces *C'est beau* at the Petit d'Orsay theater.

1976 *"disent les imbéciles" ("fools say"),* a novel.

1978 A play, *Elle est là,* is produced by Claude Régy at the Centre Georges Pompidou and is published, together with Sarraute's earlier plays, in a collection titled *Théâtre.* She begins work on a book, provisionally called "L'Usage de la parole," which is composed of short texts grouped around a unifying theme.

CHAPTER 1

"Balzac's Cane,
Baudelaire's Trousers"

I N one chapter of the novel, *Between Life and Death,* Nathalie
Sarraute gently satirizes the public's mania for inquiring into a
writer's private habits. The neophyte author, who has just published his first book, is flattered by the interest paid him by visiting
admirers, to whom he serves tea and shows off his *bibelots.* Later,
he is amazed to find that the simple occurrence has been blown up
into a ritualistic ceremony, his humble teapot transformed into a
"samovar," his everyday life metamorphosed into myth. Apparently, he is unaware of the "rules of the game"; he fails to
recognize the importance of "Balzac's cane, Baudelaire's
trousers," and the various mementos of the famous — habits, pos-
sessions, likes and dislikes, even a momentary temper tantrum —
that are greedily snapped up by the collectors of such memorabilia.

It is almost as difficult to extract biographical information from
Nathalie Sarraute as it is to ascertain the *état civil* of her characters.
She keeps the events of her life strictly separated from the public
figure she has become, refusing to lend herself to the "cult of
personality" she ridicules in *"fools say."* At a time when many of
her contemporaries — Simone de Beauvoir, Julien Green, Claude
Mauriac, and others — are busily composing memoirs that run to
many volumes, Nathalie Sarraute has not written a single word
about herself, any time, anywhere. When questioned, she insists
that her life is uneventful, banal. Some people might think otherwise. The few facts that she grudgingly imparts hint at a personal
history so interesting, so out of the ordinary, that a traditional
novelist (the kind she frowns on) might well use it as the basis of a
Balzacian-type novel: her peripatetic childhood; her cosmopolitan
upbringing in a milieu of emigrant Russian intellectuals; her

schooling in France, England, Berlin; her venture first into the field of law, then of letters, with the determination — unusual for a woman of her generation — to forge a career for herself; the necessity to hide out under an assumed name during the German occupation; the years of patient, plodding effort, crowned eventually, unexpectedly — beyond belief, perhaps — by fame and success.

There is no field day here for the psychoanalytic school of criticism (an approach to literature that Sarraute has also satirized). What she gives of herself to her reading public is uniquely what is contained in her novels, essays, and plays. When pressed on occasion to say whether or not these books are autobiographical, Sarraute hedges by replying that every writer of necessity writes out of personal experience and that she is no different from the rest. Moreover, to those who expect her to be persistently aware of "tropisms" in everyday life, she insists that she is no more sensitive than anyone else to the undercurrents in ordinary discourse.

The few facts she has relinquished about her life are sparse and unembellished. Nathalie Sarraute was born on July 18, 1900, in Ivanovo-Voznessensk, Russia. Her parents, Ilya Tcherniak and Pauline Chatounowski, had met as university students in Geneva during the early years of the reign of Nicholas II, whose religious harassment prevented Jewish students from attending universities within Russia itself. After Ilya Tcherniak obtained his doctorate of science as a chemist, he returned to Russia, where he married, settled down, and opened a dye factory in the textile-manufacturing town of Ivanovo.

When she was two years old, Nathalie's parents were divorced. She spent much of her early childhood shuttling between Russia, France, and Switzerland, and thus became fluent in French and Russian at a precocious age. For four years she lived in Paris with her mother, visiting her father in the summer months. By the time she was six, her mother had remarried and moved back to Russia, settling in Saint Petersburg with her new husband, a historian. Her mother collaborated on a literary review and published a number of novels and short stories under the masculine pseudonym of Vichrowski, a disguise that none of her readers ever penetrated.

At eight years of age, Nathalie moved to Paris permanently to live with her father, who had also remarried and had set up a new dye factory. Ilya Tcherniak had left Russia for the purpose of organizing a movement to block the extradition of his younger brother, a member of a revolutionary group, who had taken refuge in Sweden after participating in a celebrated attack against the tsarist government. (Although Sweden refused to extradite him, he was later found asphyxiated in his cabin aboard the boat that was to have taken him to Antwerp — victim, so it was rumored, of the secret police).

The Tcherniak family lived in the XIVe *arrondissement,* a mecca for Russian émigrés and intellectuals. Under the tutelage of her stepmother's mother, a cultivated woman who spoke several languages and was an excellent musician, young Nathalie studied the piano, learned German and English, and acquired an early appreciation of the French and Russian classics.

At school she was a bright and eager student, seeking and earning her father's approval by her consistently high grades and honorable mentions. Thanks to her father's encouragement and to the extraordinary milieu of Russian intellectuals among whom she grew up, Nathalie Sarraute never faltered in her ambition to make a career for herself and in her confidence that a woman could achieve success on the same level as a man.[1]

Nathalie received her *certificat d'études* from the communal school of the rue d'Alésia, then went on to the lycée Fénelon, where for a time she avidly studied physics. After obtaining her baccalaureate, she prepared a *licence* in English at the Sorbonne. In 1920 she began work for a B.A. in history at Oxford, and spent the following winter studying sociology at the Faculty of Letters in Berlin. In 1922, she entered the University of Paris Law School. It was here that she met a fellow law student, Raymond Sarraute, whom she married in 1925.

Nathalie Sarraute was a member of the Paris bar from 1925 to 1941. During this time her three daughters were born: Claude, Anne, and Dominique. She has since said that, far from being "wasted," her years of legal training contributed to her eventual formation as a writer by giving her practice in utilizing spoken language through oral arguments and pleadings and by helping to rid her writing of the convoluted sentence structure and formal elegance taught at the Sorbonne. Some readers note the influence of Sarraute's legal background in her ability to present both sides of an argument, in the claims and counterclaims of opposing voices, and in the attack and parry, aggression and defense, of spoken discourse, at which she excels.

In 1932 and 1933 Sarraute composed two short texts *(Tropisms II* and *IX)* to which she gradually added others. In 1937, she tried to peddle her book to various publishers, but without success. Rejected by both Grasset and Gallimard (the latter has since become her regular publisher), *Tropisms* was finally accepted by Robert Denoël and appeared in February 1939. It passed virtually unnoticed. Apart from a few responses by such notables as Max Jacob, Jean-Paul Sartre, and Charles Mauron, *Tropisms* was reviewed in only one journal, by Victor Moremans in the *Gazette de Liège*.

At the outbreak of World War II, Nathalie Sarraute had begun work on a second novel, *Portrait of a Man Unknown,* which continued to occupy her during the tempestuous years when she was forced to take refuge in the town of Parmain (Seine-et-Oise). Here, under the name of Nicole Sauvage and with the courageous complicity of Madame Robert Dieudonné, with whom she lived from 1943 to 1944, she hid from the Germans by posing as the governess of her own daughters.[2] *Portrait* was completed in 1946. With a preface by Sartre, whom Sarraute had come to know during the war, it was published in 1948 by Robert Marin; four hundred copies were sold, and the rest were remaindered.

Because these first books were poorly received, Sarraute was moved to explain her unorthodox approach to fiction in a series of essays that began to appear, from 1947 to 1956, in literary journals like *Les Temps Modernes* and the *Nouvelle N.R.F.* Ultimately, four of them were collected under the heading *The Age of Suspicion* and published by Gallimard in 1956. These articles, together with her many interviews and lectures, form a body of criticism, of literary theory and aesthetics, in which Sarraute has expatiated on her ideas about the development of the novel, her affinities (or differences) with contemporary fictional innovations, and her general perceptions about art.

Meanwhile, her sorties into fiction continued apace. *Martereau* appeared in 1953, followed in 1956 by *The Age of Suspicion* and in 1957 by a reissue of *Portrait of a Man Unknown* (all of these under the imprimatur of Gallimard). Also in 1957, *Tropisms* was reprinted by the Editions de Minuit, under the literary direction of Alain Robbe-Grillet. *The Planetarium* came out in 1959 and was widely received as an example of the burgeoning New Novel. In 1963, Gallimard published *The Golden Fruits,* for which Sarraute received the *Prix international de littérature*.

In 1964 Sarraute wrote her first radio play, *Silence,* which was initially broadcast in a German translation throughout Germany, Switzerland, and the Scandinavian countries. A second play written for radio, *The Lie,* was broadcast simultaneously in German and French in March 1966. Both plays were chosen by Jean-Louis Barrault as a double bill to celebrate the twentieth anniversary of his troupe and to inaugurate his new theater, the Petit Odéon, in January 1967. The novel *Between Life and Death* appeared in 1968, followed by a radio play called *Isma,* in 1970. *Do You Hear Them?,* another novel, came out in 1972. *It's Beautiful* was published in 1973, and produced the same year by Claude Régy. Sarraute's latest novel, *"fools say,"* appeared in the fall of 1976. In 1978, Claude Régy staged a new play, *Elle est là,* for the Festival d'Automne, almost simultaneously with its publication in the first collected edition of Sarraute's plays.

Since 1935, Nathalie Sarraute has traveled extensively. She has visited the USSR, Scotland, Italy, Greece, Turkey, Morocco, Spain, Sicily, Israel, Yugoslavia, Portugal, and Sardinia. Beginning in 1959, she has delivered lectures in Switzerland, Belgium, Italy, Sweden, Norway, Denmark, Germany, England, the USSR, and Cuba. She has visited the United States a number of times, lecturing and serving as "writer-in-residence" on many college campuses throughout the country. Her books have been translated into twenty-three languages, including Russian, Norwegian, Swedish, Czech, Polish, Spanish (in both Spain and Argentina), Italian, Japanese, Portuguese, Dutch, Danish, and Finnish; there is even an Egyptian translation of *Tropisms.* All her novels have been translated into English and German.

Nathalie Sarraute has produced a sizable and significant body of work. She has earned a secure niche in the history of letters and has had an impact on the literary course of an entire generation. To analyze her contribution and evaluate its importance, it is essential to turn to her works and let them speak for themselves.

CHAPTER 2

Forays into Fiction

I *"First Learn to Spell"*

A well-known story is told about Honoré de Balzac. When he was a youth, his family wanted him to study law, whereas he was determined to be a writer. He extracted from his reluctant parents the promise that they would accord him a year in which to prove himself. At the end of the allotted period, he emerged from his garret with the fruit of his labors — a verse play about Cromwell — which was submitted to a family council for a formal reading. A professor of literature who was called in to give his opinion pronounced the categorical verdict that the young man should enter any field at all, except literature. (So much for the critical acumen of academicians. . . .)

Nathalie Sarraute had a similar experience, at a far more impressionable age. From her earliest recollection she had always wanted to write, and at the age of seven she composed her first novel. She had the imprudence, or misfortune, to show it to a writer-friend of her mother's. After leafing through her manuscript, he returned it to the eager little girl, with the crushing advice: "First learn to spell, before you write a book." Nathalie Sarraute still speaks of this as one of the most traumatic moments of her childhood, which may well have set her career back by twenty-five years.[1] Marked more deeply than Balzac by this disillusionment, she gave up her writing ambition and went to law school instead.

II *Inner Movements*

Somewhere in the back of her mind, the desire to write continued to haunt her. At length, in 1932 and 1933, Sarraute yielded to this

18

long-suppressed urge and composed the first sketches of *Tropisms*. She created these fragments "almost unconsciously, just as one writes a first poem."[2] They were the spontaneous expressions of certain sensations she had observed within herself and others, "inner movements" that seemed to underlie the speech and gestures of everyday relationships. Borrowing a term from biochemistry, she dubbed these inner movements "tropisms," by analogy with the instinctive and irresistible movements whereby primitive organisms expand or contract under external influences, like light or heat. On a psychological plane, she noted similar tiny, flitting impulses ocurring in reaction to people and circumstances: "These movements glide quickly round the border of our consciousness, they compose the small, rapid, and sometimes very complex dramas concealed beneath our actions, our gestures, the words we speak, our avowed and clear feelings." They form the infinitesimal but complex dramas that hide beneath our overt words and acts. They provide the hidden clue to our admitted feelings. For Sarraute, they constitute "the secret throbbing of life."[3]

After committing these first texts to paper, Sarraute became very excited because she had the impression — perhaps the illusion — that she was not only the first to perceive these inner movements but the first to set them down in writing.[4] It was a formidable task. Since tropisms occur transiently, on a preverbal level, Sarraute was faced with the challenge of capturing in language what is felt, but is never formulated in words. Her aim was to seize these elusive flashes of sensation at the moment of their inception, before they seep into conscious awareness, and to render them palpable to the reader. Since they are not susceptible of being readily apprehended, Sarraute discovered that they could not be expressed in traditional forms — not through exposition or dialogue or even interior monologue. In order to communicate these intangible sensations, she found herself obliged to arrest their lightning movements, to break them down into their component parts. She also had to find words and images that would give the reader the impression of experiencing the same feelings as the characters, simultaneously with them. The necessity for communicating tropisms has been the basis for Sarraute's never-ending search for new modes of expression.

Tropisms provide the essential element in Sarraute's writing and the focus of her attention. Even in her first book what interested her above all were "the dramatic situations constituted by these invisible actions."[5] She wanted nothing to distract her readers from concentrating on these movements, whose development replaces plot in her novels. Even her "characters" exist only as casual bearers of tropisms. The tropism itself is the driving force in all her books.

The original *Tropisms,* published in 1939, was composed of nineteen short pieces. In the subsequent edition of 1957, one of the early texts was deleted and six new ones, written between 1939 and 1941, were added at the end. Each text was also numbered individually.

These twenty-four brief, unrelated pieces are difficult to classify by any of the traditional literary designations. Sarraute herself is reluctant to term *Tropisms* a novel. Rather, she calls it "a collection of short texts" or "fragments," with no connection between them.[6] Variously referred to as "prose poems" or "microdramas," they are essentially a series of compact vignettes, their only link being the unifying concept of "tropisms." They present fugitive glimpses of people and relationships, momentarily transfixed as if by the camera's eye. Each reveals a minuscule situation, an arrested moment of time, an indistinct place inhabited by nameless people who are caught up in the web of their interdependence.

The characters are anonymous, the situations representative, the settings undistinctive. Particularities of time, place, and character are shorn away. What remains, in this paring down to essentials, are the common feelings and experiences that are not dependent on any particular moment of history or cultural acclimatization, but belong to the common heritage of humankind, in the true classical tradition.

III   *Classical Traits*

Sarraute's terseness is worthy of a La Rochefoucauld, her faculty of observation reminiscent of La Bruyère. Her very first book is an achievement in economy of expression. Out of a microcosmic instant, she extracts the essence of a character. A partial conversation conveys the sense of an entire relationship; a lifetime is compressed into an afternoon. This concision and distillation are traits she shares with the moralists of the seventeenth century.

Sarraute may also be termed "classical" through the universality of the experiences she depicts. She is not interested in singularities or idiosyncrasies, but in the common denominator of humanity.

There are no unique or individualized characters in her work. Instead, the people in her pages are divested of all particularities of background, personal history, and physical appearance. Although occasionally, among the *Tropisms,* someone is recognizable as a child, or an old man, or possibly a grandfather, for the most part they are ageless, of no determinable occupation or social condition. They are stripped of the appendages of identity in order to emphasize their shared humanity.

To reinforce the concept of anonymity and generality, Sarraute uses a system of third-person narration. The pronoun "they" is most frequent, denoting a faceless, undifferentiated group that acts in a concerted and often predictable way. But even when the singular "he" or "she" is employed, the individual in question is merely indicative of a much broader sampling. He is like a myriad others who resemble him.

The tendency, in this generalization from the particular, is to distinguish in Nathalie Sarraute's "characters" representatives of a species. Some of her sketches are almost "portraits" in the manner of La Bruyère: the pompous professor at the Collège de France, the woman gossiping with her cook, the would-be "bluestocking," the prim little girl who grows up to be a prim little lady, the small boy afraid of the dark. Others dispense entirely with the individual, in order to concentrate on the group itself: the bevy of ladies chattering over tea, the army of women marching in high-heeled shoes through the city in grim pursuit of a tweed sports outfit. However, just as we think we have come face to face with a "type," the concept dissolves before our eyes. The person is not presented as a character sketch, but as the involuntary bearer of some "tropism," which conditions his behavior and attitudes, almost without his awareness.

There is a strong dose of satire in some of these delineations. Women, especially, are portrayed in an unforgiving light, their frivolous concerns and useless occupations underscored. Even the "intellectual" woman is the butt of ridicule: her aesthetic tastes are not sincere but donned to conform to the fad of the moment. Each individual who is held up to scorn is symptomatic of a larger group. Sarraute's irony — sometimes gentle, sometimes finely honed — derives its force from the numbers it impales with a single stroke. By virtue of this multiplicity, it strikes not only the individual whom Sarraute has momentarily isolated but all the countless look-alikes who reinforce his mediocrity.

Just as there is never the sense of being in the presence of a unique individual, so there is never the sense of being privy to a special experience in a character's life. No memorable occasion, no climactic moment, no turning-point of existence, no single scene imprints itself on the reader's mind. Rather, the particular incident that Sarraute presents is symptomatic of a repeated experience, a habitual mode of behavior, infinitely renewable.

Significantly, there are no specificities of time or place. Even in her more complex novels, Sarraute dissociates characters and situations from any socio-historical framework. Her people exist in a chronological vacuum, insulated from history. Among the *Tropisms,* references to time are of the vaguest: a hot July day or a balmy spring evening. The "settings" (without benefit of descriptive décor) are generally indoor scenes, as indistinguishable as their inhabitants. Sometimes they are outdoor cityscapes, with drab buildings and dreary public squares. One of the few "rural" scenes is not a true countryside at all, but a suburban wood, where the grass is sparse and trampled, and even the buds on the trees resemble sickly children in hospital wards (*Tropism XVII*). No place has a name. If a street is indicated, it is not a specific street: it *could* be the rue Gay-Lussac or the rue Saint-Jacques, one of the quiet little streets behind the Panthéon (*Tropism III*), representative of an entire category.

There is a basic undercurrent in Sarraute's works, implicit even in these early texts, of what might almost be termed "moral" concern. In this respect, as well, she follows the lineage of her "classical" predecessors. Almost every one of the vignettes of *Tropisms* illustrates some foible of human behavior, which a moralist like La Rochefoucauld could summarize with a maxim. It is not that Sarraute expresses a judgment or even conveys a message. She refrains equally from reprobation or approval. What she does is to posit certain truths about human behavior, based on observation. These truths are subsurface characteristics, not readily discernible. Sarraute searches them out from where they lie hidden and displays them to conscious awareness. It is because these characteristics are universal that they awake an echo in her readers, who have themselves known similar sensations, though perhaps unacknowledged. It is also because these sensations, which are common to everyone, frequently stem from the frailties of human nature that Sarraute writes of them with gentle sympathy, kindness, and humor. She assumes no patronizing attitude of aloofness.

She does not suggest what ought to be; she reports what is.

IV   *The Human Condition*

Like other twentieth-century French writers (Sartre and Camus, who give voice to existentialist anguish; Malraux, who situates the "human condition" in a historical framework; Ionesco and Beckett, who point up the absurdity of existence), Nathalie Sarraute provides a pessimistic view of life in the sketches of *Tropisms.* Just as there are no bright colors and no wide-open spaces, there is no delight or laughter or loving intimacy. There are no moments of joy or excitement, rarely even a sense of contentment and serenity. Dun-colored emotions tint dun-colored lives, moving in a routine circle of monotony and resignation. It is a humdrum landscape of the soul, with little to relieve its monochrome bleakness.

Each person is isolated in his eternal solitude. The anonymous "they" who live by themselves in some quiet street behind the Panthéon sometimes meet their downstairs neighbor, with his two pale children, silently opening his door and gliding away into the dim interior of his apartment *(Tropism III).* No one speaks, no one smiles, no one attempts to pierce the invisible partition that isolates him from others. Each is immured in the watertight compartment of his separate life, utterly alone.

The loneliness of the human condition can only be mitigated by human warmth. Since solitude is unendurable, it is necessary to enter into a "social contract" that often leads to frustration and despair. Each attempt to draw close to another human being entails a loss of independence and self-identity. There are alternate movements of approach and withdrawal, reflecting the ambivalence between an obsessive need for companionship and the contrary desire to maintain one's integrity intact.

The act of approach involves capitulation. A person becomes dependent on the good will and approbation of another. How exhausting it can be to submit to someone else's whims *(Tropism IV)*! Relationships are purchased at a dear price. In *Tropism IX,* "he" is so desirous of placating "her" that he talks on and on endlessly, revealing secrets about himself, his friends and family — anything, in order to maintain the thread of their contact and forestall some dread outburst on her part. The need for companionship can override all other concerns. Despite the realization that the people she frequents are dull and commonplace, the character in *Tropism*

XXIII literally "joins their circle." By taking part in their game —
a mournful parody of children's plays — she abdicates her
individuality and becomes the very cliché she had despised them for
being. Once surrender to the group has taken place, it is impossible
to break away. This is the "message" of a sinister little piece
(Tropism XXIV). "They" bend all their efforts to spying on
"him," seeking the slightest signal of revolt. They surround him in
a tight circle, and when they see him surreptitiously trying to crawl
out from their midst, they have only to lower their clasped hands to
block his escape.

In the subsurface region where tropisms swarm, there is a ceaseless struggle for domination and control. One person is almost
invariably subservient to another: out of timidity, or distrust, or a
sense of inadequacy, or a dozen other feelings of inferiority. An
encounter between a young girl and an older man, a friend of her
parents,' illustrates the complicity of the victim in her own violation
(Tropism XV). She seeks him out, as she has always done since she
was a child. In a scene that borders on sexual violence, he batters
and bludgeons her with the force of his questions: "Dover, Dover,
Dover? Eh? Eh? Dover? Thackeray? England? Dickens? Shake-
speare? Eh? Eh? Dover?" (p. 40). He grips her tightly in his fist,
watching her squirm, while she keeps up the pretense of smiling
politely.

Domination in its most complete and lethal form is the domination that poses as love. In the guise of affection, "they" step on
"him," stamp on him, turn him round and round and survey him.
They devour and possess him, to the last crumb of his being. Sometimes they give him slack, let him run a bit, only to snatch him back
when he ventures too far. But he is an accomplice to his own
domination. Since childhood he would reach out to them of his
own accord, offering himself up to their smothering kisses. There is
no escape, no exit, from the world where he has allowed himself to
be imprisoned *(Tropism XIX)*.

Control over others is established through various means. Sometimes material objects are used as instruments of repression. "She"
leaps out of bed early, scurries about the apartment, bangs on the
bathroom door, hurries everyone down to breakfast *(Tropism VI)*.
The children jump to attention. "Things" are her power, the
source of her strength, the devices she uses to triumph over others:
a ringing doorbell or telephone that has to be answered, an open
window that has to be shut: "You had to rush, quick, quick, be-

rated, browbeaten, apprehensive, drop everything and rush forward, ready to serve" (p. 16).

Sometimes language itself has the force to mobilize tropisms. Language can be used as a means of aggression (the older man who badgers the young girl with his questions), or to trigger an explosion *(Tropism VII)*. Conversely, words can serve to ward off an outburst, to salve an offense: words that are ground out mindlessly to cover awareness and plug up silence (*VII* and *IX*).

The basic emotions underlying these relationships are fear and misunderstanding. An undercurrent of fear is present in almost every sketch. There is the fear of overstepping an invisible boundary and provoking an explosion *(VII, IX, XIV)*, fear of being "different," of not being accepted *(XXIII)*, even the private fear of drawing attention to oneself, as expressed in *Tropism V* ("she" sits motionless on the edge of her bed, trying to occupy the least possible place, afraid of making a sound, even of turning on the bathroom faucet, lest she attract the notice of those dreaded "Others," who are waiting on the far side of the wall, ready to pounce).

Rarely is one person secure in another person's esteem or affection. He constantly feels the need to shore up his defenses, to anticipate criticism or anger, to assuage even the mildest irritation. In violation of his integrity, he grovels like a lackey, then despises his own self-abasement. In the barest outline of a relationship, "they" literally dance attendance on "him"; he is a ballet master, directing their steps with his relentless baton: backwards, forwards, turning, pivoting, they gyrate in response to his incessant questioning *(IV)*.

There is often the dread of something vague and menacing. "At times the shrill notes of locusts in a meadow petrified by the sun and as though dead, induce this sensation of cold, of solitude, of abandonment in a hostile universe in which something anguished is impending" (p. 11). *Tropism XX* depicts the terror of a young boy who is petrified of what lurks in the dark, a prey to nameless fears of the unknown. By seeking reassurance, he delivers himself over to the power of Others; even as an adult, he still cannot dispense with his dependence on "them."

Misunderstanding results from a breakdown of communications or a failure to envision another point of view. The inability to comprehend the other person — his feelings, secret fears, hopes, anxieties — sends each one scuttling back into his private burrow of loneliness. Sometimes it is adults who fail to understand each

other. "She" sits knitting, self-effacing and withdrawn. She claims
to want nothing, but they are wary in her presence; they tiptoe
around her, surveying every word and intonation, lest they set off a
myriad of tiny, sharp-tongued bells. Little do they suspect her
walled-up wishes to get close to them. Her tentative efforts to make
contact are thoughtlessly brushed aside. The attempt to bridge the
chasm that separates people ends in failure; a pervading misunderstanding prevents access and approach *(XIV)*. Sometimes it is
adults who fail to understand children, perhaps trying to give them
pleasure but not knowing how — dragging them forlornly to watch
a doll in a window display, who mechanically opens and shuts its
eyes while the children look on listlessly *(I)* — or perhaps "using"
them for their own needs, like the grandfather who cannot resist
manipulating the grandchild in his power, frightening him with talk
of old age and dying *(VIII)*.

Sarraute often depicts children as helpless, stolid victims, lacking
the verve and *joie de vivre* that children have (or ought to have) before they are molded into gray conformity, like their elders. A sad
example is the youngster taken on a picnic who refrains from joining other children in play and remains seated beside his parents
instead, solemnly absorbed in their adult conversation *(XVII)*.
Throughout the sketches there are an abundance of "obedient"
children — docile, self-restrained — who will eventually grow up
into "obedient" members of society. In their conventionalized attitudes, their prim and proper behavior, they will join the army of
self-appointed judges who seek out and reprove any eccentricity,
any departure from the established code of conduct. The guardians
of the *status quo* are often symbolized by the ubiquitous concierge,
whose all-seeing gaze can become unendurable (as in *Tropism*
XXI). These zealous guardians of society's values are the anonymous "they" of *Tropism XXIV,* who stay shut up in their apartments, spying on "him" for any signs of deviation. They are the
chorus of voices in *Portrait, Do You Hear Them?,* and *It's
Beautiful,* who express the monotonous litany of society's
reproval.

The world of tropisms is unpredictable. At any moment, the unexpected may occur. There is no permanence or stability on which
to rely. As soon as the One is faced with the Other, motives are mis-
interpreted, misunderstandings arise. No one can gauge another
person's responses. In *Tropism IV,* no matter how assiduously
"they" cater to him, he suddenly explodes in anger; however ex-

tensive their efforts, the result is unforeseeable and fruitless. In *Tropism VII,* "she" is always on the alert to distract "him" from topics that may provoke his wrath, but occasionally someone else broaches a subject that she expects will infuriate him; contrary to her fears, he is indulgent and amused. But there is no lesson to be learned from these experiences. Behavior is a puzzle, without pattern or design. One must be constantly watchful, wary, on guard, ready for all eventualities.

V *A World of Platitudes*

The anguish of the human condition is rendered bearable by the camouflage of clichés. Trite words, trivial observations, everyday expressions are used to gloss over the bitter realities of existence. Language serves the defensive purpose of maintaining a cloak, not of silence but of words, over the truth. Shopworn platitudes cover up feelings, conceal disturbing "tropisms." People chatter away incessantly to fill up the void of silence and restrain the intrusion of menacing thoughts *(IV, IX).*

Clichés reflect the tacit censorship that people are agreed to clamp on certain unpalatable facts of life, like death and old age. They are worn like blinders to shield our insight from the unbearable truths of existence. As Sarraute uses them, clichés are not what everyone thinks or feels; rather, they are "what people force themselves to think and feel in order to escape from the vertigo of reality."[7] Clichés enable people to live their lives in superficial tranquillity, without descending into an uneasy abyss of awareness.

One vignette uses clichés to underscore the sadness of old age, when life is reduced to a series of meaningless rituals *(XVI).* Old people go out for a walk, sit down in a café, choose a spot well protected from drafts, carefully select a beverage. They mask their fruitless occupations with hoary platitudes: "Youth is over, passions are spent"; they are like "old furniture that has served its purpose"; they groan as they sit down, "Ah! these old bones, we're getting old" (p. 41). Resigned to the monotony of their repetitive actions, they wait for the inevitable, the unmentionable, to occur.

Hackneyed opinions, adopted by common consensus, provide the delusion of exerting control over other people and even over life itself. A communality of banal attitudes reinforces self-identity within the group. A shared vocabulary, however trite, is a shibboleth by which outsiders are excluded (like the youngster who does not know the "password" in *Between Life and Death)*. When "she" and the cook endlessly criticize other people's habits, appearance, and life-style, their insidious chatter filters into the consciousness of the disgusted listener with the force of repetition, if not of persuasion, and he is helpless against them *(II)*. The chirping ladies who spend their afternoons gossiping in tearooms, render judgments about events, emotions, love, life, everything they consider to be their domain. By repeating the same commonplace phrases and platitudes, they knead the substance of existence into a small gray pellet — trivial, nondescript, and insipid *(X)*.

One scene is a "cliché" in and of itself, a still-life that typifies the comfortable stability of old England: a wisteria-framed cottage with a cat sunning itself on the doorstep and a white-haired lady placidly waiting for her cook to ring the bell for tea *(XVIII)*. There is not a single tropism to trouble the serenity of this self-contained universe. But the painted façade will be cracked open, the tranquillity shattered, when Sarraute probes behind its deceptive exterior in *Martereau*.

Despite the general acceptance of platitudes, occasionally a need is felt to escape from society's rigorous code. This half-acknowledged yearning is sometimes expressed wistfully or resignedly *(XIX)*, sometimes in helpless frustration *(XXIV)*, sometimes in annoyance *(IV)*. Once in a while it erupts with the force of desperation. The "docile little girl" who grows up into a "docile little woman" — always attired primly in black, always punctiliously polite, strict in her observance of the conventional amenities — one day, in the midst of paying a condolence visit, abruptly bolts from the room and flees through the streets, howling her frustration and revolt *(XXI)*. A fissure has appeared in the thin shell of surface appearances, and the roiling tropisms burst forth in an irrepressible gush.

VI   *Future Ideas in Germ*

The short work *Tropisms* contains the germ for many of Sarraute's later novels and plays. Certain basic thematic material and narrative methods are already present, in embryonic form. The anonymity of character, the absence of plot, the elimination of historical contingencies, even the paucity of décor and physical description will be intrinsic elements in Sarraute's subsequent writings. Certain fundamental concepts of human behavior will continue to characterize interrelationships: the ambivalent needs for contact and independence, for adherence and withdrawal; the seesaw struggle between domination and submission; the fear and misunderstanding that jeopardize relationships; the tendency to hold existential anguish at bay by means of clichés.

Some of the situations or "characters" in later books are pre-figured in these early sketches. The pompous professor who claims to have studied Proust and Rimbaud clinically, to have emptied them of their mystery *(XII)*, represents an attitude of bombastic arrogance that will find its place in *The Golden Fruits*. The woman who exudes rapturous admiration for all the latest cultural fads *(XI)* will have a counterpart in the host of sheeplike adherents to prescribed aesthetic values who parade through *The Golden Fruits, Between Life and Death,* and *Do You Hear Them?*; her rhapsodic exclamation of "It's so beautiful" denotes the same artificial pre-judgment that is both the theme and the title of the play *It's Beautiful*. It has been suggested that *Tropism IX* calls to mind the woman writer and young narrator of *The Planetarium, XXI* brings in the dutiful daughter of *Portrait of a Man Unknown,* and sketch *XXII* announces the hypersensitive narrators of *Portrait* and *Martereau*.[8]

Most important of all is the unifying concept of tropisms. They are the raw material Sarraute has developed in all of her works. In 1963, almost twenty-five years after *Tropisms* was published, Sarraute was still maintaining the primacy of these inner movements, which have merely been broadened and rendered more complex in her subsequent writings:

> Tropisms are still the living substance of all my books, the only difference being that the time of the dramatic action they constitute is longer, and there is added complexity in the constant play that takes place between them and the appearances and commonplaces with which they emerge into the open: our conversations, the personality we seem to have, the person we seem to be in one another's eyes, the stereotyped things we believe we feel, as also those we discover in others, and the superficial dramatic action constituted by plot, which is nothing but a conventional code that we apply to life.[9]

"Tropisms" — a word and a concept that Sarraute has appropriated as her own — have come to symbolize her distinct and unique contribution to modern-day fiction.

CHAPTER 3

A New Kind of Novel

I   Novel or "Anti-Novel"?

WHEREAS *Tropisms* was a collection of unrelated texts, Sarraute's next books — *Portrait of a Man Unknown* (1948), *Martereau* (1953), and *The Planetarium* (1959) — are distinctly classifiable as novels (or, in Sartre's terminology, "anti-novels"). In fact, in spite of the innovations they introduce into the form and concept of fiction, these three works may be considered the most "representational" of Sarraute's novels. They still retain a semblance of plot and a nucleus of recognizable characters in some kind of relationship (which may at first glimpse appear unintelligible, but is eventually clarified). The tropistic movement still serves as the focal point, out of which radiate increasingly complex situations. Instead of the one-on-one relationships of the earlier sketches, the author presents an assortment of characters interacting in various combinations. (Nonetheless, the field is still fairly limited: three "main" characters in *Portrait,* four or five in *Martereau,* perhaps half a dozen in *Planetarium* — hardly Balzac's cast of thousands!)

In his Preface to the 1956 edition of *Portrait of a Man Unknown,* Jean-Paul Sartre coined a special term, "anti-novel," to designate the experimental fiction that Sarraute and a few others had begun to compose. He was referring, as he explained, to a new kind of writing, which retains the appearance and outlines of an ordinary novel, but reflects a breakdown of traditional fiction. These "curious works," difficult to classify, are analogized to painting: they are to the great structured works of Dostoevsky and Meredith what Miro's canvas *The Assassination of Painting* was to the works of Rembrandt and Rubens. Sartre did not consider that this unconventional approach represented a weakening of the novel as a genre, but simply attested to the fact that "we live in a period of reflection and [...] the novel is reflecting on its own problems."[1] Sarraute was later to object to the term "anti-novel" as indicating that Sartre had a predetermined notion of what a "novel" should be, which he used as a yardstick against which to measure other types of fiction that did not correspond to this norm.[2] It is precisely this type of preconception (in art, as in human relationships) that Sarraute attacks time and again in her writing.

Sarraute's break with conventional fiction involves a radical change in the concept of characterization and plot, chronology and milieu, point of view and dialogue. So pervasive are the differences that distinguish her writing from the traditional novel — the sacrosanct domain of Balzac, Stendhal, Flaubert, and Zola — with its convolutions of intrigue, its well-defined characters, its omniscient-author technique, and its aim of verisimilitude, that the first exposure to a novel by Sarraute can be a disorienting experience for the reader. To claim his attention and ensure his active involvement in the fictional process, Sarraute deliberately removes from the reader's grasp all the familiar props of plot and character. She substitutes instead a strange, disturbing world in which appearances are deceptive and conventional reality is revealed as a *trompe-l'oeil* artifice of delusion and sleight-of-hand.

II *Disintegration of Character and Plot*

Instead of setting the stage with long passages of description and exposition, like Balzac, Sarraute begins each book by plunging the reader directly inside someone's thoughts, with no indication as to who the person is, what he looks like, his age, background, or profession. None of these questions matters in the least. There is no attempt to re-create flesh-and-blood characters so realistic that they can, in Balzac's words, "rival the civil registry." According to Sarraute, such characters have been described so often in literature that they are as lifeless as the wax statues in the Musée Grévin (an image that recurs frequently under her pen).

Sarrute divests her characters of all the superficial appurtenances of verisimilitude. They have no recognizable physical appearance or personality traits that stamp them as individuals. Most of them do not even bear a name. The characters in *Portrait* and *Martereau* are all anonymous, with two exceptions: Louis Dumontet in the first and Martereau in the second. Both are presented as strong-willed, opaque personalities, the kind that are incapable of experiencing "tropisms." For that reason, they are viewed externally, almost as objects. Although the characters in *The Planetarium* all have names, the attentive reader will discover that a name is used only in conversation and never when the person is the subject of somebody's thoughts. At all other times, strict anonymity prevails. Sarraute once made this analogy: If she thinks about someone — her daughter, for instance — she sees an image in her mind, experiences a sensation, but has no need to pronounce a name. The name is exterior to thought and becomes important only when she has to designate the person aloud to someone else; then she will say, "My daughter Claude."[3]

Sarraute has often explained that the anonymity of character in her books is not a gratuitous procedure, but is intrinsic to her aim of situating the reader directly inside a person's mind. She has found that the use of a name creates an impossible distance between herself and her character:

This lack of names in all my books does not come from a desire to be modern, difficult, or obscure. It comes from sheer necessity. I have some-times tried to replace the "he" or "she," which I generally use, by the character's name. I have then found out that it made me move away from that place on the border of consciousness where the tropisms can be ob-served and where no names are ever pronounced, where we see a rapid image, a vague form. It made me move away, somewhere on the outside, on to the social level.[4]

To the contrary, she feels the necessity to be situated deep inside that "undifferentiated substance" where proper names do not exist and where sensations alone matter. She also insists that the reader must learn to recognize characters without depending on the familiar indices to which he has become accustomed in the traditional novel:

Instead of letting herself be guided by the signposts with which everyday custom flatters his laziness and haste, he is obliged, in order to identify the characters, to recognize them at once, like the author himself, from the in-side, and thanks to indications that are only revealed to him if, having re-nounced his love of comfort, he is willing to plunge into them as deeply as the author, whose vision he makes his own.[5]

There are antecedents for Sarraute's amorphous, equivocal

characters. Joyce in *Finnegans Wake,* Kafka in his novels, identify their central personages by initials only, thus refusing them a distinct personality or existence. Likewise, there is a deliberate confusion of identities among certain of Faulkner's characters (the dual use of the names Quentin and Caddy in *The Sound and the Fury* is a case in point). A similar effect is achieved by the first-person narrative, the anonymous "I" who is found in the writings of Céline and Genêt, among others.[6]

Not only are characters presented anonymously. There is also no indication, at the outset, of their relationships to one another, which must be puzzled out as the book progresses. In *Portrait,* the primary characters are first referred to as a faceless, anonymous "they," whom the narrator glimpses in a crowd or whose presence he senses in a room. In a roundabout way, the reader finds out who "they" are: a "miserly old man" and his daughter. *Martereau* opens in similar fashion, with a conversation between two unidentified persons discussing the early days of "her" marriage; only gradually does Sarraute drop the clues that enable the reader to recognize them as the narrator and his aunt.

In *Portrait* and *Martereau,* where there is a central narrative consciousness, the problem of identification is more readily solved than in subsequent novels. In *The Planetarium,* for instance, there is a fragmentation of the narrative function from chapter to chapter; the reader is passed back and forth from one mind to another, and it is only by imprecise and scattered indications that he realizes inside whose thoughts he is situated at the moment. As the matter of individual identity becomes less important in later novels like *The Golden Fruits* and *Between Life and Death,* Sarraute dispenses entirely with signs for recognizing characters. Ultimately, in *"fools say,"* the only differentiation between two speakers lies in the opposing views they hold — although one person often melts into the other (and "I" can become "he" or "we" from one paragraph to the next). This virtual interchangeability of personality, increasingly prevalent in Sarraute's later works, tallies with her belief in the universality of certain human experiences, perceived on their most intimate level.

In the same way that characters and relationships are not immediately discernible but require a period of preacquaintance before they come to light, external events are never explicitly narrated but are divulged almost accidentally, through conversation or some other indirect means. The reader of *The Planetarium* learns the outcome of a fierce family feud over a pair of chairs only when a visitor admires the Louis XV bergère in a young couple's home; likewise, he finds out that the same couple have moved into their aunt's apartment (another source of dramatic conflict) only when someone pays them a call and is shown through the rooms. The reason for deemphasizing the resolution of each crisis is that the situation holds no particular interest for Sarraute, however traumatic it may be for the characters involved; what matter are the tropisms that it calls forth. Once the confrontation is over and the tropisms subside, she regards the result as of little consequence.

There is a breakdown of conventional plot in all of Sarraute's novels. Nothing "happens," nothing of any moment or interest. In *Martereau,* the narrator's aunt and uncle purchase a country villa. In *The Planetarium,* after some maneuvering, two young people take possession of their aunt's apartment. Action *per se* does not exist. The intangible tropisms form the crux of dramatic conflict. These may be set in motion by certain external causes (a Louis XV bergère or a spacious apartment), but the causes themselves have no intrinsic importance. In fact, the more trivial and inconsequential they are, the greater is the emphasis on the tropisms they generate.

III   *Family Milieu*

The family is the terrain *par excellence* for the deployment of tropisms. It is the circumscribed milieu that Sarraute chooses repeatedly for enacting her dramas. Not only the early novels — *Portrait, Martereau, Planetarium* — but some later works as well — *Do You Hear Them?, It's Beautiful,* and parts of *"fools say"* — are centered on family situations. The most oppressive experiences for the writer in *Between Life and Death* are the confrontations with his father and mother.

Among people who know each other so well that no one can surprise the other, behavior and reactions tend to follow familiar patterns. The same scenes, the same incidents, are repeated *ad nauseam.* It becomes impossible to start afresh. Each person is transfixed by preconceived opinions formed in the past and cannot present himself as he would like to appear. Perhaps that is why a character often turns to someone outside the family (to a Martereau or a Germaine Lemaire) to satisfy his need to be known in his own right.

In the shuttered precincts of family life, intimacy exacerbates the intensity of emotion. Feelings of hate or distrust, hostility or misunderstanding, assume colossal proportions. The physical and emotional proximity of the participants makes the struggle, when it comes, all the more vitriolic. The field of combat is marked off, the weapons familiar, the defenses known in advance. All possibilities of escape are sealed off. The venom and violence of familial relationships represent in microcosm the antagonisms and interdependence of the world "out there."

IV *Time and Space*   2047336

The context in which Sarraute's novels occur is a timeless, spaceless vacuum. Sarraute situates her "dramas" in a hermetic universe, isolated from whatever contemporary events may be taking place in the outside world; wars and strikes, natural and manmade disasters, all are absent from her work. To be sure, there is a reference in *The Lie* to the place where one character spent time during "the war" — but it is a hazy war that exists in memory only and has no bearing on the situation at hand. Because the action of her books is situated in some vague moment outside history, it is idle for critics to speculate about the time period intended, or to adjudge that the events of *Martereau,* for instance, represent a postwar bourgeois mentality, based on affluence and luxury.[7] In a "realistic" sense, there is no possible moment of recent history, either prewar or postwar, when these dramas could have occurred, without at some point reflecting the shadow of external events; this kind of "realism," however, is anathema to Sarraute.

The spatial dimension is extremely limited. There are no descriptive settings and no particularized places. If a locale is mentioned at all, it is an unspecified site: usually an interior, a street, perhaps a restaurant or café, as restricted as a stage set. One or two excursions into the countryside take place in *Martereau,* but the natural setting has no function other than to elicit conflicting responses from the narrator and his uncle.

The temporal dimension in Sarraute's books is a perpetual present. Her characters live entirely in their own here and now. If an incident from their past lives is introduced, it is not to make them three-dimensional or provide them with an *état civil* like the characters of Balzac; it is rather to heighten awareness of the present by showing a past precedent for the characters' inner state.

The intrusion of the past gives consistency and solidity to the present.

The banality of experience and the sameness of sensation endow the present with a timeless quality. There are no "privileged moments" like those Proust describes. There are no unforgettable peaks of experience, no pivotal dramas or crucial decisions that may influence the future course of life. There is not a single scene — not even the dramatic crisis between father and daughter in *Portrait* — that cannot be considered typical of an unlimited number of similar scenes, endlessly repeatable from the past into the future. Because the "events" that take place in the course of a book are not unique occurrences but emotional states that are inevitably relived with only infinitesimal variations, the present moment is deepened and amplified, charged with the significance of habit, laden with the emotional accretions of a symbolic experience.

Time turns on itself in a circular motion. There is no linear progression, no chronological sequence of events, except in the most general way. Even when specific incidents are depicted (e.g., an encounter in a restaurant in *Portrait,* a visit to a villa in *Martereau,* a family dinner in *Planetarium*), no necessary temporal order need be preserved. And inasmuch as everything is viewed through a subjective consciousness, in which memory, imagination, and actual events are commingled, the notion of time virtually disappears. "I do not observe any chronological order," Sarraute has stated. "Things take their place simply when they shore up sensation."[8] This disregard for a temporal sequence becomes even more pronounced in *The Golden Fruits* and *Between Life and Death,* in which the general movement is like a parabolic curve, or the undulation of a wave, with its trough and its crest — an ebb-and-flow of movement, endlessly renewable. All experience is repetitive; each experience, by itself, is merely representative.

Since Sarraute's aim is to capture inner movements at the moment they form in the mind, it is the present alone that counts. But for the reader to participate in an experience, a sensation, in that split-second instant before it reaches conscious awareness, the tropism must be arrested in its fleeting passage. Sarraute has compared her method to the unrolling of a movie film; the present moment is expanded unnaturally, while the evanescent tropisms are immobilized within the multiple frames of a motion picture, which are then projected in slow motion before the reader's eyes.[9] Time is no longer the time of real life, but of a "hugely amplified present."[10]

V   *Narrative Point of View*

From the anonymous "he," "she," and "they" of *Tropisms,* Sarraute has transferred the narrative point of view to a central consciousness, "I," through whose perceptions all actions and events are sifted. Secondary characters have no autonomous existence, being merely excrescences, experiences, or dreams of the central "I." In *Portrait* and *Martereau,* the focal consciousness is a first-person narrator; in *Planetarium,* the narrative function is dispersed among a variety of characters, although a dominant point of view is still preserved in the person of Alain Guimier; in the later books, the optic keeps shifting from one anonymous character to the next. In spite of this increased fragmentation, there are certain indices that distinguish the narrative function in Sarraute's novels.

Invariably, the narrator is a suggestible, impressionable person, aware of the subsurface movements that are apt to escape ordinary notice. It is he who probes beneath outer appearances ("cherchant la petite bête," like the father in *Do You Hear Them?*). He refuses to clap labels on people, to term the father a "miser" in *Portrait* or to call his grandmother "cute" in *"fools say."* He is the "disturber of the peace," the "misfit" in *Between Life and Death,* whose disquieting presence introduces an element of questioning into a stable universe. This highly receptive figure appears somewhere in each of Sarraute's books, obdurately combating the social forces that try to quiet him and "put him in his place." From *Portrait* to *"fools say,"* whether as central narrator or only one anonymous voice among many, he is heard — *vox clamantis in deserto* — beseeching the impenetrable Others to give heed.

The narrator is pitted as the One against the Many. Timid and uncertain in his judgments, even about himself, his sensitive antennae are fine-tuned to the reactions of Others. He is constantly reappraising himself and readjusting his demeanor to forestall disapproval, elicit admiration, achieve a semblance of superiority, or conserve the vestiges of self-esteem. His view of himself is tinged by the reflection he sees in other people's eyes, to which he inadvertently tends to conform: "I am so easily influenced, [...] so sensitive to suggestion. The impression people have of me rubs off on me right away, I become exactly the way they see me, right away

and in spite of myself" (*Portrait,* p. 51). His sense of self-identity is
blurred at the edges, as he finds himself molded by the attitudes of
the group.

His sense of self-identity is blurred at the edges, as he finds himself
molded by the attitudes of the group.

This focal consciousness placed at the center of each book functions on two levels. He is both an observer and a participant in the
action, the sensitive recipient and recorder of tropisms, and their
precipitator in other people. He is simultaneously immersed with
all his emotional strength in a given situation, and withdrawn in an
attitude of critical awareness.

The narrator of the earlier books has been called "a novelist in
search of his subject."[11] He "creates" the personalities of the people around him, as he imagines them to be, in his reactions to their
presence. But because this image of others changes in response to
his fluctuating impressions or to alterations in their respective positions, he never achieves a completed picture, but only an indistinct
outline (like the amorphous "portrait of a man unknown"). However much he would like to pin down reality, he finds it forever
slipping out of his grip.

The narrator's active role in constructing character is counter-
balanced by his passivity in serving as the subject of other people's
interpretive embellishments. As he scrutinizes others, so he is
scrutinized in turn. His personality undergoes continual modi-
fication, so that the outline of his character is no sharper, in the
eyes of others, than their contours are for him. The narrator's creative imagining is not a one-sided activity, but part of the inter-
creativity implicit in every relationship. Each person is constantly
creating and retouching the characters of those around him, according to his own internalized perception.

VI   *Reality is Subjective*

There is no objective reality in Sarraute's universe. There are
only subjective impressions in a perpetual state of flux. As Proust
pointed out, "It must be remembered that the opinions we have of
one another, our relationships of friendship and family, are fixed
in appearance only; they are everlastingly in motion like the sea."[12]

The indetermination of character in Sarraute's books stems from
the fact that there is no objective point of view, no omniscient
author to guarantee authenticity. There is only a narrative con-

sciousness that projects onto other people his own fears and uncertainties. The depiction of Martereau illustrates this tendency. At the outset, he seems to be a strong, self-confident person, with the unruffled poise of an English country gentleman — a cliché-image that is reinforced by the mental Gainesborough portrait the narrator paints, posing him in imagined harmony with his wife, his cherubic children, his pony and his setter. This inflated picture serves the narrator's inner needs, regardless of external "reality." As the book progresses, his conception of Martereau changes. The solid personality is gradually decomposed, as the narrator endows him with the troubling anxieties that infest his own psyche and identifies Martereau's reactions with those he feels himself. At the end, there are no assurances of who or what the "real" Martereau is. The character has become hazy, out of focus, like a photograph that has been double-exposed.

Moreover, the side-by-side coexistence of contradictory aspects of personality is not an impossibility. This is not the physical world, where a choice must be made between two mutually exclusive assertions: if A is true, then non-A must be false. Martereau is (or can be) both the indomitable figure the narrator pictured him to be at first, or the vacillating sycophant he later imagines he is. He can be both a paragon of honesty and an intriguing schemer. He can be the adulterous seducer of the narrator's aunt, or not. He is all and none of these at the same time. He is a composite of all the views anyone has ever had of him. He is indefinable.

Aesthetic opinions are just as illusionary as character judgments. Standards of physical beauty differ according to subjective norms. Alain Guimier and his father quarrel heatedly over the question of Germaine Lemaire's beauty. In the words of the marquis de Sade, "The mirror sees the man as beautiful, the mirror loves the man; another mirror sees the man as frightful and hates him; and it is always the same being who produces the impression."[13] A similar subjectivity governs the aesthetic standards applied to a book *(The Golden Fruits)* or a work of art *(Do You Hear Them?)*.

Since reality is subjective, physical description is irrelevant. A character's external appearance is rarely given. Occasionally, the reader is apprised of some physical characteristic (a rounded back, a "simian" face) or some particularity of speech (the daughter's habit of sniffing, or the father's clipped, staccato way of posing questions, in *Portrait*), but these idiosyncrasies serve as the tiny hints Sarraute has dropped to help the reader orient himself in an unfamiliar world; in her later books, they will disappear. Near the end of *Portrait,* the narrator catches sight of his reflection in a shop window; this is the only intimation of his outward appearance: a pot-bellied, balding little man with a bedraggled air. It is significant that he is seen merely as a reflection in a glass, just as his character is perceived in the image reflected in other people's eyes.

Even when it comes to factual data, there is no concrete reality. It is not only *The Lie* that obfuscates the line between fact and fiction by creating uncertainty as to what actually occurred and what one person insists took place. Objective reality is blurred, beginning with Sarraute's earliest books. Real events often fuse with the expectation or remembrance of their happening. A series of imagined scenes in *Portrait,* purely speculative on the narrator's part, are presented with the immediacy of real occurrences. Five mutually incompatible scenes, revealing Martereau in five contradictory guises, all bear the same degree of authenticity. A courtroom scene in *Do You Hear Them?,* patently a fantasy on the father's part, is indistinguishable from the recapitulation of actual experience. Sometimes the same conversation, the same incident, is reproduced from a different point of view, in a technique reminiscent of the films *Rashomon* and *Last Year at Marienbad.* Even two people's recollections of a speech may vary, as any courtroom lawyer (like Nathalie Sarraute) can attest. This duplication of scenes permits the acceptance of conflicting versions of "reality," all of which have equal validity.

VII   *Conversation and Subconversation*

Just as there is no black-on-white delineation of external events or character, so there is no clear-cut distinction between unexpressed and vocalized thoughts — what Sarraute refers to as "subconversation" and "conversation." "Subconversation" represents the half-formed thoughts and feelings that accompany the words we speak aloud. It is the medium through which hidden tropisms are expressed.

Subconversation is not to be confused with "interior monologue," a form that was popularized by James Joyce and Virginia Woolf. Interior monologue was always a dialogue that the subject carried on with himself, almost exactly as he might have expressed himself aloud; the words came consciously to mind, but did not escape his mouth. Subconversation arises within the subconscious regions of the psyche, where it is not yet structured in dialogue form; still groping its way into language, it is barely expressible in words.[14]

Sarraute's books consist of an interplay between subconversation and surface dialogue. There is no exposition of background and no narration of events, but merely a running series of sensations and perceptions inside the narrative consciousness, whether singular or pluralized. The passage from unspoken thought to verbalized expression is accomplished imperceptibly. Quotation marks and conventional phrases like "he said" and "she replied" are suppressed as cumbersome contrivances that create an artificial gulf between the reader and the characters. It is only by the most tenuous of indications — through subtle changes in rhythm and form — that the reader, situated within the character's mind, is made to realize that a transition has been effected from internal thought to external utterance.

Surface conversation is artificial, insincere, a tissue of platitudes that conceal genuine feelings. The prevalence of clichés in Sarraute's writing is not merely a literal rendition of contemporary dialogue, to whose idiomatic usage she is acutely attuned (if this were her only purpose — to copy "reality" — her writing would be unbearably tedious). Banalities of expression serve a more important aim. By exchanging innocuous trivialities of speech, the façade of intercourse is preserved, while nothing is actually said. Clichés are communications devoid of substance, an accepted currency with no intrinsic value. As Sartre pointed out, this is "the realm of the commonplace," in all its significance (*Portrait,* p. ix). The exchange of "commonplaces" (*lieux communs* in French) refers not only to the hackneyed words that come to everyone's lips; it also designates the common meeting-ground of the community, a neutral terrain where people can come together without engaging their inner selves.

Subconversation provides a corrective commentary on spoken conversation, which is banal and inauthentic, artificial and insincere. As Michel Butor observed in his discussion of *The Planetarium:*

Wherever we are, whomever we are with, in our conversation we lie; no sooner have we pronounced certain words than we begin to regret them: that's not what I wanted to say, not exactly, I should have said.... Thus every word we speak is surrounded, commented on or contradicted, amplified or attenuated, by a swarm of words that we fail to utter. These words have a prolonged resonance inside us which may cause them to e-rupt a few days later in a story or an echo — like a bubble that bursts on the surface of a pond and causes ripples to spread to the furthest shore.[15]

The silent thoughts and feelings that accompany conversation pervade the ceaseless murmur of subconversation.

VIII   Portrait of a Man Unknown *(1948)*

When approaching the writing of her second book, Sarraute decided that instead of continuing to isolate individual tropisms in disconnected fragments, as she had done before, she would take a familiar situation or relationship and uncover the countless tropisms that lurk beneath the surface. She chose a situation similar to the one depicted by Balzac in *Eugénie Grandet,* with two central characters who might be described in a traditional novel as a "miser" and his "spinster" daughter. It is Sarraute's aim to decompose these labels and to determine the kinds of inner movements and feelings that motivate someone whom others call a "miser." She enters directly into the relationship between father and daughter to scrutinize at close range the ingredients of their interaction: their intertwined needs for domination and dependence, their alternate feelings of affection and estrangement, their mutual possessiveness. With careful insistence, she unravels the gossamer threads that bind them more tightly than bands of steel.

It is not Sarraute the author who seeks out the secret tropisms. She has delegated this role to a first-person narrator, who functions as a recording device with an exquisite sensitivity to his own and other people's feelings. He is endowed with what he himself calls a "supernatural flair." He can sense the presence of father and daughter, even before he sees them, by the anxiety and excitement that grip him when they are nearby. All three are keenly receptive to one another's reactions. The girl has presentiments that warn her of the narrator's approach, and the father has a "subtle flair" of his own for ferreting out the narrator's weaknesses.

The book can almost be considered the story of a quest: the narrator's obsessive attempt to *know* the father and daughter, not superficially but in the deepest recesses of their relationship. His pursuit follows a circuitous pattern of approach, like the ever-narrowing circles a hound describes in chasing and finally cornering its quarry. At first "they" are merely the subject of his discussions with other people. Next, he senses their presence in public places, in a crowded room or at the theater. He glimpses them from afar. When he first sees "her" alone, it is an accidental meeting on the street, and she quickens her pace to avoid him. The narrator follows her in his mind's eye to the dingy apartment where "he" sits waiting. Unable to follow her into the room, the narrator feels he is "losing touch," and when she later emerges, red-eyed, he can only guess at what has taken place: she must have been asking for money, which "he" refused. Gradually, the narrator circles in on them. He meets the girl in a restaurant, joins them both for luncheon, visits them at home. What he cannot directly observe, he tries to visualize. Eventually he is present (in a spiritual sense) at their most intimate moments together. But in the end he comes to realize that his insatiable wish cannot be fulfilled. In the final analysis, it is impossible to "know" another person in the infinite convolutions of his personality and in the permutations of his relationships with others. The narrator's searchings, his trials and errors, the obstacles he encounters, his frustrations, his repeated endeavors, his small triumphs and his ultimate failure, provide the momentum of the novel.

The narrator's quest is also an experiment in creativity. In a way, he serves as the author's *alter ego*; his discoveries parallel her own. His frustrated but persistent attempts to define the father and daughter echo the novelist's experience in creating characters. Not satisfied with the superficial judgments he overhears, that "he's a selfish old man . . . she's just a crank" (*Portrait,* p. 19), he is determined to crack open these convenient labels and arrive at the essence of their personalities. But he finds them elusive, impossible to grasp. Alone among his entourage, he divines a world of hidden movements beneath the most trivial words and actions. Like Sarraute, he feels compelled to penetrate this miasmic region, where he guesses he will find the key to the characters he is pursuing.

As if recapitulating Sarraute's earliest experience in writing, he has a "vision" — like a scene lifted bodily out of *Tropisms* — of young girls and women enveloping aspiring suitors with the soft, curling tentacles of their hidden desires, building their nests or spinning cocoons out of the hackneyed shreds of old books, plays, films, corny advertisements, and ladies' magazines. This discovery at first overjoys him, as if it provided the means of grappling with character (Sarraute's approach in *Tropisms*), until he is discouraged by an old friend (someone he calls his "alter ego"), who minimizes the effectiveness of this technique.

The narrator's sensitivity to the tropisms underlying the three-way relationship among father, daughter, and himself enables him on occasion to imagine their feelings, even to visualize a brief scene or two between them. He senses the mask the father dons in his daughter's presence; he even surmises the reason: it is a means of containing the threatening explosion of his love. The narrator suspects that the father has always worn this mask, which he may first have assumed when she was an infant:

[...] at the moment, doubtless, when he heard for the first time her stubborn, strident cry; or perhaps, even at the moment when, as he leaned over the cradle the better to see her, he felt the downy, aggressive outline of her overwide nostrils, distended upwards as she cried, pierce through him and pain him, the way the silken edge of certain sharp grasses cuts insidiously into the flesh (p. 62).

The narrator has allowed his imagination to re-create this scene out of the past, just as he tells his friend he has pictured the encounter between them (described in the kind of imagery that Sarraute favors): "I can see [...] them with their foreheads pressed together in close combat, hunched up in their shells, in their heavy armor.... The blind, relentless struggle of two giant insects, two enormous dung beetles..." (p. 47).

The narrator vacillates between the desire to define their characters in a traditional way and his realization that this is impossible — at least for him. In a way, he would like to see the "trembling shadows" and "ghosts" he is vainly trying to seize take on the firm outlines of Tolstoyan characters like Prince Bolkonski and his daughter, Marie; he would like to view each of them as "a finished, perfect whole, entirely enclosed on every side, a solid, hard block, without a single fissure" (pp. 67–68). He might even venture giving them a name to identify them: this would provide them with substance and consistency. But it would only be wasted effort on his part: "Rich ornaments, warm colors, soothing certainties, the fresh sweetness of 'life,' are not for me," he sighs (p. 68), as if speaking with the author's voice.

In frustration and despair, he consults a "specialist," to whom he recounts the painful fascination "they" exert upon him. The visit can be interpreted as a psychoanalytic session to cure the narrator of his neurosis (though Sarraute is careful not to call the specialist a psychiatrist or even a doctor); it can also be viewed as the opposition of two conflicting theories of literature, symbolic of the writer's dilemma.[16] The "symptoms" of which the narrator complains reflect Sarraute's own artistic preoccupations: the sensitivity to hidden "effluvia" or "currents," the effort to probe behind masks and clichés, the predominant role played by (imagined) "scenes," even the tendency to omit names. Although the specialist insists that he is no art critic, the advice he hands out is like a negative "critique" of the nonconventional novel Sarraute is writing: make your characters "living," concrete, tangible; avoid "sterile musings" and "insubstantial" ideas that are not a suitable subject for art; beware of a tendency toward "introspection" and "idle daydreaming"; remain in contact with "reality"; remember that "the role of all creative effort in the arts is, precisely, to clothe abstraction" (p. 75).

The immediate effect of this consultation on the narrator is to make the "characters" harden in his mind like painted cardboard dolls. As he begins to "recuperate," he grows accustomed to moving docilely in a world of bright outlines and shapes, far from the somber, viscous regions in which he had been plunged with "them." Then, just as he seems definitively "cured," a visit to a museum in a foreign city affords him a revelation that redirects his efforts and gives his quest a renewed impetus.

He is curiously attracted to an unsigned painting entitled "Portrait of a Man Unknown." Everything about the subject is vague, fragmented, uncertain; the outlines are sketchy, as if groped for haltingly by a blind man. Only the eyes appear finished, concentrating in their intense gaze all the life that is missing from the other, half-formed features. They rivet the narrator's attention with their insistent and silent appeal. Simultaneously, he experiences a sudden feeling of liberation and joy.

The significance of the portrait is not immediately discernible, and the narrator's elation is at first as inexplicable as Marcel's surge of happiness upon tasting the *madeleine* described by Proust. The symbolism becomes apparent only when this museum visit is juxtaposed with two other painting scenes. The first is a fantasy of the narrator and his *alter ego* in which they pretend that one day, while strolling through a museum, they come across a painting, hung next to *Portrait of Madame X* or *Girl with Parrot,* which is immediately recognizable as the narrator's work — an "exquisite portrait" of the daughter, clearly titled *Hypersensitive Girl,* Fed-on-Clichés. (This episode stems from the period when the narrator still nurtured the hope of being able to capture the daughter's essense in neatly defined categories.) The second scene reveals a complete reversal of attitude. While viewing a Manet exhibit in the daughter's company, the narrator expresses his preference for works that are less self-assured and complacent, more tentative in their approach, like the unsigned portrait of an unknown man he has seen in a Dutch museum:

I believe that rather than the most perfectly finished works I prefer those in which complete mastery has not been attained... in which one still feels, just beneath the surface, a sort of anxious groping [...] before the immensity... the elusiveness of the material world... that escapes us just when we think we have got hold of it... the goal that's never attained... the insufficiency of the means at our disposal... (p. 201).

From an earlier insistence on attaining certainties about people, despite his intuitive recognition of their amorphous qualities, he arrives at the realization — through the half-finished portrait — that in order to achieve an authentic representation of character one must be satisfied with shadows, ambiguities, and wavering shapes. The joyous freedom he experiences after his visit to the museum is a liberation from the shackles of a conventional approach, as the narrator — like the author — prepares to make a new attempt at characterization.

The revelation of the portrait marks a turning-point in the narrator's quest. From being a simple observer, he becomes a creator. Whereas previously he had depended for his knowledge of father and daughter on what he witnessed for himself or what other people told him, he now realizes that he contains within himself the resources to complete the picture. In order to supplant what he cannot personally observe, it is no longer necessary to rely on anecdotes and gossip. He need no longer try to track down and surprise his quarry in a moment of weakness or abandonment in order to arrive at the tropisms that constitute their essence. He need only have recourse to his own imagination. To understand what is occurring in the subterranean zones of their relationship, it is sufficient to envision the hidden dramas taking place. Discarding the "impossible realism" he had struggled to obtain, he enters the domain of hypothesis and conjecture.[17] He thereby takes the step required of every would-be artist: he crosses the fragile boundary separating "fact" from "fiction" and becomes not the recorder but the "creator" of character (like Sarraute herself).

In taking the leap, the narrator presents the products of his imagination in exactly the way a writer presents fiction — not merely as hypothesis, but as reality, *his* reality. In a way, this is what makes the next scenes so disconcerting to the unalerted reader. There is no apparent distinction between objective reality and the narrator's imaginings. His account of scenes at which he could not possibly be present might at first appear to resemble scenes related by an omniscient author. But this is not the case. The narrator never rises above his position as a character confined within the novel, and it is up to the reader to realize that some of what he tells is purely "fictitious," i.e., his private conjecture ("fiction" twice removed, like a play-within-a-play).

The imaginary scenes that follow become increasingly ambitious and complex as the narrator exercises his newfound creative prowess. At first, he recalls something he has heard about an angry scene the father made in a restaurant — and he finds he is able to reconstruct in detail the incident, the occasion, the surrounding circumstances, and even the possible feelings that precipitated the outburst. Following this venture, he conjures up a scene between the father and an old friend, half-glimpsed in a suburban railroad station. As the smoke from the train renders the physical scene invisible, the narrator's mind takes over the function of seeing, and he continues to accompany them in their train ride to Paris, overhearing their conversation and probing it for tropisms. From this imagined incident, the narrator proceeds to others, in which he attempts to perceive the old man's motivations from *inside,* in a process of identification similar to the writer's experience in creating character. Beneath the father's pretense of calm, the narrator surmises the obsessions and torments that haunt his sleep: his worry that his daughter is fleecing him, draining him of his life savings. To verify his fears, the father springs out of bed in the middle of the night and finds irrefutable proof that his daughter has been robbing him, for a large end has been cut off a bar of soap. (This is almost like a scene out of *Eugénie Grandet,* perceived from Grandet's point of view — or rather, reported by someone trying to see with Grandet's eyes.)

These preparatory "exercises" precede the major confrontation,

the crucial scene between father and daughter that crystallizes their
relationship and brings all the narrator's creative abilities into play.
It is almost a *reprise* of the earlier incident when he tried to follow
the daughter to her apartment, only to "lose touch." This time he
is present (in spirit) throughout her encounter with her father, not
only hearing the harsh words they say, but also registering the feelings that underlie speech. He sees their battle as a combat between
two huge insects, locked in a fierce embrace: "They were standing
firmly, brow to brow, heavy and awkward, in their rigid carapaces,
their heavy armor — two giant insects, two enormous dung
beatles..." (p. 174).

Both parties are reinforced in their mutual antagonisms by the
protective forces of society. She has come to ask for six thousand
francs for a massage cure that has been recommended for her ail-
ments. He laughs at the preposterous enormity of her request, ac-
cusing her of hypochondria and self-indulgence. Each is supported
by an imaginary cohort of adherents: while she leans on a band of
gossipy crones who cluck sympathetically and call him a selfish old
miser, he is backed up by the ranks of his contemporaries,
mouthing platitudes about the ingratitude and greed of the younger
generation.

The struggle is all the more intense because it is not unique, but a
repeated situation — almost a game (a "war game") whose rules
are acknowledged ahead of time. The combat is not only consented
to, it is deliberately sought out. This typical love-hate ambivalence
is so pervasive, the interdependence so inescapable, that each person is able to attack the other in the most vulnerable part of his
being, and is least able to shield himself from hurt. There is a sensual quality to the torment inflicted. As the father humiliates the
daughter with his accusations — she is a parasite, she should look
for a husband to take care of her, but she is too homely, no one will
have her — he experiences "the painful, sickening voluptuousness
of a maniac, the kind that takes one's breath away, that one feels
when one presses one's own abscess between two fingers to make
the pus spurt out, or when one tears off bit by bit the scab of a
wound" (p. 187). His cruel words provide him with an exquisite
suffering, a sadomasochistic relish. The scene escalates in intensity
and recriminations until finally the father throws the daughter out,
physically. She wimpers through the keyhole, and he tosses her a
sheaf of banknotes, which she pockets with satisfaction.

After this momentous scene visualized by the narrator — and

which may or may not correspond to "reality" — when next he catches sight of father and daughter, they are in the company of a third party, who turns out to be her fiancé. The newcomer is endowed with a name (Louis Dumontet), a profession, and a complete physical description, down to the bunion on his toe (like the wen on old Grandet's nose), as if he were a character from a nineteenth-century novel. By his sole presence among them, he arrests the tropisms that have occupied the narrator's attention. The latter finds himself back in the "real world," where finances and mortgages are discussed, plans are made, and banalities are passed like hard currency from hand to hand.

After the daughter exits with Dumontet, father and narrator are left alone. But all the old awareness has died:

I no longer felt, as I used to, that he was palpating and probing me in order to discover my most sensitive spot. There was nothing left in me that excited him, or even incited him to try to provoke me. No matter how closely I listened, I could no longer catch the old resonances in our conversation, the old echoings and reechoings that used to plunge so deep down inside us (p. 219).

Everything the father says has hardened into the form of old gramophone records, a series of clichés endlessly repeated: Time is passing. He is getting older. It is time his daughter were married. Late marriages often work out best. The narrator feels a slight spell of nausea, a passing dizziness, as he wonders if the old man really believes what he is saying. But the mumbled words have a soothing, incantatory power, like prayer. Eventually, when he learns to recite them, the narrator will be received into the "faith." Old women will no longer be afraid to gossip in his presence. The old man is a selfish egotist, a miser, they will say, and he will nod in pious agreement. Life will take on a clear, unperturbed aspect, "akin to the air of serene purity that the faces of people are always said to assume after death" (p. 223).

Faced with the insatiable need to "know," for a brief moment the narrator had become a "creator" of character. But the exertion proved too strenuous, and he failed in his supreme attempt. Perhaps father and daughter were not what he had imagined at all. The final scene with Dumontet seemed to knock down the intricate scaffolding he had constructed. At the end, with a touch of giddiness as the last tropisms fade away, he is ready to relinquish his pursuit and retreat into the reassuring world of appearances. He is prepared to accept objective reality, with its labels and clichés. His experiment in creativity has aborted. The figure of Louis Dumontet, who effectively destroys all inner movements, consigns the characters to the realm of the superficial, the "inauthentic," back to the domain of the traditional novel.

IX   Martereau *(1953)*

Martereau begins where *Portrait* left off. Sarraute says she conceived of her next book as a continuation of or complement to its predecessor. Where *Portrait* ends with the introduction of a conventional character, impervious to "inner movements," *Martereau* starts out with a similarly solid personality, who dissolves into a mass of tropistic possibilities. Sarraute calls Martereau "the Mr. Dumontet from the *Portrait of a Man Unknown*." For some trivial reason he arouses suspicion, and this marks the beginning of his disintegration: "Through this tiny hole which has been made in the solid shell that protects all characters in life and in novels, through this narrow chink, the narrator sees that Martereau is activated by the same movements. He is as people are, not in traditional novels, but in real life."[18] It is the shifting perception of Martereau in the narrator's mind that constitutes the movement of the novel.

In this case there is a rudimentary storyline, but so scanty that a mere summary sounds lifeless and flat. The narrator lives with his aunt and uncle, who decide to buy a country villa. In a maneuver to avoid taxes, the uncle asks the narrator's friend, Martereau, to make the purchase ostensibly in his own name. Because Martereau fails to furnish a receipt for the uncle's cash payment, he is suspected of double-dealing. The narrator is tormented by his friend's imagined fraud. At the end, a letter from Martereau allays suspicion, but the narrator finds it difficult to view him in the same light as before.

The tiny threads of plot are unimportant; they serve simply as pretexts for an assortment of inner movements whose development constitutes the novel's interest. Because the field of interaction has broadened, the combinations of relationships offer rich variety. Like a novice who begins by juggling three balls, then adds a few more, and, when successful, incorporates a medley of objects, Sarraute keeps adding to her stock of characters and blending them in increasingly intricate ways.

The action is once again perceived through the eyes of a first-person narrator, who is also involved as a participant in the relationships he records. In many respects he is the blood brother of the narrator in *Portrait*: in his sensitivity, his timidity, his awareness of tropisms. His inclination to explore hidden motivations is ranked by others as a sign of weakness or illness. The narrator of *Portrait* was told to consult a "specialist" to overcome his obsession. The narrator of *Martereau* supposedly is an invalid on the path to recovery (we do not know the nature of his malady except that Martereau calls it the "rich man's disease," as if it were some shameful, parasitic ailment). His hypersensitivity is attributed to his illness:

It's because of my health that I am here, for obvious reasons of health, on the advice of my doctors that I live this sort of muffled, slow-motion existence [...] this "mother of all vice," that keeps alive in me my idle musings and gives me that sensitiveness — abetted by my physical weakness — of a hysterical woman, as well as a morbid sense of guilt.[19]

More is known about him than about the narrator of *Portrait*. He is situated in the midst of his family (aunt, uncle, and cousin), among whom he is accused of leading a "nonproductive" life. Though he bears no name, he has a professional identity: interior decorator. His profession is not internalized in any degree of aesthetic appreciation (when the family contemplates the purchase of a country home, he has no eye for color or furnishings, no flair for the possibilities of décor); rather, its effete and "feminine" overtones provide a contrast to the solid, "virile" success of his uncle's business.

In their receptivity to tropisms, the two narrators are alike. But where the narrator of *Portrait* was motivated by a desire to "know" other people, the narrator of *Martereau* is impelled by a wish to win approval and acceptance. His awareness of tropisms is a matter of self-preservation and defense. He is continually observing people, trying to discover what they are thinking and feeling about him. In his febrile attempts to secure his uncle's favor, he is alert to the slightest signs of rejection: "I keep palpating, searching him, inspecting his every cranny, I spy upon him with the anxious attention of a sick person watching for symptoms of his ailment. I feel his slightest reaction in advance" (p. 143). Like the narrator of *Portrait,* he supplies in imagination what he cannot directly perceive. In his case, however, it is not a question of

"creating" personality, but of forestalling disapproval. He endeavors to "get close" to the members of his family and to
Martereau, even if it means offering himself up to ridicule and
scorn; he ingratiates himself like a fawning dog, ready to accept
whatever position of compromise or servility will help him attain
the illusive complicity for which he yearns (like the obsequious
character in *Tropism IX*). His constraints, his doubts about himself, his hesitations and self-consciousness deprive him of self-identity. He becomes nothing but the reflection of other people's
expectations.

The narrator is not merely receptive to tropisms; he activates
them in other people. He is a "spoilsport," a "catalyzer," whose
uncontrollable agitation incites a similar reaction in others (p. 104).
He "fishes in troubled water," disturbing the calm surface and
churning up the depths (p. 60). By his very nature, he seems to draw
forth tropistic responses:

It is doubtless precisely this strange passivity, this sort of docility which I
have never succeeded in explaining very well to myself, that excites them
and makes them secrete irresistibly, when they come into contact with me,
a substance like that which certain animals eject in order to blind their
prey... (p. 2).

Once again the family is the privileged milieu for the flowering
tropisms. It is primarily in his relationship with his uncle and aunt
that the narrator's supersensitivity comes to the fore. Similarly, it is
only when Martereau becomes intimately involved with the
"family" — embroiled in the uncle's financial dealings — that his
upright character begins to break down. It is as if he were sullied by
exposure to their insidious milieu, where all motives are complex,
all actions suspect, all words layered with hidden meanings. With
Dumontet, the opposite effect took place. It was at the moment he
came on the scene to remove the daughter from her family, to res-
cue her from her intimate dependence on her father, that the
tropistic undercurrents disappeared.

The narrator cannot remain aloof, even if he tries. He is used as a
pawn in the infighting that takes place. These are no polite parlor
pastimes, but "the blood-letting games of the arena" (p. 60). One
day, while the family is dining together in a restaurant, his aunt
calls his attention to a woman in a large, outlandish hat, who is
seated nearby. Innocuous on the surface, this remark sets in motion

a multitude of alarming ripples. The uncle, excluded from the featherbrained chirpings of mother and daughter, has attempted to enlist his nephew in a virile counteralliance. The narrator suddenly finds himself trapped between two enemy camps. By the simple motion of following his aunt's direction and turning his head, he enters into a "degrading promiscuity," an "ignominious comradeship" with the women, and earns his uncle's contempt (p. 24).

There is a constant shifting of loyalties and realignment of forces. One day the aunt engages her nephew's sympathy by issuing a series of complaints against her daughter; with a smothering connivance, they "dissect" the girl's imperfections, like a pair of surgeons amputating a diseased limb (p. 58). But immediately afterwards, the mother and daughter come downstairs arm in arm. They have been "rewelded," their alliance revived, and the narrator concludes that he is the "designated prey" whom his aunt has fed her daughter to seal their bond of intimacy (p. 59).

The terms "aunt," "uncle," "cousin" seldom occur within the text. They are used here for the sake of convenience. In the narrator's mind he rarely refers to them otherwise than by a pronoun: "he," "she," or "they." The characters are introduced anonymously, in their relationship to the narrative consciousness. When the book begins, as if a door had opened, the reader finds himself, with the narrator, deep in conversation with a woman whom he apparently knows well. To the reader, their relationship is a mystery. To the narrator, the insider, everything is perfectly clear — so clear as to require no explanation. The reader, situated within the narrator's consciousness, must willy-nilly adopt his point of view, including the knowledge of who his companion is. All that is evident is the narrator's excessive sensitivity to her reactions. In fact, like a machine clicking off her pulse rate or blood pressure, he registers the stages marking her growing self-assurance and power. The question of identity is secondary. Their tropistic interactions receive the focus of attention. The conscientious reader, however, will find scattered through the text occasional references to "my husband" or "your uncle" — references which, when juxtaposed, like snapshots taken from differing perspectives, turn out to refer to the same person, and establish the narrator's relationship to the woman.

The first chapter serves to "set the scene." It is a form of exposition — not in the traditional sense, in terms of background, character description, or physical décor; rather, it is a means of conveying relationships and feelings. These are never static, but perpetually in a state of transition. Like a running stream whose waters are never still but which itself remains changeless, the attitudes and interactions among the family members are continually fluctuating, while retaining essentially the same form. It is the introduction of an outsider into their midst that precipitates a brand-new set of tropisms.

Martereau appears in the second chapter, almost in answer to the narrator's yearning:

It was not by chance that I met Martereau. [. . .] We make a mistake to think that we're going to stumble against people haphazardly. I always have the feeling that we are the ones who make them spring forth: they appear at a given spot as though made to measure, to order, and they correspond exactly (often we don't realize this until much later) to needs in us, to desires that are at times unavowed or unconscious. [...] I've always been seasrching for Martereau. His image — now I realize it — has always haunted me (pp. 70-71).

The narrator had already hinted at his longing for a more stable family relationship. In the previous restaurant scene he had glimpsed a father and son, whom he imagined walking through a meadow in idyllic harmony. In his mind, they represented his uncle and himself — not as they are, with their chaotic complex of possibilities, but as he would like them to be, simple, uncomplicated, in perfect accord. This idealized vision is followed, in the next scene, by an actual walk with his uncle through a meadow — a nightmarish outing, marked by fear and humiliation, consternation and anxiety.

In contrast to the undependable figures of his family, with their sudden metamorphoses from friend to enemy, Martereau provides the comforting assurance of stability:

He was the distant mother-country from which, for mysterious reasons, I had been banished; the home port, the peaceful haven, to which I had lost the way; the land on which I could never go ashore, tossed as I was on a rough sea, drifting constantly with the changing currents (p. 71).

There is nothing dubious or complex about Martereau. Nothing uncertain or suspicious lurks behind the gaze of his clear eyes. His hearty handshake is like the laying on of hands, the exorcism of baleful influences. His sole presence is sufficient to put tropisms to rest.

Martereau is the incarnation of a cliché. The narrator pictures him in the tranquil setting of an English countryside — always a symbol of serenity for Sarraute — feeding his pony, patting the neck of his favorite setter. His speech is a patchwork of platitudes, his sentiments a sugary concoction of commonplace feelings. The snapshots with his wife in their photograph album represent a model of marital devotion. The narrator willingly accepts this paper-mâché façade as the sign of a three-dimensional substance. He sees Martereau as a distinctive creature, a rarefied being, inhabiting a different world from his family and himself.

Tropisms are intertwined with dramatic action. Each new development in the "story" hinges on these inner movements. It is not only surface events that precipitate tropisms; tropisms themselves can activate events. This continuous process from internal to external action, and vice versa, furnishes the momentum that propels the novel forward, in the absence of a conventional plot.

Every step in this progression is preconditioned and prepared by the narrator's feelings, especially his sensitivity to his uncle's moods and his need for approval. Even his suggestion to enlist Martereau's aid is prompted by the desire to impress his uncle with his solidity and good sense. The uncle's delight with the country house Martereau locates for him is counteracted by the aunt's tight-lipped disapproval. For days she subjects her husband to the "silent treatment" (a form of punishment she has perfected). The state of siege continues between them until the uncle adopts a winning stratagem: he uses his daughter as a weapon to achieve victory over his wife. In an uncharacteristic show of confidence in the young girl's judgment, he asks her to perform an important service for him: he has to leave town on business, and in his absence he asks her and his nephew to arrange with Martereau to purchase the house in his name. The narrator is delighted at this sign of his uncle's esteem, but his elation is short-lived. When the uncle returns some weeks later and learns that they failed to ask Martereau for a receipt, his anger and incredulity cut through the narrator like an icy blast. The latter runs to see Martereau for reassurance, but his friend is not at home. When he later spies Martereau on the street, the latter passes him without a glance. The narrator fears he has been purposely snubbed, and insidious doubts form in his mind. Like a pendulum swinging from one extreme to the other, he is now sure that Martereau deliberately withheld a receipt.

Martereau had constituted for the narrator a smooth, solid

Each of these variants marks an increasing breakdown of Martereau's self-confidence, a deterioration in his relationship with the narrator's uncle, and a disintegration of his idyllic marriage. Each represents a deeper incursion into the world of tropisms, until at last Martereau enters completely into those subterranean regions from which the narrator had for so long excluded him.

Every view of Martereau is dependent on the narrator's contradictory and ambivalent perceptions. The need to assimilate Martereau into his own insalubrious element had overshadowed the desire to maintain Martereau intact. In his tangled imaginings, he had been weaving an "intangible, trembling web" in which to "catch" the other man (like the spidery father waiting to trap his daughter in *Portrait*): "I wanted to crush him slowly, to agglutinate him, to make of him the formless, mushy, ever so insipid substance that we are made of here, the same that I feed upon" (p. 202). Now, to correct this version of Martereau and reestablish his dominance, the narrator recalls their visit to the country villa; the sensation that they were reenacting a scene out of Kafka's *Trial*, with Martereau one of the dark-dressed "gentlemen" escorting him, restores Martereau to a clear-cut position of authority. The narrator is pleased to see him again as a solid entity, even if it means pinning on him a new label: "swindler" and "crook."

The narrator apprises his uncle of a "fact" he has learned, that Martereau was in collusion with the owner of the villa to dupe him:

I feel again the delightful sense of security that Martereau has always given me. From one fact to the other, my thought stretches clear, direct, the shortest road. Joining one of the exactly situated points to the other, it outlines a drawing that has all the precision of a geometrical figure. One look suffices: the definition is evident. No doubt is possible. Martereau is a crook (p. 207).

From perpetrating one crime, the narrator speedily convicts Martereau of committing another. He becomes convinced that the other man is his aunt's adulterous lover. This new role for Martereau activates a different order of tropisms, which enfold Martereau within the family milieu. This time it is the aunt who has "betrayed" her husband, just as the narrator had betrayed Martereau and his uncle before. The situation is enacted (in the narrator's mind) with all the clarity and realism of a scene from a play, with each actor conforming to his assigned role. But — as if conscious of the artificiality of this strobe-lighted certainty — when the narrator next sees his aunt and Martereau together, he finds the whole thing unreal, "a bit too stagey" (p. 216). Ill at ease among bright lights and strong currents, preferring his "natural element," the "putrid ooze that quivers on the bottom of stagnant waters," the narrator sinks into the flickering uncertainties of his fantasizing (p. 220).

There is a review and revision of earlier scenes, like the corrective retouching of memory: the excursion to the villa under Martereau's escort becomes the parade of three prisoners with shaven heads being conducted from the Tuileries to the Temple under the jeers of the rabble; the narrator's visit to Madame Martereau is no longer marked by the welcome extended to an honored guest but by the brutal treatment accorded a hostage, who is kicked into a corner by a proud and arrogant Martereau. In each of these recollected scenes, Martereau regains his lost strength, his dominance, his assertiveness. A letter he writes explaining everything — he is giving back the house as of October 15, he has only occupied it so as to watch over its renovation, the bills are all in order, etc. — restores his purity and normality in the narrator's eyes. The latter admits having momentarily indulged the fancy that Martereau was like "them," subject to their changing moods and wavering motives. But Martereau has remained as steadfast and dependable as the narrator secretly wished him to be. He is just as he appears in his actions and words; nothing lies hidden beneath the surface. He is utterly blank, like a sheet of white paper (p. 238). Martereau at the end has come full circle, back to the place he first occupied in the narrator's mind.

But not quite. The peaceful picture of Martereau fishing in the closing scene threatens once more to disintegrate, as the narrator imagines something odd in Martereau's tone of voice — a slight hissing, an acrid jet of steam — while the harmless words dissolve between them, enveloped in "heavy gases, unwholesome emanations" (p. 243). The narrator is uncertain whether the disturbance arises from his reaction to Martereau or Martereau's reaction to himself. How much is his "creation" (as in *Portrait*), how much is external reality? So completely has he tinted Martereau with his own protective coloration that they have become reflections of one another:

I absorb, I become impregnated, as usual, I reproduce all his reactions, all the eddies, the uncoilings in him, within myself, or is it rather my own reactions that find repercussion in him? — I don't know, I never have known: a game of mirrors in which I lose my way — my image which I project into him, or the one he plasters immediately, savagely, on me, the way the other man, my uncle, does, and beneath which I smother (p. 243).

This passage supplies a key to the three-way relationship uniting Martereau-uncle-narrator, a relationship that keeps decomposing and reshaping. At times the narrator senses that Martereau and his uncle are in league against him, at other times he and his uncle align themselves against Martereau, and he and Martereau even have an occasional chuckle at the uncle's expense (at the ridiculous idea of his skiing, for instance, at Saint Moritz).

To some extent, Martereau and the uncle function as "doubles." Their personalities shade into one another and blend. The strong, dominating Martereau is an idealized version of the uncle, uncontaminated by tropisms. The similarity between them is reinforced in tiny ways. When Martereau speaks, it is in the same hackneyed phrases the uncle uses — except that in Martereau's case the narrator accepts his clichés without analyzing their meaning. The model couple represented by Martereau and his wife are the obverse of the narrator's uncle and aunt. When Martereau becomes the aunt's lover, he assumes the uncle's position, even to the henpecked indulgence of her whims; the narrator pictures him cavorting like a clown or crowing like a rooster — the same images he had previously applied to his uncle. The two men are on a seesaw, evenly balanced; at one moment, the uncle is on top, dominating Martereau; the next moment, Martereau is in control, and the uncle is his pawn. There is no absolute distinction between them. Each participates partially in the other's substance.

Their duality represents the narrator's ideal of what he would himself like to be. He nurtures a "childish hope" of somehow resembling his uncle, in order to be accepted and feel at ease in his presence (p. 33). The reason he first suggests Martereau as an agent is to prove to his uncle that "I'm with him, like him, like he pretends to be, on the right side, in the world of real men" (p. 103). In the same way, he yearns to emulate Martereau, but the latter's perfection seems even more unattainable. Ironically, when he is unable to hoist himself up to this idealized image, he drags Martereau down to his own slippery level. Instead of the narrator's succeeding in becoming Martereau, it is Martereau who in turn becomes the narrator's "double" and assumes all his weaknesses — his sensitivity, timidity, self-consciousness, and self-doubt. Martereau loses the hard outlines of his identity and, like the narrator, becomes the mere shadow of other people's opinions: "He's so malleable, so dependent, tremulous, changeable... at each moment he's like the reflection of himself that he sees in people's eyes..." (p. 185). The narrator describes his own character in almost the same terms: "With me, so little is needed, I'm so malleable, a slight impulse suffices, a breath, to keep me at the desired distance..." (p. 153). He evokes his feelings and those of Martereau in similar imagery:

I have experienced exactly this before, I recognize the sensation: this uprooting, this rending, everything trembles, cracks, gapes open... I feel as though I were split in two, an icy blast rushes into me... (p. 146).

The crevice, a gaping hole, that Martereau had felt open up in him at moments during that evening, then close right away, reopened wide this time, an icy draft blew into it [...] (p. 183).

The recognition of Martereau's kinship with himself is a conviction the narrator cannot permanently sustain. In the end, a little tap from Martereau, like his uncle's sharp rap calling him to order when he tends to daydream, rescues him from the bog in which he was floundering. Forcibly, he reintegrates Martereau into the world of appearances, squelching the lingering doubts in his mind. The narrator's final glimpse of Martereau, sitting erect, absorbed in contemplating his fishhook, is of "kindliness and purity," serenity and calm. At the end, the disturbing tropisms are laid to rest, as they were in *Portrait*. Neither narrator has been sufficiently strong to overcome the gravity pull of habit and tradition. Unable to remain in the miasmic milieu of tropisms, they rise to breathe the clear, cold air of superficial "reality," and relapse once again into conventionality.

The titles Sarraute chooses for her works often have symbolic overtones. Both *Tropisms* and *Portrait of a Man Unknown* can be interpreted on two levels, literally and metaphorically. *Martereau* would appear to have no secondary significance beyond being the name of the title character. However, "Martereau" in itself evokes repercussions in French. It has a compact, "hard," definitive sound appropriate to the monolithic personality it is meant to represent. As Ruth Temple points out, it can be considered a composite of two French words: *marteau* (hammer) and *martyr*

(martyr). The "hammer" may refer not only to Martereau's blunt and forthright manner (before he has been "martyrized" by the narrator, sacrificed to ensure his relationship with his uncle); it is directly echoed in the uncle's advice that one must continually "hammer on the same nail" — a refrain he repeats six times in the text, almost as if he wanted to bludgeon or "hammer" Martereau into submission.[24]

Martereau is linked to the *corpus* of Sarraute's works through the repetition of certain situations and themes. Specific passages recall *Tropisms,* while others prefigure works to come. The gossiping aunt and cousin in the restaurant are reminiscent of the chirruping women in *Tropism X*; the comparison is strengthened by the "bird" imagery common to both. The family's tiptoeing fear of rousing the uncle's wrath recaptures the situation in *Tropism VII*. Martereau immobilized in a Gainesborough-type portrait translates the placid stereotype of *Tropism XVIII*. The narrator's futile attempt to steal down the hall and escape his aunt's watchful notice can almost be taken out of the context of *Tropism V*. His wariness of physical objects — their innate hostility and vague menace — is an echo of *Tropism XXIII*.

There are also intimations of incidents that will be developed in later books. For instance, in his subservience to the aunt, Martereau escorts her to tearooms, heaps platters high with dainty cakes for her consumption, then is cut to the quick by her razor-sharp glance at the small tip he has left (p. 246). In *"fools say,"* Sarraute holds this infinitesimal incident up to the light and examines it from a different angle, from the point of view of the humiliated bride whose love and admiration for her new husband are vitiated by her shame at his parcimonious tip. Another passage announces the subtitle of the play *Isma,* or *Ce qui s'appelle rien.* The uncle's suspiciously prompt compliance when asked to prolong his stay elicits a slight vibratory response in Martereau, which the narrator quickly qualifies, "It was nothing, what we call nothing..." (p. 188). The French words prefigure *Isma* precisely: "Ce n'etait rien, ce qui s'appelle rien." In each case, a minuscule cause triggers a momentous reaction. Elsewhere, there is a foretaste of *Do You Hear Them?*. The aunt is complaining to the nephew about her daughter's disinterest in art; while they are conversing, from the other side of the wall can be heard the sounds of laughter, "pitiless, piercing, peals of laughter and loud voices" (p. 47). This is a fleeting moment, which passes without repercussions. In the later book, Sarraute will go back and pick up this trivial incident, scrutinize it for the tropistic possibilities it contains, and inflate it into the basis for a full-scale novel.

X   The Planetarium *(1959)*

Frequently considered to be Sarraute's masterpiece, *The Planetarium* is her most popular book in English. (It is also her longest.) The novice reader is often advised to approach Sarraute by way of this novel, perhaps on the spurious grounds that it is the "easiest" to read. This assessment may be based on its superficial resemblance to a conventional-type novel. There is more of a plot than in her other works, more interwoven threads connecting people and incidents. The progression of the action is linear — events follow a straight chronological order rather than the circular patterns to be found in *The Golden Fruits* and *Between Life and Death,* or the amalgam of possibilities offered in *Portrait* and *Martereau.* There is an expanded "cast of characters" who are susceptible of being differentiated and identified, not only by name but by personality and relationships.

An immense "CAUTION" sign is mandatory at the outset. The appearance of conventionality is a deception, the kind of *trompe-l'oeil* effect Sarraute warns about in *The Age of Suspicion.* The unwary reader who takes the novel as a literal representation of reality will be as deceived as the famous birds of Zenon pecking away at a bowl of painted fruit or like an observer who accepts the artificial sky of a planetarium for the starry heavens overhead (but more about the symbolism of the title later). It is the tropisms, as always, that command Sarraute's attention, and any attempt to shift that emphasis to external events or characterization is a falsifying of her intentions.

The novel is structured around two motivational "dramas": Alain Guimier's attempt to gain possession of his aunt's apartment, and his endeavor to ingratiate himself with the writer, Germaine Lemaire. The ultimate achievement of these aims provides the "storyline," and the obstacles encountered along the way furnish the narrative "suspense." Such trifling concerns would appear to constitute the most unpromising raw material of fiction (as Germaine Lemaire herself hints to Alain). Nonetheless — like Alain Guimier holding his audience spellbound by narrating his aunt's egocentricities — Nathalie Sarraute extracts from the mediocre substance of daily living a full range of emotional possibilities. Banality itself is the focus of her fiction, cracked open to expose the tropisms underneath:

In [. . .] *The Planetarium,* the commonplaces behind which the tropisms hide, the platitudes, the clichés, constitute the plot itself. Nothing could be more commonplace than this plot. An old lady wants to put a new oak door in her flat. A young man tries to become one of the favorites of a well-known writer. But the tropisms, which make our life infinitely rich and complex, hide under any commonplace gesture or word. They can be found anywhere at any moment. Why, then, describe exceptional situations, great action, heroes? [. . .] Why try and persuade the reader that all the richness, the complexity of life is concentrated in certain chosen actions instead of going on in him, whatever he is doing, all day long in ordinary life?[25]

Because tropisms lurk in the most trivial situations, there are no "privileged moments," pivotal crises, stormy adventures in Sarraute's books, merely the humdrum cycle of existence. Whatever occurs stems from ordinary personal interactions on a tropistic level.

The more insignificant the cause, the greater is the discrepancy between the source of the tropism and the enormity of the inner reaction it produces. This disproportion is apparent from the very beginning. In the opening pages, a woman is excitedly anticipating the installation of an oak door that she has ordered for her apartment. Her mood changes to distress when the door has been hung and she finds its effect marred by a hideous nickel-plated knob. Her anger mounts in a crescendo, until she is sure that the door was deliberately ruined through the workmen's malevolence. The latter become in her mind an advancing army of conquerors, trampling underfoot the precious remnants of her world. The exaggerated metaphor transcribes the incongruity between external cause and emotional response. The inflation of a trivial occurrence into a crisis of cataclysmic proportions is characteristic of the affective nature of tropisms, which exist on a level of primitive emotions that escape the assuaging powers of reason.

No one is exempt from these excessive emotional responses. Alain tries to amuse the guests at a party by telling the story of his aunt's obsession with her oak door,[26] but his mother-in-law changes the subject, finding that her guests have grown fidgety (he is like a magician who has failed to pull the promised dove out of a hat); her attempt to silence him unleashes in Alain a paroxysm of rage. When the mother-in-law offers the young couple a pair of sturdy English club chairs and they demur in favor of a Louis XV bergère, it is her turn to react with disproportionate anger: "Her heart started to beat, she blushed, anybody else, except them, would have been surprised by the violence of her reaction, the hatred, the rage in her tone all of a sudden, in her false, icy laughter."[27] When Alain proposes an exchange of apartments, his Aunt Berthe provokes in him feelings of inordinate fury: he would like to punch her, kick her, physically abuse her. Similarly, his wife, Gisèle, becomes so enraged with her father because he disagrees with her opinion of Germaine Lemaire's beauty that she hates him, would like to have him whipped, drawn and quartered, burned at the stake (p. 121). The immoderation of the tropistic response, with its implications of physical violence, indicates the primitive region from which it springs.

The catalyst that brings tropisms to life is often some material object which is inconsequential in itself but has a symbolic importance. The leather club chairs, for example, represent to Alain's mother-in-law the stability and solidity of established values, in contrast to the menacing uncertainties of her daughter's household: "Here everything is as reliable as these chairs, everything is simple, clean-cut. But out there, at her daughter's... shadows, dark holes, disquieting swarmings, soft uncoilings, dangerous layers of ooze that open up, engulf her..." (p. 47). To the young couple, for whom the antique bergère symbolizes the beauty and harmony of their marriage, the club chairs are a covert means of asserting control over their lives. Alain realizes this fully: "These chairs, we all know what they are. But never a word on the subject. Absolute secrecy. There exists a tacit agreement, we don't speak of them.... We use all the weapons in our possession, but never an allusion to what they really are: the badge of the order they want to force upon me, of their power, of my submission..." (p. 101). Because he is aware of their symbolic nature as arms in the "bloody battle" for domination, Alain is ready to fight against having the chairs in his home — as if, he says, he were defending his life.

The struggle waged over the leather club chairs is a prefiguration of the more harrowing confrontation over the acquisition of Aunt Berthe's apartment. Each tactic in the enactment of this miniature battle is dependent on a predetermining tropism, and each tropism is set off by an external cause. The same interweaving of objective

events and inner tropisms noted in *Martereau* is a propulsive force
here. In his desire to gain possession of the apartment for himself,
Alain enlists allies, his wife and his father, whose hand-to-hand
combat with Berthe provokes tropistic reverberations. When Gisèle
approaches her father-in-law to intercede with Aunt Berthe on their
behalf, she is conscious of appearing in his eyes like a voracious
buzzard or like some wizened crone who has stolen his son. When
the father visits his sister Berthe on his children's errand, his old
jealousy and animosity surface, and he sees her as a sorceress
crouched in her cave, presiding over secret rites he fears and
detests.

Berthe's refusal to be coaxed into relinquishing her apartment so
enrages Alain that he threatens to have her evicted. This menacing
gesture precipitates a swarm of tropisms, not merely on the part of
the principals involved, but among a chorus of disembodied voices,
the arbiters of public opinion who figure in all of Sarraute's books,
for whom the delicious thrill of gossiping is like a roller-coaster
ride. At first they feel threatened by Alain's act, for in its evidence
of selfishness and ingratitude they recognize a distorted image of
themselves; but their uneasiness is quelled when one of the group,
by praising the young couple's customary devotion to their aunt,
reconstructs the charming trio of waxen effigies (as falsely reassuring as the photographic perfection of Martereau and his wife).
In Berthe's eyes, Alain's threat constitutes a "crime" against her,
and when her brother Pierre pays her a second visit, she feels
constrained to warn him against his son. In Pierre's mind, Alain's
"crime" is not mistreating his aunt, but his boyhood habit of running to her to have his whims gratified. To placate his sister, he
minimizes Alain's gesture, reassuring her of the strength of the
young man's devotion. What is for him a perfunctory dismissal of
his son's rash act is for Berthe the yearned-for-proof of her
nephew's love, which motivates her to capitulate and give up her
apartment.

Alain's maneuvering to obtain this goal has its counterpart in his
maneuvering to ingratiate himself with Germaine Lemaire. He first
approaches her in reaction to the pressure exerted upon him to accept the club chairs. His acquaintance with the famous writer
awakens a range of responses in his psyche, from awe and timidity
in her presence, to pride vis-à-vis his family, to embarrassment as
he sees her through his father's eyes. At first petrified in her
presence, Alain regains confidence by regaling her with the story of

his aunt's oak door and the family controversy over the leather chairs. This time, his narrative is a success. (He is a magician with an appreciative audience, pulling cascades of ribbons out of his hat. With this repetition of an earlier metaphor, Sarraute emphasizes the contrast in the two situations: Alain's failure in the one, his triumph in the second. In both cases, he tells anecdotes about his family to win approval for himself, "sacrificing" familial privacy to personal ambition, like the *raconteur* in *Tropism IX.*) Eventually, by conforming to her caprices and exigencies, Alain wins a place among Germaine Lemaire's accepted retinue. The seal of her approval is her visit to him at the end of the book. This final scene marks a dual triumph for Alain, the attainment of both his goals: possession of his aunt's apartment, friendship with Germaine Lemaire.

In spite of the deceptive appearance of conventionality, *The Planetarium* is in many ways more innovative than Sarraute's earlier novels. For one thing, it is distinguished from its predecessors by the disappearance of a central narrator and the dissipation of the narrative function among a variety of *personae,* none of whom is readily identifiable. This technique, which points toward the future evolution of Sarraute's characterization, leads eventually, in her more abstract novels (*The Golden Fruits, Between Life and Death,* and *"fools say"*), to the complete disintegration of character, until all that remain are an anonymous multiplicity of consciousnesses momentarily displacing one another in the spotlight. No longer confined within one person's mind, the reader shares in the fictionalizing process of a number of narrators, each of whom projects himself into other people's minds, to assess their responses and readjust his own accordingly. As Bernard Pingaud points out, "All the characters are engaged in writing the novel, all the characters take turns being the author."[28]

As always, the book begins *in medias res.* There is no exposition or external description, no background of character or situation. The reader finds himself inside someone's mind, participating in snatches of thoughts, worries, and emotions relating to the installation of an oak door. In the next chapter, he is situated inside a different mind, or else he is passed like a shuttlecock from one mind to the next, without knowing precisely where he is. He hurtles back and forth among a variety of persons, who seem to be conversing aloud on one level and expressing their unspoken thoughts on another. There is a continual counterpoint of conversation and "subconversation": the insipid platitudes of everyman's conversation, floating on the surface of a brackish, bottomless lake of inner tensions and uncertainties. If the reader tries to identify the speakers or relate them to one another, he is rewarded by bewilderment and disorientation. It is best to float with the current that Sarraute has set in motion and to *experience* each individual conscience as it drifts by.

The difference between Sarraute's method and the technique of the omniscient author, who also reveals what each character is thinking and feeling, is that the latter provides all the information necessary to the reader's understanding. Sarraute leaves the reader to fend for himself. He must learn to recognize characters from the *inside,* by internal identification with their emotional states. Claude Mauriac adopted this technique in his *Dîner en ville,* in which it is necessary to guess each character's identity from the context of his thoughts. With Mauriac, the process of identification is an intellectual puzzle to be solved by the reader (he even provides a "seating plan" of the dining table around which his characters are disposed). For Sarraute, the matter of recognition is of negligible concern. Her readers are not even assisted by the minimal designation Faulkner provides in *As I Lay Dying,* where each chapter heading denotes the identity of the character whose thoughts are otherwise anonymously transcribed. In *The Planetarium,* the majority of the chapter divisions entail a shift from one mind to another, but these changes are never signaled externally. Each takes place with no precognition and necessitates a startling readjustment of focus on the reader's part.

At first as undifferentiated as the faces of strangers at a cocktail party, the agglomeration of consciences eventually sort themselves out, thanks to subtle indices buried in the text. Among the chorus of voices, one is heard entreating another to tell a hilarious story about his aunt and her oak door. From this single clue, the first hint of a relationship is intimated (aunt-nephew) and the first strand is provided linking the second chapter with the first. The reader now finds himself viewing objectively (through the nephew's half-mocking story about his aunt's "mania") what he had previously experienced subjectively (the aunt's misgivings about her beautiful door). In an even later scene, a mother points out to her daughter her son-in-law's imperfections: his mania for expensive antiques, like his Aunt Berthe with her oak door. The jigsaw puzzle begins to take shape; additional pieces are found to interlock.

The continual shifts in narrative point of view enable the reader to see people and situations from varying perspectives. There is no single objective reality, only a multiplicity of subjective responses. To some people, Alain is a monster of ingratitude, whereas to others he is a model of devotion. Even external appearances are open to personal interpretation. Germaine Lemaire is either "ugly" or "beautiful," depending on the optic of the viewer. The violent argument that erupts over this question is a verification not of her objective appearance but of its emotional connotations for the people involved. For Gisèle's father, who insists that she is "ugly as sin," she represents the career woman, the female intellectual whom he despises; her very existence contradicts his stereotyped conception of a woman's role as ornamental, "a luxury indulged in by successful men" (p. 119). Gisèle's disproportionately furious retort is based on her inner fear of corresponding to that stereotype, of being nothing more than a "hairdresser's wax dummy" (p. 120).

Each subjective consciousness serves as an object for others. Of this painful fact everyone is aware. There is a universal tendency to doubt the value of one's own judgment and to try to perceive oneself through someone else's eyes. This uncertainty extends to the objects of one's predilection, whose value must be acclaimed by others before it can be confirmed for oneself. Alain tries to see Germaine Lemaire through his father's eyes, or to imagine what "they" (the Others) will think of the Gothic statuette he has chosen, with its slight imperfection. Aunt Berthe frets over the aesthetic impression people will have of her oak door. Even Germaine Lemaire is not immune to the need for having her subjective judgments corroborated. In fact, her sycophants' adulation provides a bulwark against the realities of stark self-assessment.

On the tropistic level a communality of experience is universally shared. Certain psychic responses — like primary physical needs — are basic to everyone: the desire for approval and acceptance, the need for security, the even more forceful wish to dominate rather than be dominated. Each of these desires has its negative corollary, which can be described in a single word: *fear.* This term recurs repeatedly in Sarraute's vocabulary (in *The Planetarium* alone it appears some seventy times). There is the fear of uncertainty and instability, the fear of being rejected or reproved, the fear of being criticized, ridiculed, misunderstood. Examples are rife throughout Sarraute's pages. Berthe is afraid of people's opinions, Gisèle fears her mother's influence, her mother is intimidated by Alain's moodiness, Alain fears Germaine Lemaire's scorn, and Germaine Lemaire is afraid, in the secret depths of her soul, that she is not as good a writer as she is acclaimed to be. These private anxieties, barely acknowledged by the subjects themselves, link them one to another on a preconscious level.

Certain resemblances among characters are explicitly emphasized, so that one almost functions as a "double" for the other, as was the case in *Martereau*.[29] Jean-Luc, one of Germaine Lemaire's disciples, is virtually a stand-in for Alain in his fanatic obsession with the writer; Alain refers to Jean-Luc as his own "wretched double" and tells Germaine Lemaire he is afraid of her, "just like Jean-Luc" (p. 153). Alain is said to "take after" his aunt Berthe; instead of denying the resemblance, he broadens it to include everybody: "Why, of course I am like her. We are as alike as two peas, did you never notice that? Otherwise, I should not be so interested by her. [. . .] Nor would you be so interested, you either, if you yourself and all of us here, didn't have a little something, somewhere, well hidden, in some well-closed remote recess..." (pp. 40–41). The fundamental similarity among all people on a tropistic level ("well-closed, remote") is a truism for Sarraute. The refrain is echoed in Germaine Lemaire's closing words, referring to someone's ill-concealed vanity: "I think we're all of us, really, a bit like that" (p. 296).

The central narrator of *Portrait* and *Martereau* provided a single optic through which the world was viewed. Fictionalized scenes, presented indistinguishably from actual experience, extended the range of the narrator's vision into the domain of imagined possibilities. There was nothing fantastic or farfetched about these improvisations. They were all equally capable of "realistically" taking place — just as the sequence of scenes between Martereau and his wife were like alternate scripts of the narrator's devising, representing differing versions of "reality." In *The Planetarium*, it is no longer necessary to supplant the narrow perspective of a single consciousness with invented embellishments of reality; since the narrative function is shared among all the characters, the reader is already provided with a variety of points of view. In fact, there is only one scene of the kind found in *Portrait* and *Martereau* — that is, a scene that takes place in imagination *as if* it had actually occurred. This is the idyllic meeting Alain describes between his father and Germaine Lemaire, which is followed by the account of another meeting completely at variance with the first. The fictitious

nature of the initial encounter is signaled by the words: "And but
for almost nothing — just a certain movement on his part, this
charming spectacle *would have taken place*" (p. 143; italics are
mine). There is no possible confusion here over what happened and
what was only wishful thinking. Nonetheless, even the "real" scene
is filtered through Alain's perception, as he endeavors to view
Germaine Lemaire through his father's eyes. In the first, imaginary
meeting, his father had remarked what a handsome woman she
was; in the course of the actual meeting, Alain *imagines* that his
father sees her as a large woman, outlandishly dressed, who looks
like a secondhand clothes dealer or an actress past her prime.
Germaine Lemaire, in the privacy of her own thoughts, has a
similar impression of the father's reaction. (Both views are like the
reflection of a reflection glimpsed in a mirror.)

Although this is the sole instance of a fictitious incident
presented indistinguishably from reality, many imaginary scenes of
a more fantastic sort are patently incompatible with actual
experience. Whether they occur in swift, short snatches or in prolonged detail, these scenes are the metaphoric means of expressing
tropisms. Alain trying to escape from family pressure by
telephoning Germaine Lemaire is a fugitive on foreign soil ringing
the doorbell of his embassy to seek asylum; as he endeavors to
interest a restive audience in his aunt's eccentricities, he becomes an
explorer leading his followers through a virgin jungle teeming with
unknown fauna; his threat to have his aunt evicted turns him into
an informer, bent low, scurrying to denounce Jews and resistance
fighters. The incongruity between the exoticism of the image and
the commonplace situation out of which it arises eliminates the possibility of confusing the "imaginary" with the "real" and once
again emphasizes the disproportion that exists between a tropism
and its cause.

Sometimes the repeated use of a metaphor serves as a form of
epithet that clings to a character, reflecting the tropisms he invariably triggers in the observer. Alain regards Germaine Lemaire
with awe, as if she were a queen, and this regal simile recurs when-
ever he sees her: she is surrounded by a coterie of admirers, like
courtiers paying homage; the most fanatic of her devotees is a
"jester" who sits on the steps of her throne; when she is troubled
she bows her "heavy crowned head," and her social call to Alain at
his home marks the arrival of a sovereign to survey her vassal's
domain.

The repetition of a metaphor in different contexts (like the comparison of Alain's storytelling to a magician's conjuring trick) can establish a parallel between two separate situations. It can also underscore the similarity of experience on a tropistic level, as in the case of the frequent military metaphors that reappear (from jousting contests to aerial warfare, from trenches to minefields to marine battles, involving swords and daggers, rifles and bayonets, tomahawks and TNT — the physical manifestations of "psychological" warfare on the terrain of tropisms).

It is seldom that the imagery associated with a specific tropism corresponds to a character's individuality. Rather, it is culled from the storehouse of the reader's experience and is intended to arouse a reaction in *him*. The frequent use of "medical" metaphors — the repeated examples of a surgeon wielding a scalpel, amputating a limb, pressing an abscess — has no relation whatever to a character's profession. Alain's figuring as an acrobat or a magician or the leader of a jungle safari is unconnected with any experience in his past. In only two cases is a relationship specified between an imaginary scene and a character's "real life," and even these associations are peripheral rather than fundamental. Both of these scenes are like stage sets mounted in precise detail, rather than the flashbulb flickerings of most tropisms. In the first instance, a dead dog is found outside a ranch, a servant has disappeared in the night, a scalped and mutilated body, pierced with arrows, is discovered tied to a tree. This graphic and grisly décor pictorializes Berthe's fear that her brother has turned into an "enemy scout" by treacherously siding with Alain against her. The scene has its source, we are told, in the Indian stories Berthe used to read as a child. Its precise counterpart is an interior pictured by her brother: the guests assembled in the drawing room of a London manor house, a fire flickering fitfully on the hearth, an assortment of strange objects arranged on the table, and an assassin hiding in the midst of the group, who will give himself away by fingering the murder weapon. This descriptive setting — a metaphoric transcription of Alain's ill-concealed greediness — is based on the old-fashioned detective stories Pierre is said to be fond of reading.

In addition to the imaginary scenes in which tropisms are evoked, one actual incident is portrayed in two variants, "two parallel tracks which meet only in the 'common place' of conversation."[30] Whereas the variants in *Martereau* were fictitious embroiderings of reality conceived by the same mind, the dual versions in this case transcribe a "real" event experienced from two points of view. The incident is Pierre's second visit to Berthe, as perceived first through her eyes and then through his. The surface conversation is identical, but the accompanying patter of subconversation signals the disparity of the partners' reactions. Even Pierre's fingering of the fringe on a rug — an "external" act — is interpreted differently. Pierre finds the upturned fringe irritating, and he absentmindedly straightens it; Berthe thinks that by concentrating on the rug he is not listening to her. The same metaphors occur in both minds: Alain as a "criminal" (for different reasons), old wounds that reopen (stemming from different causes). A last image, common to both, expresses their reconciliation, but with dissimilar emotions. Each envisions walking together across a field: Pierre, at ease and happy now, imagines them striding across a beautiful English lawn (again the British symbol of serenity); Berthe, still wary, pictures them picking their way cautiously over a recently cleared minefield (p. 252).

Although the narrative optic shifts, in *The Planetarium* there is still one dominant point of view, that of Alain Guimier. He is more of a central consciousness than any of the others, not only because more space is devoted to his thoughts than to any other character, but because he is more sensitive to inner movements, more acutely aware of the discrepancy between outward behavior and the covert truths it disguises. This responsiveness to tropisms marks his kinship with the narrators of Sarraute's earlier books. Like them, he is poised on the frontier of activity, a passive spectator of life. The thesis he is writing remains suspended. There is no assurance that he will ever complete it or overcome the tendency to lose himself, like his counterparts, in sterile speculation.

The basic theme of *Martereau* — the disintegration of an ideal — is repeated on several levels in *The Planetarium,* culminating in Alain's disillusionment with Germaine Lemaire. Every person seeks stability in a changing world. Even Alain's father expresses the need to believe in a universe where order reigns, good triumphs, and work receives its just reward; without this dependability, "everything totters, collapses, soft, crumbling ground on which we lose our footing..." (p. 262). It is especially in relationships with other people that certainty is sought. To counteract the indetermination of personality, labels are affixed to people. This is what Alain and Gisèle tend to do. In fact, they make a game of classifying their acquaintances according to mannerisms and

gestures, defining them with swift, sharp strokes; the resultant
picture, precise of contour, is nonetheless false, as Gisèle realizes
(the same conclusion to which the narrator of *Portrait* arrived).
When the preformed judgments that Gisèle has accepted prove
questionable, she experiences a physical disorientation. Her
mother's insinuation that her "Prince Charming" is less than
perfect brings on a bout of dizziness — her head reels, her legs grow
weak. When Alain in turn judges her mother harshly, she has the
sensation of falling away into space.

Alain feels a similar sense of imbalance when the support of
stereotyped preconceptions is wrenched from his grasp. He is first
disappointed in his old professor, Adrien Lebat, whom he had
always regarded with admiration and awe; beneath the pretense of
intellectual disinterestedness, he discovers a disconcerting vanity
and egotism. Moreover, Lebat's denigrating references to
Germaine Lemaire (he finds her boring and vain) instill in Alain the
first doubts ·about his idol: "He must let this sensation wear
off.... As though the ground were giving way beneath him... this
vague nausea..." (p. 279). When he sees Germaine Lemaire again,
his disenchantment deepens. He begins to wonder about the
validity of her aesthetic discernment (she has not noticed the imperfection in his Gothic statuette, but has admired Aunt Berthe's
hideous oak door). Worse still, her literary judgment is open to question. She scoffs at the possibility that those trivia on which Alain's
storytelling (and Sarraute's novels) are based — things like club
chairs, oak doors, an aunt's eccentricities — can conceivably be
converted into literature, recommending instead that a writer
"apply codes" and maintain his distance from people and things
(p. 293). Like the "specialist" in *Portrait,* she is the spokesman for
conventionality, who controverts her author's ideas about art.
Alain's faith in her infallibility totters: "The sky is turning above
his head, the stars are moving, he sees planets traveling from place
to place, a sensation of dizziness, of anguish, a feeling of panic
seizes him, everything is toppling, overturning, at once... she herself is moving away, she disappears on the other side..." (p. 294).
As the laborious structure of his idealized world collapses, Alain
yearns for the certainties he has lost. He would like to restore his
former assurance, "to feel at home once more, under the same
motionless sky in which, as before, familiar stars would shine" (p.
295), even if the price of security is the preservation of falsehood.

With the imagery of the stars and the spinning sky overhead, the symbolism of the book's title becomes clear. Alain has constructed an artificial universe centered around the stellar figure of Germaine Lemaire, with a cluster of satellites revolving in her orbit. Seen from a distance, like the heavenly bodies, she has seemed immutable, perfect, impervious to motion or change. But when Alain knows her better and begins to notice her imperfections, he has the sensation of having set a dangerous mechanism in motion — the stars whirl out of their familiar patterns, like a planetarium run amok. Alain has accepted the false sky of a planetarium — a sham, an illusion — for the true sky overhead. A planetarium is, after all, only a shadowy projection of the "real" world, a *trompe-l'oeil* imitation. Its appearance is faked, its movements a trick. To extend the metaphor, the world of the planetarium and the telescope, where relationships are perceived from afar, stands at the antipodes of the world of tropisms and the microscope, where everything is seen at close range and enlarged. For the person who concentrates on the infinitely small movements of tropisms, the celestial universe is doubly remote and out of reach.[31]

In *The Planetarium,* Sarraute touches upon the theme of art in its dual manifestations: passively, as an aesthetic experience, and actively, in the form of artistic creation. Later, she will devote a separate book to each of these aspects.

Aesthetic enjoyment, like creativity, is treated in an ascending hierarchy. Aunt Berthe's appreciation of "art" is on the most primitive level, consisting exclusively of a concern with the décor of her home. She is capable of enjoying only those things she can possess for herself; stained-glass windows leave her indifferent because they are unsuitable for personal use, and she likes only those paintings whose color combinations she can appropriate for her own decorating scheme. Her obsession with the oak door is not entirely aesthetic: she would like to consider it a "find," something that will impress others with her originality and good taste. But, like everyone else, she is unsure of her judgment and needs to have it confirmed by other people's approval.

On the next level of appreciation comes Alain, as an *amateur* of art. He is more discriminating and better educated on the subject (he is writing his thesis on some aspect of painting). He is alive to the beauty and rarity of the art objects Germaine Lemaire has amassed in her travels, and his discernment extends to antique bergères and Renaissance statuettes. His aesthetic enjoyment is not the pure contemplation of beauty (as it is for the father in *Do You*

Hear Them?), but is marred by the desire to evoke envy and admiration in others. Despite his training and expertise, he wavers in his opinions because he is afraid of what other people may think of his judgment.

There are no absolutes of aesthetic certainty, any more than there are absolutes about people or events or even — as Sarraute will show in *"fools say"* — about ideas themselves. Matters of taste are as relative and subjective as any other kind of opinion. It is undemonstrable (and irrelevant) whether the oak door is as handsome as Berthe would like to think, or as ugly as Alain considers it, or as tasteful as Germaine Lemaire finds it to be. Even within the same person's mind, judgment is unstable, for it is influenced by other people's reactions, real or fancied (even Alain's assurance about his Louis XV bergère is jolted when a member of Germaine Lemaire's entourage suggests that a pair of English club chairs might have been preferable in its place!). The fluctuation and variability of artistic judgment will form the subject of *The Golden Fruits*.

Alain also exhibits an affinity for the other aspect of art, albeit on a lowly rung. He is, in a way, an embryonic creator.[32] As a storyteller, who tries to weave enthralling tales for his audiences out of the minutiae of everyday living, he is a budding Sarraute, with tropisms as his subject matter. Oral narration is the step preceding literary expression — not merely in the history of the species (the oral Bible, the earliest *chansons de geste,* the recitations of jongleurs and troubadours), but in the autogenic maturation of the Writer, as Sarraute will bring out in *Between Life and Death.* Alain stands on the brink of artistic creativity, according to Sarraute:

Alain Guimier in *The Planetarium* could almost be a writer: he already discerns a living substance in matters that seem of no interest to anyone or are considered unacceptable, things that everyone disdains and that belong to him alone. This is the reason why Germaine Lemaire, a conventional writer, does not understand him.[33]

The creative artist is represented in *The Planetarium* by Germaine Lemaire, a writer so well known and successful that she has to dodge reporters when she wants to go out. She is enveloped in an aura of literary glory. Admission into her circle of intimates is a prize Alain covets beyond any other; entry into their restricted ranks is equivalent to acceptance as an initiate into a special religion with its shared creeds and taboos, a cult to which only the "chosen" (*élus* in French, a cognate of *élite*) are permitted access (pp. 174–75).[34] However, even Germaine Lemaire's superiority is superficial. When the reader is granted a glance inside her head, he finds her consumed by self-doubt — the same order of anxiety that tormented Berthe over her oak door and Alain with respect to his narrative ability. In one intimate moment, beyond the praise of her sycophants, beyond the range of interviewers and television cameras, Germaine Lemaire stands alone face to face with her *oeuvre*. The need for self-assessment has been sparked by a question in a magazine article: "Is Germaine Lemaire our Madame Tussaud?" — a question that embodies Sarraute's stock metaphor for everything that is conventional, stereotyped, and lifeless in literature. In privacy, Germaine Lemaire confronts the merit of her work. To counteract the untenable opinion that has been expressed about her writing, she reviews within herself her gifts and attributes: her mastery of words, her talent for creating a strong impression of "reality," even her childhood "pre-destination." For reassurance, she rereads passages from her favorite book, only to find that they are frozen and congealed, covered with "a thin layer of shiny varnish" (p. 182). Instead of vibrating with life, her writing is inanimate and inert: "It's all dead. Dead. Dead. Dead. A dead star. She's alone. No recourse. No relief from any one. She's pursuing her way in solitude beset with terror. She's alone on an extinguished star. Life is elsewhere..." (p. 183). The same anguish, the same sensation of panic and dismay will grip the Writer in *Between Life and Death*. But whereas the true Writer must have the fortitude to face the truth, however unpalatable, Germaine Lemaire reads on only long enough to convince herself anew of her innate excellence. She emerges from her bout of soul-searching with restored confidence. The reappearance of her claque, with their indiscriminate flattery, sets her mind at ease and reinstates her inflated opinion of herself. Sarraute will later decry this readiness to succumb to the plaudits of popularity as the most insidious danger to which the creative artist is exposed. Germaine Lemaire has fallen prey to the uncritical need for esteem that entraps the unwary. She has accepted the cackling admiration of her claque as an index of true merit. She, too, has fallen for the "copy of a copy" and has mistaken the inauthentic for the real.

CHAPTER 4

The Theme of Art

I T is natural that a writer, engaged in the lonely task of putting words on paper in order to communicate to an unseen and unknowable reader something of consequence to himself, will reflect on the nature and merit of what he is doing. The question of literature as art and the scope of the writer's role have always been at the forefront of Nathalie Sarraute's concern. She keeps nudging the reader that together they must be mindful of the problems of writing.

Unlike Diderot, who tried to suspend his audience's disbelief by proclaiming in the title of one of his stories, *"Ceci n'est pas un conte"* ("This is not a story"), Sarraute never lets her readers forget the fictional process in which she (and they) are engaged.

In *The Planetarium,* she had briefly considered the dual concept of art as creation and enjoyment. As often occurs in her writing, an idea or theme tangentially touched upon in one novel will become a dominant motif in another. It is as though she were to notice an interesting landscape in passing, which she had no time to visit, but which she ultimately returns to and explores at her leisure. It was while composing *The Planetarium* that the basic idea for *The Golden Fruits* came to her: "I had just completed a passage about Germaine Lemaire, the writer, and I thought that it would be very interesting to do something about the literary text itself, [...] to take a book, which would become the true hero of the novel, and follow its destiny as it rises and falls and especially to examine the tropisms which its publication generates around it."[1]

Until this point, the theme of art had been submerged beneath the interplay of tropisms on a more or less personalized level. The next three novels — *The Golden Fruits* (1963), *Between Life and Death* (1968), and *Do You Hear Them?* (1972) — reveal an increasing tendency to abstract the tropisms from recognizable personalities. In the first two, where Sarraute eliminates both plot and characters, there are only disembodied voices virtually indistinguishable from one another. From time to time, a lone voice of dissent momentarily rises above the clamor of generalities, only to be swallowed up again in a chorus of anonymity. These shadowy presences, who come and go at random, are as devoid of substance as the nebulous group who gossiped about the Guimiers in the sole chapter of *The Planetarium* where the possibility of later identification was withheld. Here, there are no longer any perceptible relationships, except of the most tenuous and evanescent kind — a throwback to the abstraction of *Tropisms,* except that the fragmentation of Sarraute's earlier book is here welded into a cohesive entity.

Because the matter of identity is not merely relegated to the background, as before, but is eliminated entirely, the result is an undiverted emphasis on the tropisms themselves, Sarraute's primary subject matter. This time they are not set in motion by a central narrator or by the participants in a family drama, but by an indeterminate complex of consciences who fulfill Sarraute's aim of serving solely as props for the developing tropisms. In *The Golden Fruits* and *Do You Hear Them?,* the tropisms arise in response to an art object — a work of literature in the first, a piece of sculpture in the latter. The tropisms in *Between Life and Death* are commingled with the essence of the creative act.

It has been suggested that Sarraute's earlier books can be interpreted as parables of artistic creation. Yvon Belaval comments that, in *Tropisms,* "Nathalie Sarraute has taken as her subject creation in its nascent state."[2] In his discussion of *The Planetarium,* Michel Butor remarks that "all the characters are potential novelists," whose creative effort aborts before it can be expressed in words.[3] Sarraute has acknowledged the accuracy of these observations, adding: "The primary substance of writing has always been the object of my search, in all my books."[4]

Each novel heretofore has been concerned with the creative urge in its larval stage. The narrators of *Portrait* and *Martereau* were seen grappling with the problem of imagining characters and events, while Alain Guimier wrestled with the question of oral narration and what constitutes a fitting subject for literature. The "parasitic" vocations of these central characters are explicable in terms of their artistic potentiality. The "extroverts" with whom they are contrasted — the fathers and uncles involved in financial transactions, their feet firmly rooted to the ground — are immersed in a bustling "busy-ness" that clouds their awareness of subsurface elements. The "introverts," withdrawn and brooding, attuned to vibrations in the people around them — the "misfits" to whom Sarraute alludes in *The Age of Suspicion* and *Between Life and Death* — are the embryonic creative artists.

The next three books revolve around the concept of art and the many questions it raises. The genesis of a work of art is the subject of *Between Life and Death,* while the work of art as a finished product is the focus of *The Golden Fruits.* The latter examines the matter of aesthetic values and the permanence of the art object. *Between Life and Death* concentrates on the creative act and the life experience of the artist. *Do You Hear Them?* is also concerned with artistic merit, not in terms of creativity but in the form of aesthetic appreciation (the second aspect of art that Sarraute treated in *The Planetarium*). Returning to the framework of a family situation — but retaining the anonymity of *Fruits* and *Life and Death* — it explores the opposing values of tradition and modernity in art.

I   The Golden Fruits *(1963)*

Nathalie Sarraute's novel, *The Golden Fruits,* is concerned with the tropisms aroused by a novel called *The Golden Fruits.* This *construction en abîme,* as the French call it — the mirror reflection of a reflection, already noted in connection with the perception of character — is reminiscent both of André Gide's novel *Les Faux-Monnayeurs,* whose title echoes the title of a book one of his characters is writing, and of Claude Mauriac's diary *Le Temps immobile* the subject of which is the writing of *Le Temps immobile.* In Sarraute's case, the use of an identical title serves to confuse her book with its subject and to blur the distinction between them, so that an unmodified reference to *The Golden Fruits* is by itself ambiguous. This duality suggests a frequent theme in her work — the uncertainty and unreliability of all systems of nomenclature.

The "movement" of Sarraute's book — replacing plot — is the parabolic curve described by the rise and fall of *The Golden Fruits'* reputation, as it is first discovered by an élite few, is championed by the critics and touted by the masses, rises to the crest of popularity, then gradually — it would almost seem inevitably — is discredited and ultimately forgotten, except by a handful of sensitive readers, through whose discrimination and independence of judgment the future of literature is assured.

Sarraute has not written a disquisition on the fluctuations of taste, the fickleness of the reading public, the ephemerality of literary fads. Neither has she composed a theoretical treatise about artistic values, artificially parading as a novel. Her book is, as always, people-oriented. It is human interplay that is of paramount concern to Sarraute, overshadowing whatever generalities can be abstracted from their behavior.

The book entitled *The Golden Fruits* serves as a catalyst for tropistic reactions. To use a subaqueous simile, it is like a foreign body that has been lowered to the ocean floor, where its alien character and strange opacity cause stirrings and scurryings among the marine creatures who inhabit the depths; intrigued by the mysterious object, they draw near to examine it, swarm around it in delight, and when its novelty has worn off, swim away to explore something new.

Around *The Golden Fruits* is waged a miniature "Battle of the Books." Opposing factions, with conflicting attitudes, crystallize in its presence. The antagonisms, the assertiveness, the bellicosity, the snobbery and timidity, the fear of appearing ridiculous, the desire to adhere to the majority — all the nuances of opinion that revolve around the book's reception — are not indigenous to art. Rather, they reflect the same order of tropistic responses that arise in connection with the most mundane of objects — a bar of soap, a dish of scraped carrots, a doorknob. Tropisms, which occur on a primitive emotional level, are always the same, whatever their source.[5] With gentle irony, Sarraute shows that everyone, however self-assured he may appear, has his own inner misgivings and anxieties.

These various attitudes and subtle shades of emotion are conveyed uniquely through conversation and the counterpoint of sub-conversation. More than ever, the dialogue form — spoken words interspersed with unexpressed thoughts — predominates. Conversation is not linked to specified individuals but is, like the protruding tip of an iceberg, the outward manifestation (or disguise) of the tropism underneath. Just as it is futile to try to identify characters, even by such intangible indices as a point of view or an emotion, so it is equally risky to attempt to establish a connection between one conversation and another, one scene and the next.

The effect of abstracting identity is to reinforce the universality of the experience depicted — an experience that is capable of being shared by everyone on the common terrain of tropisms. Paradoxically, as in classical drama, the general is achieved through the particular. It is by concentrating on individual quirks of receptivity — egocentricities, fears, fallibilities, self-effacements — in an uncountable number of unidentifiable cases that the quintessence of experience is distilled. As the faceless, nameless presences melt indistinguishably into one another, what remains in the reader's memory are not individual characters, but the sweeping breadth of human possibilities.

The responses to a work of art or literature are of two kinds: "genuine" and "inauthentic." The first is a direct and intimate contact between the reader (listener, spectator) and the art object, unaffected by any external influence. It is a symbiotic relationship: something transmitted by the work is picked up by the reader, as if by a sensitive antenna. Nothing deflects the pulsation from the source to its receptor; no stereotyped or preconceived judgments interfere with the reader's spontaneous appreciation. The alternate response is "inauthentic," inasmuch as it is an indirect reaction, preconditioned by elements extraneous to the innate value of the art object itself, but which impede a true perception of its worth.

In tracing the waxing popularity of a work like *The Golden Fruits,* it is primarily these "inauthentic" reactions that Sarraute catalogues. Often it is not a question of liking or disliking the book; what matters is what other people think of one's judgment. For some, appreciation of Art is contingent on belonging to an élite minority. In the first chapter of the book, a small group of initiates, like members of a select club, are united by the consciousness of enjoying a communion of spirits, a fusion of tastes not shared with the rabble — whether they are exclaiming in ecstasy over a painting by Courbet which they have spied in the corner of an art gallery, or launching a book called *The Golden Fruits,* with the same enthusiastic snobbery. When the object of their taste has achieved popular acclaim, it becomes *de rigueur* for these self-styled connoisseurs to hold themselves aloof from the admiring multitude, viewed like a herd of "bleating sheep." For others, there is a contrary need to conform, an attraction in belonging to a powerful majority, for whom recognized artists like Verlaine, Rimbaud, Gide, and Courbet provide "familiar images of a homeland revisited,"[6] the security of a shared civilization.

The beckoning appeal of the Group almost always proves irresistible. Micheline Tison Braun has pointed out the religious symbolism that pervades the book, according to which the Group is godlike in its preeminence, the sovereign good is to belong, and exclusion is "hell." The spokesmen for the group (the godhead) are the literary critics (prophets or shamans) who rule by force, after exterminating their rivals. The "faithful" communicate through veneration, or execration, of certain symbolic objects and fetishes. According to this analysis, art objects like *The Golden Fruits* have no intrinsic value, but serve as talismans whereby coreligionists can recognize and fraternize with one another.[7]

Cowardice and capitulation are customary reactions, even among those who make a pretense of thinking for themselves. One character who has formed her own judgment of *The Golden Fruits* revises her opinion to conform to that of a friend. Like Germaine Lemaire rereading her book until self-criticism has been dissipated, "she" rereads *The Golden Fruits* with a preconceived attitude, until she succeeds in stifling her genuine convictions and adopting a false acquiescence. Another person fails to give voice to his true feelings because he fears the mockery and ridicule of the crowd. If he remains silent while others praise the book, he is considered suspect; he therefore hypocritically pays lip service to the common cult, while worshiping his private gods in secret (p. 62).

It is risky to move in a direction counter to the herd. Any hint of nonconformity is met with expulsion, or worse. The woman who refuses to acknowledge that *Fruits* is "the best book written in fifteen years," without having this statement "proved," is adjudged to be "mad" (p. 71). And another, who tries to point out a misstatement by the critic Mettetal, is called a disturber of the peace, a "mad, exalted creature," who is expelled from the circle of the faithful, lapidated by their looks, closed out of their ranks (p. 97).

Disagreements over the book's importance or merit can have violent repercussions. There are frequent clashes of personality in which one party tries to establish his authority and subjugate his adversaries. This form of intellectual domination is sometimes so brutal as to acquire sadistic overtones. One opinionated reader takes pleasure in forcing others to accept his views:

[...] protected by his carapace, his face in which nothing is divulged but the most placid impartiality, the most perfect indifference, he spies on them, rejoicing in the effectiveness of his blows which no one can foresee, no one is able to parry, delighted to watch his victims, taken unawares by the rapidity, the brutality of his attacks, give way, force themselves wretchedly to remain on their feet, repress their contortions of pain, contain their groans [. . .] (p. 66).

The violence of his aggressiveness is matched by the anger and frustration with which someone else reacts to the pretentious intellectualism of a self-styled expert. He would like to grab the other man by the throat and roar in protest, to handcuff and arrest him for administering a poisoned drug, but he cannot utter a sound, and his choked rage emerges as a mild remonstrance (pp. 57–58).

At the apogee of its popularity, praise of *The Golden Fruits* rises to peaks of hyperbole. Each passage is explored for its richness and resonances. The book is described in exaggerated terms as an earthquake, a tidal wave, a force of nature, a miracle. It is said to mark a turning-point in literature (p. 101). The unanimity of its acclaim is balanced by the unanimity of its subsequent repudiation. Both extremes imply a totalitarian intolerance of dissent. The period when *The Golden Fruits* was most vociferously praised is later recalled as a time of "absolute terror" when any hint of disagreement was instantly quashed: "Nobody dared to budge. Those who took the liberty of expressing the slightest reservation were immediately eyed contemptuously, accused of being callous — brutes, mental defectives. Even between themselves, in the strictest intimacy, the greatest secrecy, they hardly dared to whisper. . ." (p. 134). Again, after the book has fallen into disfavor, a similar proscription awaits anyone who fails to agree with the common consensus. The injunction is plastered like a placard on every wall: "Ignorance of it excuses no man: those who from near or from far, openly or secretly, even in the uttermost depths of their consciences, continue to look upon *The Golden Fruits* with admiration or even mere liking, a bit of fellow feeling, all those who today still consort with it, uphold it, seek excuses or discover extenuating circumstances for it, those who by word or thought give it any support whatsoever, are fools. . ." (p. 148). Except for the relatively innocuous import of the final appellation (the same term used to brand people for their ideas in *"fools say"*), the rest of the pronouncement has the sinister resonance of a fascist proclamation. The tyranny of public opinion is literally that.

The existence of a pontifical hierarchy that hands down pronouncements on Art tends to obfuscate the reader's subjective experience and obliterate his powers of discernment. His opinions are premasticated: he is told what to like and what to dislike. How much easier it is to swallow this spoon-fed pabulum than to make the effort to think for oneself: "We are so eager, aren't we, to safeguard our tranquillity, to nestle down, like everybody else, packed close together in the nice, soothing mildness of innocence, of ignorance..." (p. 75). In their ermine-trimmed robes and judges' toques, the critics render indiscutable verdicts; the more abstruse their opinions, the more inclined are the masses to nod in addlepated agreement.

The critics are as hypocritical as those they lead, as subject to hidden and inauthentic motivations. Each sees in *Fruits* what he wishes to see, using it to underscore preconceived attitudes or as a means of wielding intellectual power. One critic, in an unguarded conversation, has called the book "superb," and now finds himself chained to this initial pronouncement. Another agrees that *Fruits* is a "flawless gem," but for completely contrary reasons. Still another (Parrot by name), who has written an enthusiastic article, is discomfited when he cannot find a single example in the book to support his assertions. He has broken the "golden rule" of criticism — ironically proffered in *Between Life and Death* (p. 102) — that prescribes sticking to generalities and never alluding directly to the text.

Two critics hold themselves aloof from everyone. They define the beauties of literature in a private language of their own, while their listeners are hypnotized into sanctimonious ecstasy. Barricaded behind the locked gates of their palaces, these initiates into a secret mystery are enthroned high above the worshipful multitude; as the ranks of their followers swell, they withdraw deeper into their hermeticism to preserve their majestic inaccessibility. With their arcane jargon and willful exclusivity, these obvious exponents of the new structuralist criticism are nicked by the shafts of Sarraute's wit.

Her satire of critical pretentiousness is summed up in one character's fatuous assertion about another, a painter and author who has expounded his own theories about *The Golden Fruits*: "Ah, if he hadn't painted and drawn, if he hadn't written such marvelous poems, what an amazing critic he would have made!" (p. 92). This subjugation of the creative to the critical process — quite different from Balzac's feeling that "every critic is a failed creator"[8] — carries the implied conclusion that the critic is a better judge of a work of art than the creative artist himself.

The personality of the artist is introduced irrelevantly into the evaluation of his work. After the popularity of *The Golden Fruits* has waned, the author's eccentricities are cited as proof that he could not possibly have written a masterpiece. His detractors produce tidbits of gossip from personal acquaintance or hearsay: Bréhier was cowardly on a mountain-climbing expedition; he is boastful and vain; his collection of comics and jazz records betrays a "platitudinous mind." The attempt to demolish the writer as a person answers a need to reduce the artist to the common denominator of mankind. If he resembles the rest of "us," if his work is only an accident, a curious "excrescence" of his personality (p. 158), then it follows that any one of us is equally capable of producing a work of art (a conclusion echoed in *Between Life and Death* and *Do You Hear Them?*).

To further diminish the artist's importance and his claims to originality, he is classified and pigeonholed according to resemblances with his predecessors. In an amusing juxtaposition of names, Bréhier's work is said to bear the imprint of such heterogeneous influences as Anacréon, Mademoiselle de Scudéry, Lautréamont, Sterne, and Thomas Mann (pp. 166–67). Above all, the author's consciousness of having made a discovery that belongs to him alone, something that has erupted spontaneously from deep within him, is quelled by the chilling proclamation: "Everything has been said. There is nothing new under the sun" (p. 164).

Counterbalancing the numerous inauthentic reactions to a work of art are the few genuine responses which, ignoring the pontifications of the critics and the fickle reversals of favor, insist on hewing to their private standards of judgment. A single dissenter maintains his "purity" of taste, despite the adulation of the group, and tries in vain to shake the others out of their trance. Discerning one other lone defector among the crowd of worshipers, he is heartened in his belief that, thanks to a few isolated individuals like themselves, "truth" will some day triumph (p. 83). One woman claims that her husband is a bulwark of sincerity because he never admired the book, even in the heyday of its success, never allowed himself to be fooled or deceived by its transient popularity:

It's thanks to people like him, pure, upright, strong people, that true values have always succeeded in asserting themselves. They are the rocks against which the waves of conformity, inertia, hysteria, break.... As their number increases, with the passing of time, through the invincible force of their conviction, works either perish or survive. Thanks to them, art goes on (p. 135).

The genuine response to art is of an immediate and intimate nature. It is not rationally directed, but affectively perceived. In fact, on the preconscious level at which it manifests itself, the authentic reaction to art is a form of tropism. It is expressed as an "emanation," a "vibration," a "pulsation" — the same terms Sarraute applies to tropisms themselves. With respect to art, it is not only the recipient who must be sensitively attuned. The work of art, if it is of real merit, must also be capable of producing a vibratory response. When an early reader first picks up *The Golden Fruits,* he finds the sentences stiff and frozen, without the slightest tremor. But after a while he detects a faint resonance: "from one word to the other, from one sentence to the other, the waves spread" (p. 31), until all he wants is to be left alone to read on undisturbed. Much later, after the masses have abjured allegiance to *The Golden Fruits,* one reader insists on casting a last look at the book. In rereading it, "a sort of emanation, a radiance, a light" flow toward him; a current passes between the book and himself. "It's like a vibration, a modulation, a rhythm [...] it's a naïve and skillful arabesque... it scintillates faintly..." (p. 153).[9] An intangible link is forged between the art object and himself. He cherishes this relationship like a secret love affair (the same feeling experienced by the person possessively attached to an "idea," in *"fools say"*): "No word from outside can destroy so natural, so perfect a fusion. Like love it gives us the strength to face anything. Like one in love I should like to hide it" (p. 153). Nonetheless, despite his private inclinations, he feels a sense of mission, like a revolutionary or a messenger of God, to spread the word and acclaim *The Golden Fruits.*

At the end, a single voice is heard questioning the certainties of the group, who are now vaunting other works in the same passionate terms they formerly reserved for *The Golden Fruits.* He feels the need to experience certain sensations for himself, sensations he can only express in halting metaphors:

It's something like what you feel in the presence of the first blade of grass that timidly sends up a shoot... a crocus not yet open... it's that perfume they smell of, but it's not yet a perfume, not even an odor, it has no name, it's the odor of before odors... It seems to me that it's that.... It's something that takes me gently and holds me without letting me go... something untouched, innocent... like a child's slender fingers clinging to me, a child's hand nestling in the hollow of my own (p. 171).

It is this barely perceptible, unsullied emotional experience that is the cachet of genuine aesthetic enjoyment.

This last, anonymous reader seems to serve, if anyone does, as Sarraute's spokesman. Unaffected by the book's popular success or failure, he meticulously searches out its qualities on his own. To overcome his doubts he returns again and again to the source, refusing to dissect the work or to judge it out of context. Through his honesty and sensitivity, he invalidates the specious attitudes assumed by other readers. Their ephemeral enthusiasms vanish before his steadfast loyalty.

In tracing the fortunes of a specific book, Sarraute touches upon certain abstract questions of art. These take the form of discussions that divide the characters into warring factions. The subjects raised are vehicles for tropistic eruptions. The resultant arguments are never conclusive. If anyone "wins," it is by the force of his personality rather than the logic of his persuasion. The characters debate each issue with a pretentious earnestness and superficiality that neutralize (for the reader) both sides of the argument. Among the questions considered are matters which are of concern to Sarraute, but which are here treated as the subject of trite remarks and simplistic solutions: the question of realism in fiction; the extent to which art reflects life, or vice versa; the matter of imitation versus originality; the evaluation of art as a whole or in its parts, etc. The most pressing question concerns the permanence of a work of art. Beyond the undulating waves of popular opinion, which transport first one work then another to the crest of success, then dash them into oblivion, are there any objective criteria for determining a work's enduring value? From the wide spectrum of reactions to *The Golden Fruits,* with its inexplicable ascendancy and equally inexplicable decline, it would appear at first glance that the vagaries of fortune are haphazard and that there is little if any relationship between merit and success.

In the pseudointellectual discussions that are paraphrased and satirized throughout the book, traditional stances are opposed. One reader asks another whether *Fruits* is a work of art, and the clarion reply is yes, because it is "extraordinarily accurate, more real than life" (p. 49). People believe in the magic of the written word, in the writer's omniscience and assurance. The reader tends to rediscover in real life what he has read about in novels: people see life through literature. According to this analogy, art does not imitate life as much as life copies art.[10]

The matter of originality in art — a capital topic for Sarraute — is debated, with burlesque overtones. A character named Jacques is so intent on proving the mediocrity of *The Golden Fruits* that he composes a pastiche, which he attributes to Bréhier. An eminent critic hails the counterfeit page as the best thing Bréhier has ever written. This incident is interpreted as proving Bréhier's (not the critic's) incompetence: if an imitation surpasses the original, it is concluded that the initial text cannot be a masterpiece. Someone argues that a pastiche can be made of any work, it proves nothing. But what if the imitation is better than the original, another voice asks. Perhaps the imitator was a greater genius than the first writer, is the answer. But that conclusion is impossible, according to Jacques. Such an argument is a defense of "academicism." An imitator cannot possibly be a greater genius than the artist he imitates, for a copy is necessarily dead — it contains no new, spontaneous sensation, no direct contact with an unknown substance (p. 143).

In the same context, there arises the question of judging the part or the whole. Because Jacques's pastiche is only one page long, it is considered irrelevant for purposes of assessing the book. A work of art must be judged in its entirety, as a composite structure (p. 144). Just as Alain was preoccupied with one arm of his statuette, someone isolates a single gesture described in *The Golden Fruits* and endows it with a symbolic significance. He is condemned for artificially isolating a segment from the entity to which it belongs. A movement separated from the whole has no meaning, he is told: everything must be integrated in a work of art (p. 54).

At the turning-point in the credit of *The Golden Fruits,* one person poses the question: What is the reason for the sudden change in its popularity? There seem to be no objective criteria on which value judgments are based. It is rather as though a signal were issued, the word passed around. The "collective hallucinations" and inexplicable "infatuations" of the public vanish as mysteriously as they arose. No one seems surprised or perturbed by this metamorphosis, except for the lone questioner. The horrifying answer he receives is that there are no sure values in art. People make mistakes. Tastes change. Even among the masterworks of antiquity, there have been eclipses of vogue. People have different needs at different times. And besides, what does it matter? (pp. 132–33)

The above character is castigated for insisting on "truth" and "absolutes" and imperative rules. He is one of many who make futile attempts to reinstate concepts of order and justice that have no relevance in a world of inauthentic values and mass opinions. People feel an invincible need "to enforce justice, to make truth shine forth" (p. 137), as if objective standards could guarantee stability and permanence in a fluctuating world.

The deep-rooted yearning for certainties in the domain of art mirrors the search for security that has agitated the characters of Sarraute's previous books. The hope is equally fallacious. How can there be objective truth or absolute value in art and literature when innate worth is so debatable as to be indeterminate, when the art object is subject to the inexplicable caprices of fashion, and when extraneous factors of many kinds subvert judgment? The assurance that each person is seeking remains out of reach. In the last analysis, all that counts is direct, personal contact with a work of art. A subjective, soul-felt experience is the only valid determinant. Long after the furor has died down and *The Golden Fruits* has been forgotten, a single persistent admirer wonders if it is not people like himself — timorous, self-effacing, but stubbornly tenacious — who are ultimately responsible for the survival of art (p. 176).

It is impossible to divine the nature or content of the book, *The Golden Fruits,* which is the subject of such diverse and contrary opinion. Sarraute concentrates on the repercussions and ripples it sets in motion, but the book itself is left deliberately ambiguous. It is viewed in much the same way that people are seen — from the outside, through the perspectives of different minds. We never know its essence, only the way it appears to others. Like a mirror, the image it reflects is that of the perceiver. As one reader observes to another, if he does not care for *The Golden Fruits,* this judgment is a "reflection" on himself, not on the book (p. 130).

At times, it seems as though *The Golden Fruits* is the epitome of what is traditional, hackneyed, imitative, and sterile in literature; at other times, it would appear to be a modern, even an "avant-garde," novel. Among the arguments it engenders are to be found all conceivable shades of opinion. Such conflicting views denote the variegations of subjective response and the latitude of interpretation possible with respect to a work of art. For one critic, its appeal lies in its classical language and structure, in the old-fashioned elegance of its style (p. 35). For another, its style is not classical at all, but heavy, awkward, and baroque; what he likes is its modernity, the way it reflects the spirit of the times (p. 44). It is said to be a difficult work that must be read several times to be understood. The "provincial" reader finds it pretentious, full of false mystery and grandiose themes that mask banality of thought and feeling (p. 106). One reader praises its "realism," its structure and organization (p. 49). Another considers it a work of pure contemplation, unrealistic, ambiguous, filled with vaguely sketched characters lacking in depth (p. 91). Still another calls it a fine "metaphysical" novel (p. 155). Various assertions are contrasted in short snippets of contradiction: The book is comic, tragic, boring, engrossing. It is like an empty container into which the reader can pour whatever substance he wishes. "Clear. Dark. Biting. Confident. Smiling. Human. Pitiless. Dry. Moist. Icy. Burning. It transports me into an unreal world. It's the realm of dreams. It's the realest of all worlds. *The Golden Fruits* is all that" (p. 99). (Similarly, the Writer in *Between Life and Death* is dismayed by the variety of reactions to his work and by the meaningless labels with which it is branded: Symbolist, Surrealist, Impressionist. Like a magician's hat with several false bottoms, it yields whatever the reader is looking for.)

Indications are that *The Golden Fruits* is not a New Novel — not the kind Sarraute writes, at any rate — but such an assertion is risky[11] and can be undermined by contrary implications in the text. Indeed, one critic admires *The Golden Fruits* because it contains no "profundities," no swarming larvae, no putrid ooze and miasmic swamps (metaphors Sarraute regularly applies to tropisms). But — as if to contra-indicate a too-hasty appraisal — another reader observes that Bréhier has taken banality as the raw material of his book (the same substance Sarraute uses, and for which Germaine Lemaire castigated Alain Guimier). Bréhier is said to have left platitude in its natural state, "formless" and "dubious"; the reader discovers it as he does in real life, by himself; he has to do the work (p. 115). Is this not precisely what Sarraute and the New Novelists require, that the reader make his own discoveries from the text and lend his cooperation to the creative process?

Just as the essence of *The Golden Fruits* is a ragbag of possibilities, the symbolism of the title is also open to debate. The very name has a classical, almost a mythological ring, with echoes of Atalanta and the golden apples of folklore. One reader calls them "priceless objects... pure golden fruits" (p. 91), round, solid, and flawless. Bréhier's original title was supposedly "Pléonasmes" — an old rhetorical term, meaning superfluity, redundancy, excess of expression. Stylistically, *The Golden Fruits* may exemplify the formal elegance of classic French prose, for one reader exults in its archaic beauty: "Like those large artfully distributed flowers that hold aloft their stiff, serried petals on a faultlessly mown, velvety, thickset lawn, a long, ponderous imperfect of the subjunctive unfurls with regal assurance in the middle of a page read at random, of a smooth, closely knit sentence, the clumsiness of its enormous ending" (p. 34). Bréhier is said to have chosen the title "The Golden Fruits" precisely because of its *trompe-l'oeil* effect: "I wanted my readers to starve to death with that. [...] I want everybody who expects to bite into juicy apples, all the starving ones, to break their teeth on it" (p. 91). Indeed, one woman complains of this very effect: "You expect to bite into juicy pulp and you break your teeth on hard metal..." (p. 44). Someone else is disappointed to note that the substance of the novel has been drained of life, the words have become hardened, varnished, shiny, coated with metal (p. 125). The metallic image is double-edged. The varnished surface may well refer to the hard shell of appearances that Sarraute is bent on cracking, and the book may be an atavistic anachronism. On the other hand, Sarraute has introduced a sufficient number of suspicious hints to splinter *that* façade of certainty along with the rest. Bréhier's stated purpose in writing *The Golden Fruits,* with its allusion to the symbol of fraudulent realism that Sarraute cites in *The Age of Suspicion* — Zenon's painting of a bowl of fruit so lifelike in every detail that the birds were fooled into pecking it — points to a conscious intent to trap the unwary reader. Bréhier may deliberately have created the illusion of reality in order to mislead those literal readers who are always ready to mistake the artificial for the real.

Speculation about the fictional author's intention is idle and irrelevant. It is adduced merely to indicate the danger of adopting any positive position with respect to Sarraute's works. Just as Bréhier's *Golden Fruits* gave rise to contradictory interpretations, so Sarraute's *Golden Fruits* are open to innumerable shades of meaning.

It is perhaps an ironic postscript to this portraiture of the fallibility and fragility of a book's reputation that the pontiffs of opinion, so spryly satirized in its pages, saw fit to award *The Golden Fruits* the International Prize for Literature in 1964.

II Between Life and Death *(1968)*

Like the second part of a diptych, of which the first panel emphasized the critical reception of a work of art, *Between Life and Death* explores the creative experience itself. Nathalie Sarraute had approached this subject obliquely in her previous novels; she now confronts it head on. "Having discovered it progressively in the course of my other books, I believe that the situation of the writer 'between life and death' is for me the most revealing of all. It is an ultimate experience [*expérience limite*] that joins the partial experiences of all my novels."[12]

Where *The Golden Fruits* described a parabolic curve, the movement in *Between Life and Death* is roughly circular. The book begins with a writer who is already successful and famous, and then backtracks to trace his tentative beginnings, his childhood sensitivity and promise, his initial attempts at writing, the submission of his first manuscript, the reaction of parents and friends, the first glimmerings of success, and his ultimate renown — at which point we have come full circle, back to the book's opening scene.

This is not the life story of an individual writer. In fact, there is no indication that the writer in the first scene is the same as the one in the scene's recapitulation, or in any of the other encounters along the way. Rather — just as *The Golden Fruits* was representative of a book, any book, whose nature was kept intentionally vague — so the central figure here is a Writer, any Writer, as he undergoes, either in fact or fantasy, the totality of experiences that are likely to confront him as he fulfills his vocation. Because no particular writer is designated and because his experiences are broadened to include a gamut of possibilities, the figure of the Writer attains a mythic stature, and the incidents of his life cycle acquire a symbolic importance that supersedes the significance of any individual history.

Stages in the Writer's development appear subjectively, from his private perspective, or through the image reflected back to him from other people. The reader is submerged, as always, inside the character's consciousness, seeing and feeling everything on the level of tropisms. The Writer's experience in pursuing his craft is entwined with his experience of life as a person. Because he is an artist, however, he will be among the "hypersensitive" recipients of tropisms who feel everything more keenly and imaginatively than the people around them.

As the book opens, the Writer is performing certain quasi-mechanical gestures: inserting a sheet of paper in his typewriter, tearing it out, crumpling it up, throwing it away. Dissatisfied, he repeats the gesture again and again. Consciously playing to an audience of admirers, he delineates his uncompromising work ethic, while maintaining a careful distance between himself and "them" — all those who may nurture the illusion of being kindred spirits, including the timid soul through whose eyes the scene is viewed, and who hastily refutes any suggestion that he shares the Writer's aim, covertly rejoining the "circle" and melting into anonymity. It is possible that this registering consciousness may in turn develop into a writer himself, or may merely be illustrative of the statement someone makes, that "one Frenchman out of two hides a manuscript in his drawer" (p. 57).

The Writer is unable to explain his creative process. He waits for the words to form on the page: a "miracle," a "mystery" he himself fails to understand. All he can do is expose to his audience the unending effort he is forced to exert, or recall the early signs of his "predestination." The attempt to trace the roots of his writing leads to a contemplation of early childhood experiences (his own or another's) that may (or may not) foreshadow an eventual career.

If anything seems to indicate an early gift or talent, it is a preoccupation with language, which manifests itself in various ways. There is the hypersensitivity to words and their usage, even to variant forms of pronunciation — a tropistic reaction on an instinctive, emotional level. Certain words seem to exude a noxious emanation, an "effluvium" to which the writer, as a child, reacts violently. The slurring of particular vowel sounds brings about a physical revulsion. This sensitivity to quirks of pronunciation — the basis for the tropism-induced tension in the play, *Isma* — is not merely an attribute of the incipient Writer, but becomes the impetus for the act of writing itself, as he privately explores the sensations aroused by his aversion to what others label a "vulgar" accent.

Language can be a source of delight as well as pain. The Writer-as-child is infatuated with words. He plays with them as if they were toys. Mumbling a series of homonyms to himself, in rhythm with the moving wheels of a train (*"Hérault, héraut, aire haut, erre haut"*), he revels in the imagery that each word conjures up: a lavender landscape, an eagle's eyrie, a knight on a richly caparisoned charger... (pp. 16–17). His mother's reactions reveal divergent possibilities. Either she calls him back to "reality" by pointing out sights of interest, emphasizing facts, insisting that the essential thing to possess is the gift of observation (talents associated with Balzacian-type realism). Or alternatively, she cultivates his sensibilities, teaching him to appreciate colors, textures, and odors — the feel of a rabbit's fur, the down on a chick's back, the velvety petals of springtime buds.

His early sensitivity to language is noted as a sign of the child's "predestination." Words are the unhewn stuff of literature — a block of marble that has yet to receive the imprint of the sculptor's chisel. When one person suggests that words are of primary concern to a writer, he is acknowledging only half — but an essential half — of the components of creativity: "A poet is not, as people think, someone who knows better than others how to look at heaven and earth, listen to the sound of the sea, the trilling of brooks and birds, a poet [...] is the man who knows how to make a poem out of words" (p. 26). Observation and sensibility are insufficient by themselves; the writer must in addition manipulate language, the raw material of his craft. Later, it is by the "magic" of words forming almost of their own volition that the Writer acquires the first taste of his creative powers. As one character in *The Golden Fruits* remarked: "Without words, there's nothing. With words, its the sensation itself that emerges, that is set in motion [...] Words create [...]. Words can induce sensation in the writer" (*Fruits,* p. 57.)[13]

Language has deleterious powers, as well, apart from the joy it can induce in an impressionable young mind. In the alien world of childhood, words serve as passwords, a "secret language" used to exclude "him." Words can inflict pain more sharply than weapons — hurled like harpoons to embarrass and wound. Words are affixed to him like tags to denote his uniqueness: "child prodigy" and "misfit." The terms are used synonymously.

The equation of these two characteristics has Romantic overtones. The implication that the creative artist is a breed apart, unadapted to life in society, echoes the notions of the nineteenth-century Romanticists, for whom the man of genius was marked by a special "sign" (like the precocious child, p. 25); not only did he display uncommon sensitivity, but he was a martyr in a hostile society that failed to comprehend him,[14] just as Sarraute's Writer-to-be feels defenseless inside the enemy camp (p. 28).

Prognostications of his "predestination" evoke ambivalent reactions in the would-be Writer. Even as a child, he is torn between the consciousness of being "different" and the yearning to be "one of them." Pitifully he wails that he is "exactly like them" (p. 28), and again cries out, "We're exactly alike" (p. 55), but he convinces no one, least of all himself. He recognizes the fallacy of what he keeps on insisting: "He is made of a more porous, more absorbent material. . . . Each drop secreted by them, a simple word with no importance, an accent, anything at all, penetrates him, provokes disturbances, makes him lose his sense of proportion, of moderation, blurs his eyesight, his mind. . ." (p. 55). His supersensitivity sets him apart, even as he tries to deny it. His dilemma — preserving self-identity while belonging to the group — is not unique to the creative artist. It is the same conflict that Sarraute has abstracted as a universal preoccupation, magnified in the case of the would-be creator by the extent of his uniqueness and the acuity of his sensibility.

As he develops into a Writer, the young man is adamant about asserting his individuality. Artistically, he resents being compared with other writers. Like Bréhier, he is convinced that what he has written is a spontaneous revelation unique to himself: "It's his own sensation, fresh, intact, new. . . nurtured on what is hidden in his heart of hearts. . . . It is his most intimate substance which, unaided, is finding its form, as though it burst out in spite of him" (*Fruits,* p. 162). The masses prefer to prove that, like all writers, he is the victim of a delusion. Everything has already been said, every terrain prospected and occupied, every rosebush and hawthorne already described (p. 59). The neophyte's publisher (or agent) discerns the influence on him of a writer whom the author has not even read — just as far-fetched influences had been noted on *The Golden Fruits.* Again there is the contrast, limned in *Fruits,* between two opposing attitudes: the critics' insistence that it is impossible to be new and inventive, versus the writer's confident belief in his originality.

As he enters the confrérie of established writers, the newcomer resents being classified as one of them. He is especially unwilling to share the ineffable experience of creation — something as private and incomparable as love (an echo of Bréhier's sense of intimacy with his inspiration). The other writers assure him that they have known the same feeling. He is not alone, nor is he unique. "Even that, believe it or not, we have in common. So you see, we are alike" (p. 84). Ironically, the assurance of resembling the others and being accepted into their "circle" — something the Writer had sought in vain in his childhood — is a condition he is loath to admit with respect to his art.

The Writer is ambivalent about exposing his work to the public. Fearful of revealing it to the indifference of strangers, he would prefer to hide it from profane eyes. But the only way to confirm his belief in himself is to subject his writing to the scrutiny of the world. His self-confidence must be bolstered by impartial corroboration. An artist cannot exist in a vacuum, hugging his work to himself. In order to live, a book needs a reader. This is the "terrible ambiguity" with which the Writer is faced, tossed back and forth between his wish for solitude and the contrary need for other people's approbation.[15] He vacillates between a yearning to be admired and a pretense of unconcern. He resents being ignored, but trembles when his work is read. Upon hearing his book praised, he becomes humble with gratitude, like a man who has escaped death. Ironically, what is admired most resoundingly is not even present in his book. As in *Fruits,* criticism is seen to be a hollow exercise, bogged down in irrelevance and generalities. The adroit critic can extract whatever he wishes from a work of art. "No need to make an effort, to read, even to leaf through — why waste one's time? Everybody knows that [. . .] you can show anything anywhere. . ." (p. 102).

As the Writer begins to achieve a modicum of success, he finds himself further and further removed from the solitary experience of writing, more and more on public display. Pressures on his life take many forms, all detracting from his spontaneous relationship with his work. Friends insist on ferreting out his sources or recognizing themselves in his book. Psychological explanations are bandied about — defense mechanisms, childhood traumas, subconscious needs — labels designed to divest his writing of mystery and reduce the Writer to human proportions. The resemblance he had previously sought becomes a badge of mediocrity: "Look at him. He is made, that's quite true, in our image. Just like us" (p. 110). His father mocks him as a renegade who has always derogated society's values and who has now, by accepting money and signing a contract, become a part of the system he had previously disdained. His mother's reaction is equally oppressive. She takes credit for having guided him through his future kingdom like a young crown prince, convinced from infancy of his "predestination." He finds her simpleminded faith suffocating.

Further obstacles beset the Writer as a result of his increasing renown. He discovers, to his surprise and discomfiture, the public's mania for peering into his private life and habits (he has yet to learn the importance of Balzac's cane and Baudelaire's trousers). The simple act of pouring tea for a visitor is transformed into a ceremonial rite; his spurt of anger on a bus becomes part of the folklore that has begun to surround him. As a necessary stage in his apprenticeship, he is told he must exchange his natural timidity for assurance and authority. His admirers turn him into an automaton who performs the mechanical gestures they teach him to use: he extends his arm, bends it, clenches his fist, and repeats the singsong chant: "I take a page. I tear it out. I crumple it. I throw it away" (p. 148) — the same words he (or his prototype) pronounced, accompanied by the same gestures, in the opening chapter. The circle is complete.

The Writer has now arrived at the apogee of his career. With mastery and self-confidence have come arrogance and tyranny. He is considered a seer, a sage, a sphinx, a sorcerer, "the creator who only complies with his own laws" (p. 151) — another Romantic notion. He tolerates no criticism, demands total adhesion. To test his powers he clacks his whip and shouts, "Debout les morts!" ("Arise the dead!") His listeners tremble. Fearfully they remind him they were speaking of "Moors," not *"morts,"* of events in Mauritania.[16] He raises his whip once again. "Debout les morts!" It is his right and his pleasure to say what he chooses. They acquiesce. They are trained (pp. 149–50).

This is the moment of greatest danger for the Writer's future course. He has reached the same stage as Germaine Lemaire,[17] applauded and successful; like her, he has lost touch with the humble fountainhead of inspiration. Either he is doomed to go round in circles, endlessly repeating his gestures like a mechanical doll, emptied of his creative vitality. Or else he will find the strength to renounce the artificial trappings of fame and return to the wellspring of his original talent.

In the midst of his gesticulations and sententious pronouncements, he detects "her" presence — the one person he cannot deceive. She acts as a catalyzing force that obliges him to confront the torpor to which he has succumbed, to abandon the comfort of his entrenched position. He sees himself as a corpse lying in state in a funeral home — an image that calls to mind all those dead writers before whose embalmed and waxen figures the silent generations filed past, in *The Golden Fruits* (p. 165). Unlike Germaine Lemaire, who stifles the small voice of self-doubt, this writer has the courage to turn his back on success. Fleeing the blandishments of his friends, the false adulation of his fans, the metallic quavers of the critics, he reverts to the privacy and solitude of his artistic labors.

There are two instances in the novel when Sarraute probes the mystery of the creative act. The first time the writer was in his novitiate, this time he has already achieved the goals of success. In each case, he must withdraw into himself to face the unnameable "mystery," the "miracle" that the posturing writer in Chapter I found himself unable to fathom. It is not the method or technique of writing that Sarraute attempts to convey, not the mechanical gesture of the writer at his machine or the superficial recipe for success *he* recites. Instead, she examines the writer's sensations at the instant of creation, transcribing the creative impulse itself, like a tropism at its incipient stage. Mary McCarthy has enthusiastically described this section of the novel: "Nothing of the sort — a rending of the veil — has been attempted before, and one would have said in advance that it was impossible, short of demonstration, to show how an author composes, that is, to create with words a sort of program music imitating the action of other words as they assemble on a page."[18]

The two scenes presenting the Writer in the very act of creation are variations of what is essentially a repeatable experience. In the first, he functions as a passive receptacle, floating and drifting in a dreamlike trance, waiting to recapture an elusive sensation. Words form in his mind of their own volition, independently of his effort. Like a mounting geyser, they erupt in an irresistible propulsion, spouting new words in their wake. He becomes fascinated by the exotic shapes they assume. They are like smooth round pebbles, strung together. They reverberate in strong cadences, move in graceful arabesques. He admires the artful effects of their combination. Sometimes a word projects a beam of blinding light; it is strident and brilliant, or opaque and dim. Words become particles of steel aligned in a magnetized design. They reflect and refract one another in a maze of mirrors. From afar, they form a block of chiseled stones fitted precisely together (pp. 66–67).

Afterwards, the Writer considers the structure the words have assumed. This is the moment when the artist must divide himself in
two, to render self-judgment on what he has accomplished. There is
no one who can replace him in this awesome moment of evaluation.
As Sarraute has explained:

I think that each writer, each artist [. . .] has a kind of double, who, from
time to time as he works, stands back and looks at his painting or rereads
his text. He is both himself and someone else. He often becomes a
completely merciless judge. [. . .] There are times when he can be mistaken, but when it comes to the work, it is almost imperative that he have
faith in his judgment, since he is the only judge.[19]

The process of autocriticism is rendered fictionally in the form of
a dialogue between the artist's twin halves: his critical and creative
faculties. The one is severe and uncompromising, the other
apologetic and self-justifying. One pronounces an implacable
verdict on the other: what he has written is dead, without a breath
of life. No matter what other technical terms may be used, only two
words matter: it's "dead" or it's "alive." The artist's creative half
begs to be allowed to salvage some part of the beautiful monument
he has erected. His critical self is intransigent; he must begin all
over again. This is the obverse side of the mechanical act of
Chapter 1: "I tear it out, I crumple it, I throw it away." Here, the
act is repeated, but the words and feelings occur on a more
authentic and introspective level: "You give up, destroy, forget,
and start over" (p. 71).

When asked if the Writer is deluded or if his work is really alive,
Sarraute once said:

It is very hard to say. This is what makes writing almost agonizing. The
more you polish the form and perfect it, the more it hardens, becomes
frozen, and dies. [. . .] It is often almost dangerous to polish the writing
and the form too much. It often happens — precisely when the polishing
has been intense and the form has taken on an aspect of great beauty
which delights the writer when he first reads it — that when he comes back
to it a few days later he sees that it is a corpse, entirely dead and meaningless. The reason is that, having lost all contact with his initial feeling, he
has been carried away by the charm of language as such. Language has
taken over and has necessarily sought harmony and an extremely
dangerous aesthetic form; the surge, the aggressive force, and the expectation of something which is about to be born have all been lost.[20]

Like the child fascinated by homonyms, the Writer in his first attempt had been captivated by words, had allowed words to take over; the result was lifeless. He sets out once again in search of his initial sensation, the imperceptible vibration he first felt stirring in the darkness. He wanders alone in frozen, limitless regions where no one has set foot before, his entire being concentrated on a single goal. When at last he detects a minuscule movement, he reaches out toward it with all his strength; again and again, it eludes his grasp. Finally, he takes hold of it, with one wrenching effort — and is carried away.... This time he allows no frivolous ornaments of style to encumber the "particle of living substance" he has so laboriously ensnared; he works until he is satisfied, even with his own dissatisfaction.

The pompous self-importance that often accompanies success stifles talent and destroys that intimate contact with a fresh, spontaneous sensation that is the sole guarantee of vitality in art. Even at the moment of gesticulating for his audience's benefit, the Writer recognizes in his heart that he has taken liberties with that indefinable something that can only be approached with precaution and respect — that "something" which he personifies, in the same way the Romantics personified their "muse": "May her ladyship deign to make an appearance... everything will be done to serve her" (p. 162). The Writer realizes he was mistaken in dressing her with the elegance of a grand couturier model, for she has acquired the stiff, anonymous grace of a waxen mannequin (like the *oeuvre* of Germaine Lemaire/Madame Tussaud).

For the second time there comes a renewal of the creative act. Now the Writer has to contend with his mastery over the language, with the icy images that arise under his pen. It is more difficult to break the mold of habit and more painful to descend to the initial sources of inspiration. Once again he addresses his "double," the critical half of himself — but something has changed between them. Formerly two words sufficed: "dead" or "alive." Now his double indulges in a potpourri of critical expressions that grotesquely imitate the metallic falsetto of the critic on his pedestal. The Writer discovers in the end that only one thing matters: to follow inspiration wherever it leads, "this untouched, living thing," whose presence is the sole object of the artist's pursuit. The only criterion he considers valid, regardless of critics and readers alike, is the living breath that emanates from his work, like the fine mist that forms on a mirror, attesting to the presence of life.

At the hub of the circular movement governing the Writer's experience is the creative act, which must continually be relived and renewed. The title Sarraute eventually selected has a dual significance.[21] It refers both to the writer himself, poised on the brink "between life and death," and to the work of art, which is either "dead" or "alive." The writer's grappling with his art takes the form of a life-and-death struggle in which all his vital energy is engaged (p. 158). When the Writer first emerges from the throes of creativity, his joyful sensation is equated with the "euphoria of those about to die" (p. 75). After his book is well received, he feels like a survivor who has narrowly escaped death (p. 98). When his creative impulse is stifled, he becomes a cadaver, embalmed in a funeral home. The Writer's experience as an artist is epitomized in the imagery of life and death: when he writes he is alone, "as at the moment of his birth, as at the moment of his death" (p. 84). The experience of creativity is as profound as life, as final as death, and as unfathomable as both.

More than anything, the metaphor expresses the fragility of creative expression, threatening at any moment to become ossified and inert. The vibration of life is the criterion Sarraute has always used to determine the value of a work of art — in the case of her own reading pleasure, in Germaine Lemaire's assessment of her work, in the father's aesthetic enjoyment in *Do You Hear Them?*. A barely-perceptible pulsation is a signal of *The Golden Fruits'* vitality; a throbbing beat is the Writer's aim in his burgeoning work — an indication that it is vigorous, natural, and, above all, alive.

Perhaps *Between Life and Death* is the most "personal" of Nathalie Sarraute's novels, not because it is in any way autobiographical (she takes pains to assure the reader that it is not), but because it transcribes an experience she has lived intimately as a writer herself. She has said she feels a "particular predilection" for this work,[22] in which she has attempted to reveal the experience of literary creation "as sincerely as possible, just as I myself live it or just as I believe other writers live it. It is something that is very difficult to re-create. I have only been able to pluck out a few fragments." She closes her ears to theoreticians who discuss the creative process, trusting only her inner feelings. For Sarraute, as for the Writer she depicts in *Between Life and Death,* the point of departure is something she feels (*"le ressenti"*), a tremulous vibration she tries to transmute into language. There is the constant risk that language will depart from the living source, that it will become empty and cold, will cling to old conventions of beauty and harmony, or assume a false air of originality or obscurity. When this happens, the writer must destroy everything he has written and begin his quest all over again: "The sensation still intact which impels him to create is something that belongs to him alone, that cannot be compared to anything else, a fragment, however slight, of absolute value. It is this thing that he must transform into words, that he must cause to exist in language. The fusion of sensation and language is a unique experience."[23] As the neophyte Writer discovers after his enchanted play with words, language divorced from feeling is glazed and dull. There must be a mysterious alliance of words and sensation, a rhythmic alternation in which first one element and then the other assumes the ascendancy. Sensation propels words and helps them take shape, but sometimes the reverse is true, and language itself precipitates feeling. An ongoing struggle takes place between the initial sensation and the ensuing "verbalization," a continuous interaction between two opposing forces, as language attempts to concretize feeling, and feeling threatens to escape the strictures of language. Sarraute believes in the existence of what she calls a "prelanguage": a sensation, a perception that seeks expression in words. As she explained to Alain Robbe-Grillet: "For me, something is stirring in the darkness, and I have a desire to bring it into existence in the form of language, because I love language."[24]

Whatever the medium he chooses, the creative artist must somehow "give form to the unformed, expression to the inexpressible, rhythm and movement to existence."[25] The creative act is both a paradox and an enigma. As Balzac once suggested: "Perhaps works form in the soul as mysteriously as truffles amid the perfumed plains of Périgord."[26] Sarraute has gone as far as anyone before her in attempting to resolve the enigma, pierce the mystery, and grasp the fugitive tropisms that accompany artistic creativity.

III Do You Hear Them? *(1972)*

Still concerned with the overall question that has preoccupied her since *Fruits* — "the relationship between the work of art, the environment into which it falls, and its fate in general"[27] — Sarraute focuses this time not on the creator but the art-lover, the recipient of the creator's productivity. Her attention centers on the nature of aesthetic appreciation and the conflict of attitudes between traditional and innovative approaches to art.

The arena of dramatic action is once again restricted to a family enclave, where the issues of aesthetic pleasure, artistic values, permanence and durability, originality and inventiveness, are scaled down to the modest dimensions of domestic interaction. The opposition between two aesthetic attitudes, represented by the contrary tendencies of a father and his children, are evinced not in intellectual discourse but in the myriad emotion-packed tropisms of everyday living. Both parties are motivated by love and a desire to transmit to the other what is most precious to each. This wish — and its frustration — is what endows the abstract issues with human pathos.

The father has tried to reconcile his two conflicting passions — tenderness for his children and devotion to art — by instilling in his children his aesthetic appreciation, but to no avail. They find his values old-fashioned, favoring instead an unrestrained freedom of creative expression. The father's desire to share his aesthetic enjoyment is similar to the artist's need to communicate his creative enthusiasm to others. It is a means of confirming his belief and ensuring its survival, like a precious inheritance he wishes to bequeath.

The movement of the book rides up and down on geysers of laughter that erupt, subside, and then burst forth afresh. The scene opens with the sound of ringing laughter. The father and an old friend are seated in front of a coffee table, admiring together the primitive sculpture of a small stone animal. The children have gone upstairs to bed. Suddenly, peals of laughter are heard overhead; the father surmises that the children are making fun of his precious stone statue. With each renewed outburst of merriment, he is beset by an assortment of tropismatic responses to their suspected mockery. The act of running up and down the stairs, in response to the repeated eruptions of laughter, corresponds in a physical way to his emotional oscillation between his two loves: the children in their bedroom upstairs, the stone figurine in the living room below.

To the extent that he is affected by the tropisms emanating from upstairs, the father vacillates in his feelings about the little stone animal. When he is interrupted in the midst of his enraptured contemplation by what he interprets to be the youngsters' scoffing, the priceless statuette loses its "vibrations" and becomes a crumbly piece of stone. He even begins to doubt its authenticity as a work of art, and in the end he "sacrifices" it by handing it over to his children.

The father's attitude toward the latter is equally ambivalent, alternating between waves of affection and anger. He pretends at first that their laughter is natural and innocuous. Sarraute's descriptive metaphors — a series of poetic clichés — connote the soothing effect of prefabricated concepts:[28] "Tiny bells. Tiny drops. Fountains. Gentle water-falls. Twittering of birds" (p. 1). The laughter is as limpid as "living water, springs, little brooks running through flowering meadows" (p. 14). As the father's suspicions begin to fester, the metaphors become correspondingly sinister. Soon the "titters" grow "sharp as needles," and the water drips on its victim like a Chinese torture (p. 63). The laughter turns into the cracking and stinging of narrow whips (p. 114), the hammer of boots marching down a street (p. 126). The father ends up sinking into a morass of tropisms, "manufacturing from this laughter miasmas, asphyxiating gases, deadly microbes, a river of rottenness, a sea of muck" (p. 127).

Like the narrators of the earlier books, the father has created "something" out of "nothing." *Creatio ex nihilo.* The children's laughter is what he interprets it to be. He constructs entire scenarios based on his creative imaginings. The friend accuses him of wallowing in his misconceptions. All the father need do is sweep his hand through the air and "nothing" will remain but the innocent laughter of children — another prefiguration of *Isma, ou ce qui s'appelle rien.*

The father's fanatic convictions occasionally falter in the face of his children's merriment. Their exhilaration and gaiety exert a powerful attraction against the counterweight of traditional values. He flees to join in them that secret part of himself that he had thought buried but that has been revived in them: a quiescent rebelliousness, a refusal to compromise. He would like to share in their laughter, even at his own expense. At moments like these, he turns to his friend for help in resisting them: "They're sucking me up . . . save me, protect me" (p. 23). The old friend, reflectively chewing the stem of his pipe (another "English" characteristic?) exhibits a phlegmatic composure that comforts the father. He is the unflappable "witness" whom Sarraute has inserted into all her books, the voice of reason and common sense, impervious to inner movements, untroubled by tropisms. Like Dumontet at the end of *Portrait,* he is the guarantor of a false stability, an apparent permanence. He is an impregnable fortress, insensitive to the wavelets lapping against its walls, "to the tiny creatures moving about in the ooze of the moat" (p. 119). For him there is nothing insidious in the children's bubbling laughter; it is the spontaneous exuberance of youngsters at play.

The father's devotion to art has all the hallmarks of religious fervor; hence he perceives his children's indifference as a form of heresy. The recurrent religious symbolism denotes, as it did in *Fruits,* reverence for acknowledged values in art. The stone figurine is looked upon as their father's "sacred object," which the children are expected to approach "reverently," in "religious silence," before trooping upstairs to bed, "steeped in devotion" (pp. 7–8). But they do not share in their father's sterile cult; they are free from flagellations, prosternations, long hours of vigil (p. 117). In their emancipated view of art, "All are chosen. All are called" (p. 117). There are no initiates and no precepts of indoctrination. Nonetheless, the father has attempted over the years to "convert" them to his concept of beauty and love of art. He has dragged them to museums and exhibits, sugarcoating his instruction with anecdotes, carefully couching his value judgments in the casual idiom of the young: "All the same, it's not a bad job, that little number. All the same, that's damned fine..." (p. 26).[29] In order not to rebuff their sensibilities, he has pretended the merest lip service to the cult of art: "A pure formality, a brief genuflexion, a gesture of the hand that dips into the holy water and makes a rapid sign of the cross..." (p. 26). When gentle coaxing proves ineffectual, the father turns virulent and sarcastic; as Sarraute explains, "the emotion he feels is akin to religious fanaticism, for it is a question of imposing an absolute, and punishing blasphemy."[30]

Scenes escalate in the father's imagination, as he broods over his children's suspected mockery. Tiny tropisms are magnified into full-blown detail. The first scene takes the form of an interrogation by a social worker, instigated by complaints of the father's abuse. One little girl sobs that he flew into a rage and "bit" her when she failed to show proper respect for that awful stone creature. The father demands proof of her allegation, but his are averred to be the kind of bites that "don't show" (p. 69) — like all familial bruises, the scars they leave are invisible, albeit indelible. The social worker reprimands him in turn for coddling his children and turning them into sensitive hothouse plants. In this fictitious scene, she is the mouthpiece for the forces of society represented elsewhere in Nathalie Sarraute's novels by cohorts of concierges and gossips whose collective opinion often shores up a faltering conscience.

The second imaginary scene is a courtroom trial, based on the friend's reference to the children as "mean natures" — an appraisal the father has elicited by his own complaints about them. The dispute revolves around the hair-splitting interpretation of the friend's comment: did he say they *are* or they *would be* "mean natures"? The friend testifies from the witness stand that he said they *would be,* out of politeness, though he would have liked to say they *are,* in order to teach the father a lesson, for he finds it shocking to hear him speak ill of his children in the hypocritical hope of being contradicted (a devious aim that will again be castigated in *The Lie*). As for the laughter that upset the plaintiff, he personally would have paid it no attention. "Live and let live," is his motto. "Live and let live," is the ensuing verdict. The father finds this a comforting conclusion. With this platitude as a guide, the children can be expected to tolerate the foibles of their elders, and vice versa. "Live and let live" means that what is "alive" for one (the stone animal, for instance) is "dead" for the others — the basic symbolism of *Between Life and Death*.

At this juncture, when is he ready to "live and let live," the father experiences a temporary sensation of deliverance and peace, a lull in the battle for his children's adherence. Free from the nagging awareness of *their* reactions, he immerses himself in aesthetic pleasure, and for a brief moment he knows a joy that exists outside time, "a motionless instant" that partakes of infinity (p. 84). The tranquillity he seeks and finds in the contemplation of art depends on the permanence of his cherished values; it is the serenity Alain sought from an immutable universe. The children perceive his devotion to art differently, as a futile attempt to immobilize the inevitable process of change: his art treasure, "an obstacle set on the path of time" (p. 45), is the sacred vessel in which he hopes to capture an absolute and arrest the passage of time.

The father's visceral feeling for art is incapable of being explained on rational grounds; it is an emotional response, a sympathetic "vibration," a subjective delight of the highest order. Whereas the aesthetic judgments voiced in *Fruits* were largely "inauthentic," the father's veneration for art is sincere and absorbing. The art lover's withdrawal and communion with a work of art resembles the artist's solitary immersion in the act of creation. For both, it is an experience that transcends the everyday concerns of existence — a private and personal means of acceding, if only

transitorily, to a meaningful reality. The amateur of art, especially
when he comes across some rare object, feels the breathless sense of
discovery that the creative artist knows, for what he has done is to
"create, to confer life a second time. To snatch from death, from
decay..." (p. 10). The creator and the art-lover — the two major
figures of *Life and Death* and *Do You Hear Them?* — participate
in the inseparable duality of the aesthetic experience, the one
creating and the other responding to creation, while both vibrate in
unison through the art object that links them.

The purity of aesthetic enjoyment is not without its seamy under-
side. If the response to beauty is sensual and voluptuous in nature,
the father's fascination with art has obscene connotations. When
he pretends to be working, he often sneaks off to a museum to in-
dulge in his solitary pleasure, his "secret vice." Implied in the
children's attitude is the view that he and his friend are two "dirty
old men," roués, rakes, hedonists, who smack their lips in immoral
delight over some treasure they have tracked down, or lasciviously
assume the pose of a statue they have seen.

The children emerge from their room to catch their father red-
handed, "buttoning up" in embarrassment at having been detected
at his artistic orgy (p. 88). An alternate interpretation of their motives is possible. Perhaps they have come down to admire the little
animal in reverent silence. Or is this only an "idyllic vision" born
of the father's "senile desires" and his "miserable dissolute
imagination?" (p. 95). There is no way of reading the children's
thoughts, no way of knowing if they came downstairs, or if the
father only pictured their doing so. There is no delineation between
"real" and "imagined" events. It is possible that everything in the
book takes place in the father's mind and that what appear to be
the friend's or children's thoughts are merely projections of his
own. There is an ambiguity of optic throughout the novel — an
ambiguity that is reinforced by the interchangeability of the
characters.

An anonymous resemblance blots out all distinctions. Of course,
there are no names or individualized traits; this the reader of Sarraute has come to expect and accept (she has said she was obliged to
resort to one bit of "trickery" in using the designation of "old
friend" to distinguish one "he" from the other).[31] The children,
for instance, are an amorphous group, of indeterminate age,
number, and gender. Their attitudes and identities often blend with
those of the father, despite the contradictory positions they sup-

posedly hold: "I wanted to show a kind of interaction between consciousnesses which are extremely close to one another to the extent that they almost fuse and communicate by a kind of continuous osmosis. [...] What each one feels and attributes to another becomes blurred in a sort of kaleidoscopic conflict in which each becomes any one of the others at any given moment."[32]

The resemblance is reinforced by frequent transpositions, in which the parent becomes a child, and vice versa. For instance, when the father visits them humbly in their bedroom, he is "like a child who has come up to his mother to get a kiss, then goes back, reassured, to play with his little friends" (p. 104). (As always, there is a basic ambiguity: is it the father who feels like a child, or the children who treat him that way, or both?) In another breath, he fulminates against the modern generation, complaining that nowadays a parent has no right to criticize his children: "You walk on tiptoe, you shrink in size" (p. 107) — in French, "on se fait tout petit," i.e., you become little, like a child. The father thus articulates the present-day inversion of roles that finds parents catering to their children and children ruling their parents — a metamorphosis that is represented symbolically by the father's *turning into* a child in their presence: smiling a little boy's sheepish smile as he attempts to join in their games (p. 107), or looking so forlorn that they give him back his "rattle," the stone animal, which they have bedecked in a paper ruff (p. 115), or eyeing his friend with "the look of an embarrassed child asked to recite his poem before the assembled family" (p. 117), or, frustrated by his children's supercilious attitude, beating his little fists against their powerful chests (p. 123).

Just as there is a fusion (or confusion) between father and children, so there is an overlapping of identity between father and friend. United in their attitude toward art, they are specifically yoked as "two old lunatics" (p. 21), a pair of twins (p. 41), two high-priests, two tyrants (p. 43), members of the same caste and sect (p. 55), belonging to the same rank and species (p. 87). Like the *alter ego* in *Portrait* and *Planetarium,* the old friend functions as the father's "double." He is precisely what the father would be if he could shake off his anxiety and rid himself of tropisms. The children refer to the friend as their father's "brother," his "double," his "very image," the mirror in which he can see himself reflected (pp. 100–101). The two men are allied in their attachment to the clumsy stone figurine, to which they bear an implied resemblance.

The children tell their father he is "as heavy and lifeless as this animal" (p. 116), and refer to the friend in similar fashion: he is like a cumbersome bear (p. 74), heavy and squat (p. 42), with a "fat torso" (p. 45) and "pudgy hands" (p. 51). The "animal" imagery applied to both men underscores their similarity and contrasts their ponderous inertia with the youngsters' mercurial temperament and insouciance. The father is the "big bad wolf" who stops the rosy piglets in the midst of their dance (the same image was used in *Martereau*); he is an "angry cur" who barks at his daughter (p. 68), a "beast" that is finally smoked out of its lair (p. 103). When the children prevail on their father to free himself from his set ways, to whirl lightly as they do, he feels like a "pachyderm" starting to dance (p. 118). The stone animal comically clad in a dancer's tutu and the father clumsily gyrating like a trained elephant are parodies of one another, implicitly connected.

The children's act of adorning the stone animal with a paper ruff — like drawing a mustache on the Mona Lisa — is not just a nose-thumbing gesture directed toward the sanctity of Art. It is a form of creativity in its own right. When the father demands to know who perpetrated this outrage, the children calmly reply that it was a "collective effort," achieved in "a moment of inspiration" (p. 113). They take no pride in authorship, partake of no cult of perfection. Their creation is joyful and free, unfettered by rules. For them, everyone has the potential to become an artist; all are "equals," all are "geniuses" (p. 115).[33] Spontaneity and innovation are the hallmarks of their art.

The children reach out in tenderness to their father, as he had tried awkwardly to reach out to them. They urge him to abandon his inhibitions and share their exuberant unconstraint. In the end, he capitulates in the name of the "togetherness" they have gropingly attained. Their laughter has finally been emptied of its sinister content. It has escaped the confining strictures of labels: Innocent. Mocking. Sly. None of these sclerotic terms is adequate or appropriate to retain the essence of their relationship — a fluid, boundless quality that circulates between them. The father seals his "surrender" by handing over the stone animal.

Ironically, it is the children who donate the statuette to the Louvre. It is they who display it to out-of-town visitors as a rare object that once belonged to their family. Remember when one of us called it a Cretan sculpture? Father was ready to kill us. . . . Poor papa! They bustle off on their sight-seeing rounds. There is the

sound of carefree laughter fading away.... A door closes overhead, and nothing more is heard.

This ambiguous ending can be interpreted in two ways. Either
everything that preceded has taken place in the father's mind, the
drama has come full circle, and we are back where we started: the
children's laughter dies down, their door is finally closed, they have
gone to sleep.... Or else, more fancifully, the ending refers to a future time when the father has died (the children say they must make
a pilgrimage to the Père Lachaise cemetery) and the stone figurine
is relegated to the status of a mummified object enshrined in a museum. Having paid lip service to their dead father's dead cult of art,
the younger generation hurries about its business, laughing as always: "Laughter for no one. Laughter in space" (p. 147). From
some observation post, outside time and space, it is as though the
father's spirit were watching; with absolute finality, it is as though
a door "up there" were to close. The permanent aesthetic values he
cherished have become part of history, a closed and forgotten chapter, while art has accomplished its inevitable course. As the father
had already intimated to his friend, it is possible that they are "the
inhabitants of Pompeii entombed under the ashes" (p. 100) and
that "life" has passed over to the other side, among the young.

The ancient stone figurine is an apt symbol of a traditional, even
an atavistic, concept of art. As a piece of primitive sculpture whose
aesthetic merit remained eclipsed for centuries, it represents the
concrete recognition that tastes change and that the first part of
the dictum, *ars longa vita breve,* is only relative. As in *The Golden
Fruits,* the question is posed but remains unresolved: What constitutes an enduring work of art? The little statue has an additional
symbolic significance. Because it may once have been a mythic
beast that was used in some ancient religious rite, it appropriately
represents the sacred cult of art at whose shrine the two older men
worship but which the children abjure. As an extension of the
French saying, *chercher la petite bête,* the "little beast" also
concretizes the father's mania for spying on and judging his
children, constantly seeking out the disruptive tropisms they may
be secreting. When the friend is interrogated in the imaginary
courtroom, he says he is a simple man who dislikes complications:
"Je ne cherche pas la petite bête." (The English translation — "I
don't split hairs" (p. 70) — though accurate, forcibly ignores the
extended symbolism of the French cliché.). Sarraute's use of this
commonplace expression is cleverly expanded into a literal rendi-

tion of its metaphoric content. *Chercher la petite bête* is precisely
what the father does — figuratively, in his obsession with his
children's reactions, and literally, in his preoccupation with "the
little beast."

Although some critics interpret the conflict in *Do You Hear
Them?* as the "generation gap,"[34] the real clash is between two antithetical conceptions of art. The differences that divide the father
and his children are more a question of temperament than of age.
What Sarraute has emphasized, rather than a generational dispute,
is the disparity between two attitudes: an iconoclasm which claims
it is impossible to create without first overthrowing the past, and a
contrary reverence for established values, which would like to
maintain an aesthetic *status quo*. When questioned about her own
position in this controversy, Sarraute has said she can sympathize
with both points of view. At times she identifies with the father in
his joyful contemplation of art, as he experiences "those delicious,
extraordinary sensations" she has known herself, "when time
stands still and you feel yourself to be eternal."[35] At other times,
she sides with the children, with those for whom the cult of art is a
crushing burden they must shake before they can create something
viable and new.

In her own case, the act of writing *Tropisms* was a rebellion
against the entire body of sacrosanct literature that lay behind her
— and that she intensely admired. In fact, she has stated that the
most insidious threat for the would-be writer (or artist) is to be intimidated by the great works of the past:

These demand of the writer a difficult type of conduct, a painful, dual effort. For he must at the same time impregnate himself with them, feed
upon them and discard them; be familiar with them and forget them; see
with their eyes a universe enriched with all the complexity with which they
furnished it, and yet see it intact and new.[...] The real danger for all
writers [...] is not that of being crushed by mediocrity but rather of being
dazzled by genius.[36]

The act of rebellion is characteristic of all genuine artists.

As always in Nathalie Sarraute's books, the minuscule situation
with which she starts radiates outward until it encompasses questions that range far beyond the surface scope of her subject. A
father's reactions to his children's ambiguous laughter become the
focus for a forum on aesthetic values, the subjective experience of

art, the dynamics of family intercourse, the creative needs of the artist, the forces of conservatism versus modernity, the struggle between submissiveness and freedom, guile and innocence, age and youth. The arena in which Sarraute's drama is enacted is diminutive, the participants ordinary, the cause of the conflict exceedingly minor, practically "nothing." But the clash of aesthetic attitudes precipitated on this modest scale is the age-old Battle of the Books, the Quarrel between the Ancients and the Moderns, the ever-renewed opposition between the champions of tradition, reverently turned toward the past, and the revolutionary innovators, resolutely facing the future.

CHAPTER 5

Language and Ideas

I Genesis of Sarraute's Plays

OVER the last ten or fifteen years, Nathalie Sarraute has come to public notice as a playwright. Her radio plays, first broadcast throughout Europe and then performed on the Paris stage, have achieved a resounding success. Ever since completing *The Golden Fruits,* Sarraute has interspersed the writing of drama with fiction, as a form of "relaxation" at the end of each novel and as a means of tying up whatever loose threads she may have left dangling. A tight interweaving of themes and modes of expression knits all her work — fiction and drama alike — into a cohesive unit.

Sarraute never contemplated writing for the theater, and she might have confined herself to fiction indefinitely had it not been for the perseverance of a young German named Werner Spies, who was commissioned by Radio Stuttgart to solicit radio texts from French writers. In 1963, Spies approached Sarraute with this aim in mind, promising her free rein to write in whatever form she chose. Intrigued by this challenge, Sarraute composed the two playlets, *Silence* (1964) and *The Lie* (1966).

Because theatrical dialogue seemed incompatible with expressing unspoken tropisms, Sarraute at first feared that the dramatic form might pose insurmountable problems. On stage, everything is conveyed through speech and action; over the radio, where action is also eliminated, dialogue alone must sustain the full weight of the drama. However, dialogue by itself was inconceivable to Sarraute, without the unspoken "predialogue" that underlies and prepares it. In her novels, tenuous inner movements on the threshold of conscious thought are communicated to the reader through rhythm and imagery or by means of subconversation; spoken conversation is only the end product, the surface eruption of tropisms produced in the depths.

Sarraute therefore found herself faced with the problem of integrating subconversation into conversation itself, of revealing internal movements externally; she had to turn the "inside" outward, as it were, like an inverted glove (*a gant retourné*).[1] As a result, the characters in her plays speak in a way that seems entirely natural on the surface, but actually they say things that people never utter aloud. Their speech is a mixture of outward conformity and inner commentary. Just as the reader of a Sarraute novel must make the transition between external dialogue and internal sensations, so the spectator or listener must differentiate between what a character is apt to articulate to others and what remains in the province of unvoiced tropisms.

Despite its plunges into taboo and secret zones, and however untoward the sentiments it expresses, Sarraute's dialogue remains commonplace and banal. This effect is deliberate. In the first place, because her characters are trying to communicate interior movements whose very nature and existence may seem doubtful, they must use the only language that "others" are liable to understand — colloquial speech. Secondly, Sarraute wishes the spectator to participate directly in the same experience as the characters, "to feel completely at home in these lower depths, like a fish in water. It is necessary for the unexpected to appear self-evident, to have the convincing force of an everyday experience that can be accounted for in everyday language."[2] This contrast between an ultrafamiliar form and an unaccustomed content emphasizes the dramatic nature of the tropisms that propel the action, both in her plays and in her novels.

The characters themselves are merely the generalized media for expressing tropisms. Lacking specifics of identity or personality, they function anonymously, even in the rare instances when they are equipped with a name. One character in *Silence,* who sets himself apart from the group, is further differentiated by alone possessing a name; the remainder of the roles are distributed generically among two men and three women (M. 1 and 2, W. 1, 2, and 3). The characters' names in *The Lie* appear only on the list of *personae* at the beginning of the play. Except for "Pierre" and "Simone," whose conflict provides the crux of the drama, these names are never used; in the context of the play, they become nonexistent. In *Isma,* a slight distinction is effected by calling the couple who precipitate the tropisms "he" and "she," while the anonymous group with whom they interact are vaguely designated, as in *Silence,* by gender and number. The characters in *It's Beauti-ful,* forming a family nucleus, are "he," "she," and "the son."

These characters, like their counterparts in Sarraute's novels, are shadowy supports for the tropisms that activate them. They are not flesh-and-blood creatures, but instead are "faceless beings without identity; so many *presences,* not in the old sense of the word, with form and substance, but *transparencies* based on an ever altering world of images."[3] Especially over the radio, the medium for which they were created, they are transmitted as disembodied voices, de-void of any particularizing traits. Even the distribution of roles is not a means of introducing varied personalities or points of view, but a way of forestalling monotony by presenting a random ex-change of male and female voices.[4]

The staging of the plays necessitated corporealizing what Sar-raute conceived of as "voices" that came to her as she wrote. In fact, she was skeptical when Jean-Louis Barrault first spoke of producing *Silence* and *The Lie*; it seemed to her an unrealizable project, for she felt that the substance of her plays — language it-self — could not lend itself to visual presentation.[5] Since she never pictured her characters or their actions, she was at a loss to reply when Barrault asked specific questions about their age or ap-pearance. Beyond supplying indications about the actors' intona-tions and her intentions in the dialogue, she left the question of staging entirely to him. The results took Sarraute by surprise. She has said that seeing *Silence* performed was almost like watching someone else's play.[6] Barrault had placed Jean-Pierre (the silent one) at the center, in three-quarter profile, with the other actors grouped in a circle around him. Their movements and gestures were hugely exaggerated. M. 1, for instance, gesticulated broadly, screamed, cried out, even clambered up a ladder. Although Sar-raute is inclined to view bodily gesture as a much cruder, less pre-cise form of expression than speech, she was nonetheless amazed by the way the actors' byplay amplified her text and brought the tro-pisms into sharper and yet more subtle focus. The theater was like an additional lens superimposed on the magnifying glass through which she views reality.[7]

Language is at the heart of Sarraute's plays. The catalyst that ac-tivates tropisms in each case is not an external object (like a Louis XV bergère or a primitive stone figurine), but an element of speech — a lie, silence, a hackneyed phrase — which, when injected into the dialogue, forces the participants to become aware of the mechanism of communication. Silence and lying are subversive elements that affect not only the subject but the texture of conversation, by undermining the nature and reason for social intercourse. A lie annihilates discourse by calling into question the good faith that the participants in a dialogue implicitly share. Silence — the negation of speech — destroys conversation by erecting a blank wall that stops the speakers in their tracks.

In all Sarraute's plays, language assumes the role of "detonator." Conversation ebbs and flows in response to key words, intonations, or evocative phrases. Some words are appended as labels, to categorize what is unformed and unformulated. Others are used as weapons, to attack people or parry their words in self-defense. Words are used as propitiatory formulas, to ward off unseen evil. Even the way a particular syllable is pronounced may be fraught with emotional significance.

Of course, it is not new for Sarraute to emphasize the hidden power of language. That words can wound deeply, however anodine on the surface, has been self-evident to Sarraute since her earliest novels. In *Tropisms VII* and *XIV,* care was taken to avoid dangerous words or topics, and the narrator of *Portrait* was circumspect in conversing with the daughter:

There are certain words — as innocuous in appearance as pass-words — which I never pronounce before her, I am careful not to do so. I always skirt around them from afar, I take precautions to avoid them, when she is there I continue to watch all approaches, in order to keep them from turning up, and if anyone, through ignorance or innocence, pronounces them in her presence before me, I pretend, in order to put her at her ease, to have seen nothing, I assume the unconscious, absentminded manner that tactful or easily embarrassed persons affect in a sickroom when the commode or the enema bag is brought in (*Portrait,* pp. 53–54).

Examples in Sarraute's novels can be multiplied endlessly. In the plays, where there is less visual imagery, the words themselves must carry the full brunt of Sarraute's meaning, including every innuendo and inflection.

Silence itself becomes more palpable in a play than a novel. To express silence in the written text, Sarraute resorts to visual techniques, frequently using three dots to suggest a pause in conversation (or subconversation), and inserting a blank space to separate one section from another. In a novel, if a particular character does

not express himself vocally — aloud or in thought — he simply disappears. The reader cannot be in all minds simultaneously. He is
plunged inside a character's consciousness only so long as that consciousness functions; when it falls "silent," it ceases to exist. Only
in a play is an actor's silence immediately noticeable. The distinctive sound of his voice, when not heard, is missed. On stage, this
auditory impression is reinforced by the visual confirmation of his
nonparticipation, and his silence becomes all the more obvious to
the spectator. In a similar fashion, the emphasis on intonation and
pronunciation in *Isma* — also an auditory situation with emotional
overtones — is well suited to the theatrical form.

The subjects she chooses are deliberately trivial — almost
Always, at the base of the dramatic action, are the tropisms that
Sarraute insinuates into conscious awareness. A continual struggle
is waged between two kinds of minds: those that prefer to remain
on the surface of things, on the neutral ground with which they are
familiar, which poses no threats, conceals no surprises, churns up
no anxieties; and those that are drawn irresistibly to the murky regions where tropisms flourish, and are not satisfied until they drag
others down with them into the depths. For the latter, this realm of
inner experience is a natural setting, unquestionably real; for the
others, it is a hell of anomaly and madness that they instinctively
fear and wish at all costs to avoid. From the interplay of these two
opposing attitudes comes the constant movement that passes from
the depths to the surface and back again in Sarraute's plays.[8]

The subjects she chooses are deliberately trivial — almost
nothing at all ("ce qui s'appelle rien" — the alternate title of *Isma*).
It is only by the tiniest of pinpricks that Sarraute pierces the hard
shell of appearances — but through this minute fissure is discovered a world of hidden movement and agitation. The lie that
precipitates the tropisms in her play is not a momentous untruth,
with shattering implications; it is an inconsequential falsehood,
that in no way impinges on the life or character of anyone. It
produces nothing more than a disagreeable sensation that could
easily be overlooked, just as an awkward silence could be passed
over and forgotten. However, the trivial lie, the unobtrusive
silence, become the springboard for an escalating range of emotional responses. Beginning with apathy, tolerance, or good-
humored acceptance, reactions to the initial situation swell, from
discomfort to annoyance, then to anger and full-scale rage. The actors suffer, rant in frustration, beseech one another, call their very
lives and values into question. And then — when they have run the

gamut of anguished conflict and tension — they return to the surface and find that nothing, literally nothing, has taken place. "A tempest in a teapot," as Sarraute is fond of saying. Again, as in the novels, it is the insignificance of the precipitating element that emphasizes the disproportion between cause and effect, between catalyst and tropism.

II   Silence *(1964)*

As the scene opens, M. 1 has apparently interrupted himself in the midst of describing a picturesque scene in some unspecified, but exotic, locale. Though his friends urge him to continue, he refuses, suddenly embarrassed by the "lyricism" that has left him open to ridicule. And, indeed, he seems to detect a slight snicker, which makes him jump up and exclaim: "Did you hear? Do you hear that?"[9] Like the father in *Do You Hear Them?,* whose very words he repeats, M. 1 is incensed and disturbed by the laughter he has heard (or imagined).

He thinks it was Jean-Pierre who laughed — Jean-Pierre, who has said nothing all along and who continues to say nothing, while the pressure of his silence builds up unbearably. At first, M. 1 alone is sensitive to this intimidating silence, but ultimately he communicates his discomfort to the others. It is by the frenzy of his reactions, the violence of his agitation, that he awakens their corresponding receptivity and unease. Without the presence of this delicate barometer, wildly oscillating in their midst, the others might have noticed nothing. M. 1 resembles the author, pointing out tropisms to the reader, who by himself might never have suspected their existence. M. 1 "interprets" Jean-Pierre's silence, for which he imagines a range of possible explanations, many of them contradictory: Jean-Pierre is timid, or he is arrogant; he is sensitive, like M. 1, or perhaps he is pragmatic and anti-intellectual; he understands everything, he understands nothing.

Like the narrators of the early novels, M. 1 figures as a potential creator. Through his subjective reactions, he composes, rearranges, and revises a personality for Jean-Pierre, depending not on what he observes but on what he imagines. In addition, he possesses an acute aesthetic sense, which evidently transported him at the beginning of the play onto a level of poetic description inappropriate to conversation; later, he hints that his impressions might be more acceptable if presented in the proper "form": in a "well-worked"

style within the pages of a beautifully bound book. To carry the
analogy one step further, Jean-Pierre, shrouded in his impenetrable
silence, is comparable to the silent readership whom the writer addresses, whose reactions can only be surmised, constantly questioned but never known, and who embodies the artist's hope, fever-
ishly and pitifully repeated by M. 1: "You have understood everything. I always feel that you understand everything" (p. 57).

By turns angry and sarcastic, or coaxing and cajoling, whatever
M. 1's diverse reactions may be, of one thing he is incapable: ignoring Jean-Pierre. All his emotional gymnastics (like Alain Guimier's
tightrope walk) are desperate efforts to establish contact. But he is
constantly rebuffed by a "wall" of silence ("You are walled up in
your silence," he complains to Jean-Pierre; p. 55). So eager is he
for some reaction, no matter what, that when he thinks he hears
Jean-Pierre laugh a second time, he is delighted; he will consent to
anything, if only Jean-Pierre will respond, "if only he will laugh"
(p. 63).

M. 1 wavers in allegiance between the One and the Many, between Jean-Pierre whom he courts, and the group whom he enlists
to support him. At first he tries to align Jean-Pierre in solidarity
with himself, appealing to him as to a kindred spirit who is more understanding and sensitive than the rest. When the others seem mer-
cilessly obtuse, he turns pleadingly to Jean-Pierre: "Pardon them,
they don't know what they're doing, pay no attention, have
pity..." (p. 54). These words contain the echo of Jesus's prayer:
"Forgive them, for they know not what they do." And indeed, like
Vigny's poetic evocation of Jesus in Gethsemane, entreating God
to break his implacable silence, M. 1 begs Jean-Pierre for a sign, a
token, to restore his peace of mind: "One little word from you and
we would feel saved" (p. 55).

Gradually, the others begin to reflect M. 1's perturbation. At
first, they try to distract him from his obsession, but Jean-Pierre's
silence becomes more and more obtrusive — an "emanation" that
engulfs them (like the black ink the son is felt to secrete in *It's
Beautiful*). They attempt various stratagems to induce Jean-Pierre
to descend from his pedestal of silence — they try to tease him into
talking, they ignore him, implore him. When all else fails, they play
the child's game of pretending to imitate his silence (how often Sarraute views adult behavior in terms of child's play and fairy tales!),
but soon dissolve into laughter, unable to achieve the weighty effect
of Jean-Pierre's "pregnant" silence.

What makes his muteness so oppressive and beguiling? It seems to denote a strength of mind and aloofness that instill admiration, even awe. Whether Jean-Pierre's behavior signifies scorn (p. 59), disapproval (p. 64), or snobbishness (p. 67), it is sensed as a sign of his superiority. By not speaking, he has effectively become the center of attention.

Paradoxically, silence has germinated speech. Jean-Pierre's taciturnity has been the impetus for discussion, speculation, explanation. "You never talked so much before," M. 1 is told (p. 68). There is an obsessive need to plug up silence with words. The trite, familiar phrases of everyday speech hold mystery at bay, stave off the unknowable, the unnameable — just as the diarrhetic flow of words in *Krapp's Last Tape* fills an otherwise unbearable void, and the spate of meaningless chitchat in Ionesco's plays, the contrapuntal dialogue of noncommunication, is a way of avoiding the terror of silence (the killer's deadly silence in *Tueur sans gages*).

If the essence of human relationships is the desire to make contact, then language is the link through which this aim is realized. It is through the appeal of words, the solicitation of language, that individuals are induced to emerge from their fundamental isolation and to unite in a semblance of collectiveness. Silence, on the other hand, betokens a rejection of companionship, a withdrawal behind the ramparts of the self. It is a denial of social contact, of a "social contract." In *Martereau,* silence was a form of punishment; in *The Planetarium,* it was a sign of disapproval; in *Fruits,* it betrayed a position of nonconformity. Always, it signifies separation from the group.

The figure of Jean-Pierre remains, till the end, retrenched behind a façade of silence. He is the one character inside whose mind we cannot peer. We have no way of knowing whether he is enjoying his position of eminence, deliberately prolonging the mystery, relishing his importance — or whether he is even aware of the commotion he is causing. Like Martereau before his personality decomposes, he is a monolithic block against whose opacity tropisms bounce off like harmless rays. By his silence, he remains uncommitted. He makes no gesture toward the group, no attempt to bridge the human gap. He is the Other, the Outsider, who alone seems to have the force to function independently. For that reason, he instills a tremor of fear in the members of the group. "Jean-Pierre-the-terrible," they call him, "the redoubtable bandit" (p. 54) — their mockery barely concealing an undercurrent of anxiety.

Certain clichés that cluster around the concept of silence are applied to Jean-Pierre, like familiar talismans to exorcise his mystery. One character suggests that Jean-Pierre is fully aware of the value of not speaking: his "silence is golden," in the sense that it endows him with qualities he may not even possess (p. 58). Perhaps he is basking in the aura of being the "strong, silent type" who appeals to girls and young women (p. 60). In a reversal of the popular dictum, "Silence is consent," it is suggested that Jean-Pierre is really registering his indignation, and that in his case "silence is non-consent" (p. 64).

The moment that Jean-Pierre breaks his silence, he breaks the spell. It is ironic that when he finally speaks, what he says is so trivial that in effect he says nothing. The banality and insignificance of his remark empty him of his mystery. Far from revelling in the power his silence had conferred on him, he was evidently oblivious to its effects. Hence, the others' reactions were entirely subjective; their fears had no basis outside their own imaginings. The very act of speaking erases the memory of his silence. M. 1, who was most exercised on the subject, now disclaims any awareness of it at all. Once the Outsider has been reintegrated within the group, the frenzied need to reach out to him ceases to exist, and the tropisms momentarily activated by his silence subside into nothingness. M. 1's denial of their existence suggests that the whole situation has been enacted on a preconscious level. Or perhaps the subterranean drama that has seemed to unfold in slow-motion actually transpired in the rapid blink of an eye, so swiftly that when it was over it was as if it had never taken place.

III   The Lie (*1966*)

A superficial resemblance links *Silence* and *The Lie*. In each play, a trivial occurrence in the course of ordinary conversation, unremarkable in itself, is blown up to gigantesque proportions through the hypersensitive reactions of a single individual, who succeeds in transmitting his suspicions to the group. Both dramas erupt over a question of language — in one case, the absence of speech, and in the other, its inauthenticity.

Pierre functions as a "lie-detector," unearthing truth wherever it is buried. He cannot endure falsehood in any form — not merely deliberate misrepresentations, but exaggeration, self-deception, the myriad tiny distortions of truth that people resort to when they want to impress others or evoke sympathy or — in a more complicated process — elicit a contradiction of their own self-professed faults. Like Molière's Alceste, Pierre finds it impossible to be tactfully indiscreet, to tolerate human foibles with composure or compassion. Pierre's role, like that of M. 1, is to sensitize the group to a situation of which they are at first unaware and which they later would prefer to overlook — either because it fails to disturb them, or because politeness dictates a pose of pretended ignorance, or because they are afraid to churn up uncomfortable feelings. Pierre does not permit anyone to lapse into indifference. Through his persistence, he forces his obsession on everybody, enlisting sympathy and support to remedy an intolerable situation.

The stage has been set for Pierre's receptivity even before the curtain rises. He has apparently already shocked his friends by certain forthright remarks (offstage) contradicting a statement somene had made. He claims repeatedly that he cannot control his reactions: lying is something he cannot endure. The mere suspicion that someone is veiling the truth causes him physical and mental anguish. The distress he feels is like a tiny cactus needle implanted under his skin that stings and scratches without relief. Like many of Sarraute's hypersensitive characters, he is literally in torment. "I can't stand it," he groans. "I'm at the end of my rope" (p. 91).

This compulsive reaction becomes a contagion that spreads and infects the rest of the group. Like an intense nervous disorder, it escapes the bounds of reason and interferes with "normal" living (p. 82). In fact, it is insinuated that Pierre's fixation verges on insanity. "It's like a madhouse here," Yvonne complains (p. 95),[10] and recommends he be put in a straitjacket (p. 99). Jeanne is afraid his madness is catching (p. 99), and Simone suggests he belongs in a padded cell (p. 100). Pierre himself admits to Simone that he's "nuts, completely nuts" (p. 100). This remark gives rise to a play on words, when someone tells Simone (whose "lie" has triggered the situation) that Pierre is "nuts" about her (p. 101). Their readiness to brand him as "crazy" is another instance of clapping labels on whatever is felt to be unexplained or threatening. In the same way, the appellation *fou* is applied indiscriminately in *It's Beautiful* to anyone whose behavior is incomprehensible or out of the ordinary, while a major theme of *"fools say"* is the tendency to call people "fools" whose ideas differ from one's own.

The drama begins with a game — a children's game that carries dangerous implications. To help Pierre overcome his aversion to lying, the others suggest play-acting; one of them will take the part of an acquaintance who is in the habit of making false statements, and Pierre will "practice" tolerating this person's assertions (it's a question of training, like gymnastics or boxing, they assure him). Among the varied reactions to the trumped-up prevarication is the common consensus that "truth will out." This soothing cliché is corporealized — like the physical pressure of silence that "weighed" on M. 1 — in Pierre's sensation that truth is an explosive force contained within him. The more it is restrained, the more powerfully it will erupt. Jacques illustrates the "truth" of this conviction by citing the example of a collaborator during the war who could no longer endure "living a lie" and finally confessed his identity. This anecdote reminds Simone of something that happened to her during the war, when she was living near Paris. Pierre interrupts: Simone is not telling the truth, she spent the war in Geneva (not Paris), she has assumed the role of liar in order to fool them.

The game that began in jest turns into a dead-serious contest between Pierre and Simone. Simone has violated the "rules" by refusing to say whether she is playing or not, and Pierre is adamant in his insistence on ascertaining the facts. He begs Simone to admit her lie — just as M. 1 had implored Jean-Pierre to break his silence. When cajolery fails, Pierre resorts to more direct and intimidating methods. The others, changeable as weather cocks, end up abetting him. In concert they interrogate Simone, trying to wheedle her into submission or, more brutally, to compel her to confess. Sensitive Lucie cannot stand their accusations: they want to destroy Simone, loop the noose around her neck, shave her head (like a thief forced to admit his guilt, like the collaborator mentioned by Jacques). Pierre assures Simone that "this is not true" (another word-play on the idea of truth and falsehood); they have no wish to degrade her; all she need do is say, "Yes, I was in Geneva, I was only joking...." Simone repeats his words, parrot-like: "I was only joking.... Now are you satisfied?" Although this assurance suffices to calm the others, Pierre remains dubious. There was a trace of mockery in Simone's tone of voice. He keeps repeating her words to himself, testing them with varied intonations, to determine whether she was telling the "truth" when she said she was "lying." The paradox causes him unrelieved distress. He recognizes that Simone has avenged herself: she submitted and gave him what he wanted, but with a "worm" in the apple — the self-perpetuating uncertainty of ever knowing the truth. The question of Simone's veracity, like Martereau's honesty, remains un-solved. It continues to haunt Pierre as the curtain comes down. Like Tantalus's torment, his craving for certainty can never be satisfied.

The germinal concept for *The Lie* may be traced to a minuscule incident in *The Golden Fruits,* when the woman who has con-fronted the critic Mettetal with his contradictory appraisals of Bréhier's works is scandalized by his "lie" — his present denial of what he had once asserted. In the end, she is castigated for "disturbing the peace," much as Pierre is reproved for stirring up a needless fuss.

The play as a whole raises questions about the relative nature of truth and its role in social intercourse. It is commonly accepted — except by Pierre — that small doses of deceit are inevitable: "Everybody does it more or less. Tells little white lies" (p. 83). Minor deceptions must be swallowed, for the sake of tranquillity. The game the characters play — the *pretense* of lying — makes a mockery of the concept of truth. Moreover, the search for ab-solutes — absolute truth, absolute certainty — can lead to the in-sidious evils of excess. Pierre's intransigent need to extirpate "truth," if carried far enough, fanatically enough, can result in vi-cious abuses of power (abuses hinted at in Lucie's imaginings): the third degree, the screw and the rack, all the bestial measures of in-terrogation that man has devised to extract forced confessions. The scope of Sarraute's minuscule "psychodrama," based on an in-nocuous incident in a conversation among friends, is open-ended in its implications.

Even more than silence, a lie constitutes the definitive rupture of social intercourse. The pretense of a shared pact is vitiated when one of the parties to the agreement subverts its meaning. If words are emptied of their implicit promise of truthfulness, they become nothing but windy sounds in the night, a meaningless gibberish containing no comfort. In the search for "authenticity," a lie is the ultimate denial. It indicates that the search itself is useless, for there is no knowable reality. When fact and fiction merge, the quest for truth is doomed to failure. When the secret of certainty resides in one person's mind — as in Simone's case — there is no alternate course except suspicion, or belief.

This situation is not without parallels to the novelist's art. Hasn't the domain of the novel always been that shadowy area where real-ity depends on one person's perception, where truth is what the novelist says it is? And hasn't the reader's "willing suspension of disbelief" traditionally signified his acceptance of whatever fantasies, fables, and "lies" the writer offered him? But Sarraute has evoked a new kind of reader in *The Age of Suspicion,* a reader who has grown wary of the writer's imagination, a reader who is more apt to accept the journalist's reporting as "truth" than the fictional products of the novelist's mind. In his caution and distrust, this modern reader resembles Pierre, who only wants to be assured that "truth" is not masquerading as "fiction," that there is an acknowledged distinction between the two.

IV   Isma (*1970*)

This play, like its predecessors, was originally written for radio, and was broadcast in German and French in January 1970. It was performed in 1973 at the Espace Cardin in Paris, in a production mounted by Claude Régy, who also directed *It's Beautiful* at Barrault's Petit d'Orsay theater, in 1975. Régy's staging of *Isma* was quite different from Barrault's dynamic interpretation of *Silence.* The actors — seated side by side, facing the audience — barely stirred during the play, merely rising briefly when circumstances called for some reaction on their part, then sitting down again. It was a highly stylized presentation, with scarcely any movement to detract from the text; the emphasis was on the minute and sensitive unfolding of each vibration of language.[11]

In *Isma,* the provocation for the drama is even more inconsequential than before; it is nothing more tangible than a disagreeable sound. *"Isma"* refers to the infinitesimal accentuation of words ending in *"isme,"* like *capitalisme, structuralisme, syndicalisme* — a mannerism that provokes a repulsion among certain listeners and gives rise to a chain of tropisms. These are, by the way, rather bombastic words — labels, in effect, that serve to categorize and define. But it is not their content or meaning that matters here, only their pronunciation. Language is still the tropistic catalyst — language reduced to its physical properties, amputated from its function and significance. Words are emptied of their meaning; their hollow shell alone remains.

Echoes of this idea can be found in many of Sarraute's works, where sensitivity to individual words and expressions ("straw man" in *Martereau,* "mean natures" in *Do You Hear Them?,* certain uses of the word *"faire"* in *Between Life and Death*) is extended to the *sound* of words as well. When one reader calls *The Golden Fruits "ad-mi-raable,"* his lingering emphasis on the long "a" sound reinforces the incontrovertible authority of his verdict. The father's self-conscious pronunciation of the word *"baalaade"* (which he uses instead of the more formal *"promenade,"* in *Do You Hear Them?*) is immediately pounced on by his children as a sign of surrender. A mere accent can set off a violent emotional reaction. In *It's Beautiful,* the father becomes almost irrational with fury when his wife slurs the word *"feignant,"* instead of articulating it clearly as *"fai-né-ant"* (lazy). In *"fools say,"* individual words and phrases are broken down according to the emotional associations of their syllables.

This sensitivity to the sound of words is a sign of the writer's "predestination" in *Between Life and Death* — evidenced not merely in the series of homonyms he plays with as a child, but also in his morbid revulsion to the elongated vowel sounds of words like "vaalise" or "vaaacation" or worst of all, "Meeediiter-raaaneeeean," which he finds as nauseating as the tentacles of a jellyfish. In much the same way that He and She are obsessed with the Dubuits and their pronunciation of *"isma,"* the young writer has a fixation about a couple called Ballut and their nasalized accent; in both cases, the sensitive parties are accused of entertaining an *idée fixe.* An entire chapter in *Between Life and Death* is devoted to the budding writer's attempts to overcome his obsession, until he realizes that he can put his hypersensitivity to artistic use and make the objectionable accent the focus of his creative effort.

In *Isma,* He and She participate to some degree in the artist's awareness, for they are conscious of the undercurrents that swirl beneath the platitudes of everyday conversation. Whereas the other participants prefer to remain on the surface of things, on the level of *commonplaces* (a common meeting-ground), He and She continually try to force them down into tropistic depths. When talk is steered away from "dangerous" tropisms to the safety of clichés, He and She complain that their conversation is only a sterile imitation, the "copy of a copy" of what has so frequently been portrayed in novels and plays — as if life were imitating art. "That's art, this is life," one of the characters says (p. 16) — an ironic commentary on Sarraute's *composition en abîme,* for what she is presenting is "art" that pretends to be life imitating art, like the reflection of a mirror-image reflecting itself.

As in the previous plays, the drama is set in motion before the curtain rises. The dialogue begins *in medias res* and the reader (or spectator) must make an effort, by reconstituting the prior conversation, to understand what is happening. The group has apparently been gossiping about the Dubuits and has been called to task by M. 1, who accuses them of disparaging the absent couple. They shamefacedly try to change the subject, but can find no other topic to discuss; either they fall silent, or they proffer mindless banalities to keep the conversation from dying. The titillating temptation to gossip proves too strong to resist. Because of his disinterest in picking apart the Dubuits, M. 1 is considered an oddity, "lukewarm," "indifferent." Thus labeled, he is rendered impotent; there is nothing for him to do but leave, thereby releasing the others from further constraint.

By reverting to their own experiences, they attempt to analyze the violent aversion He and She feel for the Dubuits, but nothing can explain this deep but indefinable dislike. Finally, She confesses the secret reason for their antipathy: what they find excruciating, intolerable is the Dubuits' habit of pronouncing is*ma,* of waving the final syllable in the air like a scorpion's tail. Though the others may share their dislike of the Dubuits, it is for different reasons. M. 3 insists he has no need for "embellishments": his loathing is based on *nothing.* He even goes so far as to imagine some hideous crime that the Dubuits may have committed — whereupon the others feel a delicious thrill of horror (like the joy ride of slandering Alain and Gisèle, in *The Planetarium*). He and She, however, cannot concur. Although *isma* may be an "embellishment" for M. 3, for them it is the essential element, the crux of their obsession, all by itself.

They are ashamed of their feeling and try to overcome it but, like all Sarrautian manias, it is beyond their control. One of the characters proffers some well-meaning advice: ignore the Dubuits, suppress them as if they did not exist — which is what she does in the case of people with "cauliflower ears." Moreover, she says, everyone does the same thing (just as everyone "lies a little"): if something is offensive, it is eliminated, eradicated. But He and She are incapable of diverting their attention from their chosen mania. The strength and venom of their revulsion penetrates their inmost being, degrading and destroying thought itself. "It's senseless, it's crazy!" He exclaims (p. 39) — echoing Pierre's helpless acquiescence in his own irrationality.

By repeating *isma* over and over, hopefully observing the effect, He and She make one final effort to convert the others to their repugnance. For a moment it seems as though they may have succeeded. But no, says M. 3. "No. . .it's really nothing" (p. 43). He repeats what he had said previously, when he appeared closest to sharing their feeling; now the same words — "ce qui s'appelle rien" — are used to deny his empathy and to ring down the curtain on a play that has been effectively constructed out of "nothing."

Isma is not as dramatically intense as its predecessors. Despite the violent sensations He and She experience, the dialogue tends to be sluggish and uneventful. Perhaps because the parties on whom hostility is focused are absent from the scene, we miss the dramatic interplay of approach and retreat, thrust and parry, that is carried out before our eyes in *Silence* and *The Lie*. The conversation often seems merely to be reflecting upon itself, creating its own momentum through intermittent propulsions of speech and silence. Sentences are left unfinished, suspended in mid-air, while thought trails off like vapor, and the auditors (on stage or in their armchairs) must supply the missing clues for their own comprehension. This can become an intellectual exercise, engrossing but sterile.

It is in the rippling implications of the subject, in its undercurrent of possibilities, that the play achieves a significance that extends far beyond the limited perimeters of the incident from which it springs. The tropisms aroused by this most tenuous and trifling of causes have their roots in the virulent depths of the human psyche, where irrational hatreds and prejudices arise. Just as Pierre's obsession in *The Lie* is the seed from which can sprout tyrannical abuses of power, so the indefinable sensation He and She entertain is capable of engendering acts of violence and cruelty. This potentiality is repeatedly implied in the text. At one point, He admits objecting to the Dubuits for no more logical or admissible reason than that "they exist." Indeed, He and She actually wish them out of existence, for they scan the newspapers daily in the hope of reading that some accident has befallen them. The nature of this prejudice is entirely unreasoning. It is not even a question of ideology: it is not the Dubuits' *ideas* about "capitalism" or "syndicalism" to which they object — though such abstract "isms" are often the cause of conflicting opinions — but something illogical and subjective. What drives them to distraction is a mannerism, an alien accent, that suffices by itself to brand the speakers as outcasts. Is it farfetched to detect a *rapprochement* with certain tenuous bases for anti-Semitism? Or to note Hitlerian overtones in Her willingness to line them up against the wall, "destroy" and "exterminate" them without pity (p. 36)? He and She long for a social order (a Third Reich?) where such people would be incarcerated, recognized as the "enemy," where the very act of saying "is*ma*" would be punishable by law (pp. 40–41).[12]

At the beginning of the play, He furnishes reasons for the group's pleasure in dissecting the Dubuits. The listing escalates from innocuous diversion to cruelty, in a capsule recapitulation of the successive stages that can lead from gossip to the gas chamber:

Come, come, there's no need to exaggerate. We wanted to be amusing and clever, enhance ourselves, release our aggressions and guilt feelings.... We wanted to be tickled, titillated ... to commune together and separately ... to kill, devour, exorcise.... I don't need to enumerate everything, it's all very well known. It's common practice (p. 12).

The one person who raises his voice in protest against their slanderous accusations is forced to leave, his objections overruled by a unanimous vote. The forces of reason and common sense abdicate in the face of passion and prejudice.

By intimations buried within the text, Sarraute once again hints at the thread of causality linking a trivial episode with consequences of epic proportions. While seeming to focus on the microscopic examination of an individual case, she opens the reader's eyes to its universal ramifications. In the best tradition of the classical theater, she passes from a contemplation of the particular to a consideration of the general. But so subtly is the message disguised, so discreetly is it implanted in the play, that the reader must perform the same act that the sensitive recipient of tropisms is required to execute. He must decompose the dialogue for its hidden meaning, probe gestures and actions — even intonations — for their unavowed motivations. He must dig beneath surface appearances to unearth the buried tropisms that activate human conduct and that may lead — if pursued to their ultimate possibilities — from anodyne amusement to unspeakable horrors of prejudice and brutality.

V   It's Beautiful (*1973*)

In this three-character play, Sarraute reverts to the intimate family situation of *Portrait, Martereau,* and *Do You Hear Them?*. The hothouse atmosphere is unrelieved by the presence of an outsider's consciousness, which provided a measure of distantiation in the novels. The characters are immersed in the eternal triangle of mother-father-son, engaged in lightning-swift shifts of allegiance that pit One against Two in varying combinations. The specific theme around which the drama unfolds is almost a *reprise* of *Do You Hear Them?*: the "culture shock" of opposing aesthetic values and the parents' futile attempts to impose their standards on their child.

Language is again the tropistic catalyst — in this case, a simple phrase, "It's beautiful," which the parents are afraid to say in front of their son, because it is laden with emotional nuances. "It's beautiful" is a value judgment that encompasses all the music, art, and literature, all the conventions of politeness, all the ideas and principles that govern the parents' lives. Like the father in *Do You Hear Them?,* they would like to instill these principles in their son, to mold him in their image, but they fear his mockery and "ignoble scorn." While they rail against his fondness for jazz and comic books (like the father in *Do You Hear Them?* and the aunt in *Martereau*), they hesitate to assert their own aesthetic judgment. If they were to say "It's beautiful," they would be exposing their dearest convictions to profanation, to the danger posed by the kind of people who "degrade and debase everything...everything that makes life worth while."[13] Because they dare not pronounce these words in their son's presence, "It's beautiful" becomes one of those "forbidden expressions" that are sown like minefields throughout Sarraute's books.

The phrase is a carryover from *Tropism XI* and *Do You Hear Them?*. In the earlier sketch, the aspiring bluestocking rhapsodizes, "It's beautiful," over every new book and painting; in her mouth, the words merely parrot other people's opinions and indicate an incapacity for independent judgment (precisely the reason for the son's objections, in the play). The father in *Do You Hear Them?* once made the mistake of telling his children, "It's beautiful," when he wanted them to appreciate a particular painting, only to find them obdurate in rejecting his superimposed values. The parents in *It's Beautiful* are so fearful of their son's reaction that they refrain from saying the phrase aloud, even to each other, lest it filter through the walls and reach the boy's ears.

The parents perceive their son's very presence as a paralyzing force that stifles their own being. In a half-conscious way, they would like to suppress him, to erase him from existence (just as He and She longed to eradicate the Dubuits). The father wishes him away, to the ends of the earth: "Let him end up in prison...in reform school. Let him disappear...let him go to the devil" (p. 9). And even the mother hints at having entertained a dreadful thought when she was carrying him — the unspeakable wish that he might never be born.

In his rage and frustration, the father attacks his son with the most accessible weapon he finds — a weapon of language, naturally. If the parents are prevented from saying "It's beautiful," then the son is equally forbidden to refer to his mother as "she" — an old-fashioned convention of politeness that the father digs out and brandishes, like a World War I bayonet.[14] By shouting, "Who's 'she'?" the father momentarily cows his son and sends him scurrying off to finish his homework; he has achieved a temporary triumph through the power of words.

The father and mother alternate between friction and solidarity. At times, they present a united front of indignation and righteousness; at other times, their alliance dissolves in mutual recriminations. The father is brutal and willfully obtuse. He seems impervious to the tropistic undercurrents awash all around him, preferring to remain on the level of everyday concerns (business phone calls, his son's homework) rather than descend to the insalubrious depths where his wife wallows. When besieged with disturbing intimations, he reacts by retreating into rage, hurling insults like projectiles (his son is "crazy," "good-for-nothing," an "idiot") or assailing his wife with sarcastic innuendos. The son points out that these are merely defense reflexes, a means of camouflage. What sort of camouflage? What is the father desperately seeking to hide, behind his blustering insults and badgering deprecations? Is it some dismal fear he will not admit even to himself, an unavowed terror of his son's tyranny (the black ink his son secretes, like an octopus)? When his wife insinuates that he is afraid, he pounces on her furiously: "Scared? Me? You're dreaming..." (p. 5). He disclaims responsibility for the way their son turned out: it was all his wife's fault, dating back to the boy's infancy and the way she made him wait for his bottle when he cried, removed his thumb from his mouth while he slept, deliberately abstained from cuddling him.[15]

The mother vacillates between self-incriminatory admissions and plaintive denials. She was the one who first found it impossible to say, "It's beautiful," just as she could never call her baby "little one" or "my little man." This would have been as grave an insult, she feels, as saying "kike" or "wop" or "female" — a degrading assumption of superiority, an application of the kind of disparaging label that leads to racism and prejudice. She insisted, instead, on their "perfect equality." But the concept of "equality" between parents and children proves to be a chimera; the relationship is a seesaw in which the balance is weighted on one side or the other.

The son is perspicacious enough to recognize the leverage he wields. Aware of the tropisms his father prefers to ignore, he uses his knowledge to impose his own power. He seems to delight in defiance, in daring his parents to say, "It's beautiful." As in *Do You Hear Them?*, the roles are reversed; the son assumes the authority of a parent, while the parents cower in submission, "like children" (p. 19).

The mother makes several attempts to repair the breach caused by her husband's pell-mell attacks. She approaches her son in tip-toeing apprehension, hoping to win him over by gentle wiles: praising his perspicacity (at her husband's expense), aping his youthful terminology (deliberately adopting his slurred pronunciation of *feignant* for *fainéant*), intimating an intuitive understanding and a shared resemblance by which the father is excluded. Again, the father is piqued by her disloyalty; again, he has the last word. This time he fells his son with a parting shot that reestablishes his parental supremacy: "Who's 'she'?'"

The conflict in *It's Beautiful* echoes the underlying opposition in *Do You Hear Them?* between tradition and innovation, authority and independence — extended beyond the domain of aesthetics into any area where values are dictated or imposed. In the play, positions are drawn up along generational lines: the son's refusal to accede to his parents' recommendations corresponds to youth's age-old need to set its own standards. By labeling something "beautiful," the parents are preventing their son from thinking for himself; they are preestablishing his principles, premasticating his opinions, denying him the opportunity to exercise his own judgment. The son fights to maintain his integrity and independence of mind. He also reacts to what he finds artificial and conventionalized in his parents' attitude, as summed up in the term they use. "It's beautiful" is a sterile formula, clapped on an aesthetic experience like a bottle cap. It stultifies imagination. Its triteness renders it meaningless. The son rejects his parents' language in favor of a *new* mode of expression that will give voice to his youthful approach to life and his own view of reality.

The irony at the end is that he merely substitutes one convention for another. Still unwilling to say, "It's beautiful," at his mother's urging the son grudgingly admits, "It's neat." Despite his jealous assertion of independence, his insistence on the right to think and judge for himself, he is as hidebound by convention as his parents whom he derides. He, too, reduces aesthetic taste to a barren cliché. The only difference is a question of modishness. He is using the up-to-date terminology of his own generation — which risks becoming as sterile, imitative, and sclerotic as that of his elders.

VI "fools say" *(1976)*

This is Nathalie Sarraute's most abstract and hermetic work to date. With its publication, she comes closest to accomplishing in the realm of the novel what contemporary artists have achieved in the domain of painting — an evolution toward increased abstraction. In this objective, she approaches Ionesco's stated aim of creating a type of drama that would resemble nonrepresentational painting, like the dramatic equivalent of a Klee or a Kandinsky.[16]

Not only does Sarraute's novel deal with intangibles — the attribution and propagation of ideas, the question of self-identity — it also dispenses more completely than ever with characterization and a traceable story line. It is composed entirely of dialogue (and subdialogue) occurring with vertiginous rapidity in a multiplicity of consciences. The "characters" are as anonymous and unidentifiable as any Sarraute has created. For the most part, they are disembodied voices emitting opinions, promoting arguments, struggling to escape inner conflicts of their own. No one has any social function whatever, nor any discernible relationship, except in the most evanescent of glimpses (a child and his grandmother, a pair of newlyweds, a pregnant widow at her husband's graveside — figures momentarily flashed on a screen, dissolving into other images, other scenes).

In its fragmentation, *"fools say"* almost recalls the sketches of *Tropisms*. However, unlike the earlier book, it contains a powerful unifying theme which — like the tropisms themselves — lies buried within the text and requires considerable effort to extract (Sarraute has never solicited a passive reader, and in this book less than ever). The central concern is with the free flow of ideas. One idea will be denigrated as something only "fools say," while another will be accepted as incontrovertible. "In both cases," Sarraute explains, "the same murky and totalitarian attitude tends to congeal and destroy thought, which is no longer considered on its own merits but only according to the person who produced it, or, even more seriously, according to the label attached to that person: he is a 'fool' or a 'genius.' "[17] In the life of the mind, the tendency toward external categorization creates hierarchies — ranging from "genius" to "fool" — and leads to what Sarraute terms "the disastrous cult of personality" at the top and the "persecution" of those who are classed as "fools" at the bottom.

From branding an idea to branding the person who upholds it is only a step — but a step of calamitous consequences. "Fools say" is the phrase that effectuates the treacherous passage from ideology to personality. Sarraute has called this expression a "typically fascistic" sentence. Ideas should be fought by ideas, not by insults. To be effectively demolished, even the vilest, most unsavory concept must be analyzed and combated by reason; it cannot be crushed by an epithet.[18] Otherwise, language degenerates into a tool of repression. By labeling an idea as something that only "fools say," words are reduced to a constraining formula that impedes the free-moving potential of the mind. Misapplied in this way, language becomes the instrument for suppressing man's rational faculties, those very faculties it was developed to serve.

Whether applied to ideas or people, labels are inflexible and "false." This is an old motif in Sarraute's work, rung on new changes. There are countless phrases, deliberately or carelessly uttered, that pronounce an instantaneous verdict with no possibility of appeal — appeal, that is, to reason and reflection. These expressions are as dogmatic when they are complimentary (an old grandmother is "cute") as when they deprecate and stigmatize (a boy is "jealous" or "unintelligent," a bridegroom is "stingy," some people are "fools"). Just as Martereau objected to being tagged a "straw man" and the Writer resented being called a "predestined child," there is always some sensitive observer who is averse to the inauthentic oversimplification of labels.

The book opens with a charming tableau of a grandmother and her adoring grandchildren — as idealized and artificial as the tableau of the Guimiers and their Aunt Berthe. But one of the grandchildren refuses to define his grandmother by saying, "How cute she is... couldn't you just eat her up?" His objection is twofold: he refuses to treat his old grandmother like an object devoid of sense or feeling, or like an undiscerning infant (two common attitudes toward the aged in contemporary society); he also objects to pinning on her a label of language. His recalcitrance arouses the antagonism of the Others, who feel threatened by the risk that the sugarplum confection they have concocted around their grandmother may dissolve, perhaps exposing a lubricious harpy underneath! It is necessary for their peace of mind that she remain the ideal grandmother of their delusions.

Every individual feels that he constitutes his own universe, with limitless horizons and infinite possibilities. The discrepancy between his private view of himself and the opinion of other people invariably comes as a shock. The little boy who is startled to learn that he has an "undershot jaw," like his Uncle Frank, fails to recognize a snapshot of himself — just as most of us cannot see our features in a photograph or recognize our voice on tape or acknowledge any image that controverts our subjective view of ourselves. But often, when that image is brought to our attention, we have a perverse tendency to conform to its reflection. The old grandmother who is described as "cute" at once turns into an insipid china doll; the little boy who overhears that he is "unintelligent" becomes convinced of his own ineptitude; an esteemed authority who is referred to as a "monster of pride" thereafter patterns his conduct on this epithet.

The book follows a progressive movement which may (or may not) be linked to the development of a personality. Even more tentatively and ambiguously than the life pattern in *Between Life and Death,* there is a tenuous advance from childhood to maturity, from incipient awareness to full-fledged sensitivity, from intellectual groping to mastery of thought. It is irrelevant whether or not the same person is involved. Just as the writer in the earlier book was not a single person but a representative of the species, so the impressionable "character" in *"fools say"* is an abstraction founded on all possibilities. What matter are the general contours of an experience, rather than the details of an individual life.

The little boy who is adjudged "unintelligent" is convinced that he is incapable of handling "ideas." An adult figure — perhaps his father — assures him otherwise and furnishes him with a weapon to fend off his detractors: he has only to label them "little fools." At a youthful age he learns the lesson that words can be used to combat other words and that one insult disarms another. Later he (or his prototype) insists on the right to examine ideas on their merits, however inane or unpleasant they may be. But when he tries to analyze a particularly repugnant idea, in order to disassociate himself from those who venerate it as a precious relic, he has no alternative but to call them "fools." One poor fellow (the same or another) tries to persuade the group that "We are all alike. There are no fools."[19] He, too, insists on the necessity of concentrating on ideas rather than on the personalities of those who expound or accept them. He tries to interest the others in an idea of his own, which he insists they must judge for themselves. But when they remain obtuse, deform his idea, cover it with a sticky mucosity, he is finally constrained to consider them "fools." He retires to enjoy his idea in solitary contemplation and "voluptuous intimacy" (p. 62), like a beloved mistress. But he soon realizes that thought cannot exist in a vacuum; ideas clamor to be communicated. He must share his idea with the world, else it will perish and be lost — just as the creative writer in *Between Life and Death* found it necessary to expose his cherished work to the public.

With the passage of time, an idea that was formerly greeted with disdain is surrounded by an aura of respect (and those who at first underestimated it are in turn considered "fools"). Its originator is hailed as a "Maestro" in his own right. Although at heart he feels like an impostor occupying the prince's palace by mistake, he tends to conform to the lofty image of himself that is held up to his gaze. He falls prey to the dangerous "cult of personality," displaying the same arrogance and pomposity, the same arbitrary whims and colossal self-assurance evinced by the successful writer in *Between Life and Death*. He skirts the same danger posed by uncritical adulation — the risk of losing his sense of self. The resemblance between both situations is emphasized by a reenactment of the scene in which the Writer (here the "Maestro") intimidates his disciples by bellowing the (senseless) words: "Debout les morts!"[20] Once again, there is the same tentative correction ("Master, we were talking about Moors... about inhabitants of Mauritania") and the same willful persistence on his part. No one dares murmur or even seem shocked. He has fallen victim to the self-corruption of absolute power, handed him by those very souls whom he (or his prototype) had previously exhorted to think for themselves.

The same scene is repeated from a different perspective. Like an "inverted glove," what was formerly experienced subjectively, by the Maestro himself, is subsequently viewed externally, through the grandmother's eyes, as she tells about "his" irascible moods and the time he struck his fist on the table and shouted, "Debout les morts!" This recapitulation of the previous incident postulates a link between two episodes whose relationship the reader may have inferred, by supposing the child originally sitting at his grandmother's knee to be the same who has grown up to be the authoritative Maestro. This conclusion is demolished by a chronological contradiction: the Maestro is someone the grand-mother used to know, and therefore cannot be the same person as the young boy at her side (perhaps he is a different Maestro, or she a different grandmother). This deliberate connection and dis-connection between the two scenes reinforces the characters' ambiguity and the futility of attempting to identify them.

The ultimate lengths to which the cult of personality can lead is the mania for memorabilia (already satirized in *Between Life and Death*). It is possible to reconstruct personality out of artifacts alone. Without direct acquaintance or contact, solely on the basis of letters, documents, and anecdotes, the history and character of a famous person can be fabricated — all his traits deduced and cata-logued (is this Sarraute's personal satire of "psychoanalytic criticism?"). In the end, it is impossible to resolve all the facets of a great man's complexity. Better to replace him on his pedestal and venerate him from a distance — so it is suggested.

With even less substantiation, on an even flimsier foundation, there is the tendency to judge people on the basis of gestures alone. This is not a new theme for Sarraute. The narrator considered Martereau's deliberate way of wiping his feet on the doormat to be a sign of self-assurance. Alain and Gisèle had a habit of classifying people according to their mannerisms and tics. Aunt Berthe interpreted Pierre's obsession with straightening a corner of the rug as an unwillingness to talk to her. The importance of gestures is further amplified in *"fools say."* The Maestro's tiny act of flicking a thread off his sleeve is construed as a sly way of looking at his watch, and his visitor takes this (or mistakes this — the motivation is ambiguous) as a signal to leave. Sarraute devotes an entire chapter to the towering assumptions that are founded on the slightest of actions. She gives three examples: Two lovers are clasped in each other's arms; surreptitiously, one of them wipes a moist palm on trouser or skirt, and this single motion sounds the death knell of love and happiness. A young bride notices her husband counting out change into a cabbie's waiting hand; the miserly gesture turns her Prince Charming into a skinflint. A third person is stigmatized according to the revolting way he stabs a piece of food with his fork and holds it in the air, inspecting it. A single phrase (like an appended label) summarizes this basis for prejudgment: *Ab ungue leonem.* The lion is known by his claws. A single gesture sums up the man.

Sarraute has explained that she took these examples from three different novels — *Strait Is the Gate* by André Gide, *A Life* by De Maupassant, and *The Brothers Karamazov* by Dostoevsky — magnifying the initial scene and expanding its repercussions in order to illustrate the way that literature has "taught us" to construct a character on the basis of rudimentary gestures.[21] As she puts it in *"fools say"*: "Great masters have shown us how to go about it. They have furnished us perfect models. We've an embarrassment of riches" (p. 115).

From the idyllic vision of the china-doll grandmother at the beginning of the book to the terrifying scene at the end, there is a heightening of significance. The child who senses the inadmissibility of defining his grandmother gives way to the adult who claims the right to judge ideas for himself. In each case the sensitive, thoughtful person finds himself alone, cast out from the common consensus of the crowd. If he persists in thinking he is free to consider an idea on its merits or to challenge some sacrosanct theory cherished by the masses, he discovers that this is an impossible aspiration. By his nonadherence, he is convicted of the modern equivalent of heresy: he is a "fool." Eventually, instead of attacking ideas, he may attack their proponents. By descending to the level of personal combat, he then enters the world of personalities and hierarchies, of labels and prejudices. He abandons dispassionate contemplation and rational analysis for emotional entanglement in irrelevancies. "From this moment on," Sarraute explains, "he is lost, he plays 'their' game, he has accepted the cult of personality, he is totally integrated into their totalitarian universe."[22] The book ends with a brief scene, almost an epilogue, which exudes what Sarraute has called "an atmosphere of terrorism,"[23] in which thought itself is stifled, and nothing is left but numb and obsequious acquiescence.

Nathalie Sarraute forces our attention, requires us to notice what we might prefer to ignore — like the funeral guest in one scene of *"fools say"* who not only observes the young widow's self-conscious posture, but also insists on rousing her awareness. In spite of Sarraute's insistence that her works contain no message, preach no lesson, it is difficult not to see in her a relentless moralist. True, she makes no hard-and-fast judgments of right or wrong and offers no precepts of behavior. She neither condones nor condemns. Instead, she depicts the world as she sees it and human nature as it is. But this has always been the way of the classical moralists, whose portrayal of human frailties contains no overt message but rather an implicit ethic.

Sarraute has herself reduced the subject of *"fools say"* to a single but basic concept: "My purpose is simply to call for freedom of thought, separate and apart from its author, that's all."[24] In order to think and judge clearly, one must forget the authority figures who dictate the validity of ideas. Thought must be liberated from the stamp of social approval or intellectual renown. This is the implied morality that underlies the book.

The problem posed here is the continuation, on a broader plane, of the rebellion against externally imposed criteria of aesthetic appreciation that preoccupied Sarraute in *The Golden Fruits, Do You Hear Them?* and *It's Beautiful.* However, the issues at stake here are of far more critical concern. Whereas the condemnation of a work of art on aesthetic grounds, however trifling, is in the long run confined to the realm of art, the condemnation of an *idea,* together with the person who holds it, leads to the annihilation of the individual and his innate capacity to reason. In a world where truth is often twisted and propaganda is rife, where authoritarian regimes dictate what people must think as well as how they must act, a novel that delves into the subconscious emotional processes that precondition individuals to accept such a world contains a strong and necessary dose of moral concern. For all Sarraute's insistence on keeping art divorced from social and political issues, it is nonetheless apparent that in her most recent works she has passed from a contemplation of aesthetic problems to issues that reach into the broader areas of human rights, human freedom, and human dignity.[25]

CHAPTER 6

An Aesthetic for the Novel

I The Novel as an Art Form

I N the course of composing her early books, and later, as an
established writer whose opinions were solicited about "the state
of the novel," Sarraute has had frequent occasion to reflect about
the nature of fiction as an art form. Her conclusions, expressed in a
variety of media — collected in a book of essays, published in literary journals, aired on the radio, voiced at writers' symposia and
from the lecterns of college campuses, repeated in numerous personal interviews — could, if compiled, constitute a corpus of aesthetic theory. However, Sarraute is not a theoretician; she is a
novelist. Almost all her ideas — even her critical analyses of other
writers, like Flaubert or Valéry or Dostoevsky — are not the
appraisals of a critic or historian, but the reflections of an artist
concerned with the problems and possibilities of her métier.

Sarraute has always objected to the term "experimental" when
applied to the novel, as though writers were technicians in white
coats, testing their ideas in a laboratory before exposing them to
the public. In her own case, she had no preconceived theories about
fiction when she set out to write. It was only after her first novels
went unnoticed that she began to ponder her methods and wonder
why she could not bring herself to write like other writers. The
result of these meditations was a series of essays in which Sarraute
explained her ideas about fiction, the new directions it was taking,
and the bases for her own innovations. These articles generated
little interest when they first appeared in the 1940s and early 1950s.
It was not until they were published in book form, in 1956 (the same
year as *The Planetarium*), under the title *The Age of Suspicion,*
that they suddenly attracted wide notice. Many of the concepts they
expressed — with respect to characterization, narrative point of

view, the breakdown of plot, the necessity for the reader's active collaboration — were embraced by a group of young novelists of similar inclinations who formed the nucleus of what was eventually called the New Novel (cf. Chapter 7).

Sarraute has always been convinced of the novel's vitality, in spite of those prophets of doom who for decades had been predicting its demise (even Emile Zola, rereading Balzac in 1872, had signed that the novel of his day was in its death throes).[1] Rather than foreseeing a future abandonment of the fictional form, she feels that it has not yet attained its full flowering, that its possibilities are limitless because of its protean nature as "the genre that is most open, most free, most apt to transform itself and to assume all possible forms."[2] This optimism is predicated on the belief in fiction's endless capacity for renewal — a belief fostered by the revolutionary changes that had been effected by writers like Proust and Joyce. Sarraute tells of the revelatory experience of reading *Swann's Way* in 1924 and *Ulysses* the following year, after which she was convinced that it was no longer possible to write, or even to read, in the same way as before.[3]

Although this perception was to orient her own approach to fiction, at the time she began writing, shortly before the war, her viewpoint was far from universally shared. In fact, she found fiction at that point to be fixed in an immutable mold, the innovations of Joyce and Proust largely forgotten or ignored. The novel was considered to be a story with characters, designed to provide a faithful image of life and reality and to enlarge the reader's experience by enabling him to partake vicariously of other existences. Intended to inform and educate, perhaps to help solve social problems as well, it was closer to being a documentary than an art form. This utilitarian emphasis was anathema to Sarraute. She felt strongly that the novel was not a tool of social progress, was not imbued with a message, had no moral purpose or educational function, but was as much an art form as music or painting.[4]

Sarraute insists that "the only morality for the novelist consists in trying to preserve for the novel its quality as a work of art."[5] This attitude virtually echoes the doctrine of "art for art's sake" that was the rallying cry for the Parnassian and Symbolist poets of the late nineteenth century. In her own practice of fiction, Sarraute has continually repeated that hers is not a moral but an aesthetic focus. "I must insist," she has said, "that at no moment have I sought to deliver a message, to give the slightest moral instruction, to rival psychologists or psychiatrists by any psychological discoveries whatsoever. No, all that I have wanted was to capture in language a minute fragment of the 'unnameable.' "[6] In this resolve, she tends to consider that all the arts share similar aims and endeavors: "The artist creates a world which enlarges known reality and expands the domain of the visible. This world established by the creative act does not serve or illustrate anything. It suffices unto itself."[7]

Although Sarraute believes in the correspondence of all forms of art — painting, literature, sculpture, music — she seems to feel the greatest affinity with the visual arts. She has frequently analogized fiction with painting (and not only in the implicit symbolism of the "Portrait of a Man Unknown"). Her favorite imagery for expressing what is conventional and trite in the novel is taken from the plastic arts: traditional characters are compared to the lifeless figures of a waxworks museum — the most degenerative form of "sculpture" — while the hackneyed "realism" that pretends to imitate life is referred to as *trompe-l'oeil* (a term derived from painting). She considers her own writing to be closer to the plastic arts than to any other,[8] and has even intimated that, had she been a painter, she would have tried to represent with color and brushwork what she has achieved in her writing through the use of words. She works in this medium because — like the child in *Between Life and Death* —she has always felt a sensitivity and love for language, with its sonorities and evocative qualities; another artist may choose to work in marble or clay.[9] The aim is the same; it is only the method of expression that varies.

Like the other arts, the novel is constantly undergoing a process of transformation, which ensures its vitality and prevents it from falling into sterility and decay. Sarraute does not preach Revolution, but Evolution. She has no wish to destroy the past, which she loves and admires, but only to renew what has become calcified through imitation and overuse. Past discoveries can serve as steppingstones to future achievements. The writer must "impregnate" himself with the great works of the past, and then discard them; familiarize himself with them, and then forget them; "see with their eyes a universe enriched with all the complexity with which they furnished it, and yet see it intact and new. While studying the admirable implements forged by his predecessors, he must never forget that these implements could only be used by them,"[10] and that he must develop his own means of viewing reality and expressing his vision to others.

Because of her admiration for the masterworks of the past, Sarraute rejects the idea that there can be "progress" in art, as there is in science and technology: "Great works remain great, even in their simplicity and candor, for they retain that density, that force of attack they had in the past."[11] Their continued vitality in the present springs from the freshness and spontaneity of their inspiration at the time they were conceived. Even when it comes to Balzac, whose name has become synonymous for the New Novelists with all that is trite and outmoded in the novel, it is not in his own works, she feels, but in their countless imitations, that they have become hopelessly conventionalized. In his own time, Balzac's vision was absolutely new. In the title essay, "The Age of Suspicion," Sarraute suggests that the reader of a novel by Balzac was willing to follow him through his meandering descriptions and meticulous categorizing of characters, not out of a predilection for the "solid reality" he was presenting, but because the reader knew that beneath these familiar appearances the author was exposing a hidden subject matter that was innovative and unexplored. Since Balzac's day, the "intensity of life" that he succeeded in rendering has deserted the forms in which he captured it and moved elsewhere (*Suspicion,* pp. 58–60). Every novelist worthy of the name creates a new form in which to encapsulate his own vision of reality. This form, spontaneous and original at the outset, becomes rigidified through imitation and is eventually abandoned in favor of new forms and new experimentation: "Today's discoveries will be tomorrow's conventions. The need to overthrow them will stimulate new revolts, new experiments, and hence eventually new conventions."[12] The evolution that Sarraute discerns in fiction is so natural, so continuous, and so persistent a movement that she has called it "a traditional struggle against tradition."[13]

In an early article entitled "Paul Valéry et l'Enfant d'éléphant" (1947), Sarraute posed as the "devil's disciple" — or rather, as the baby elephant in Kipling's *Just So Stories* whose naïve curiosity prompts him to ask inconvenient and embarrassing questions — to discredit the cult of veneration surrounding Valéry's poetry. Resolved to confront the poet's work on its merits, divested of the many layers of preconceived ideas with which it was coated, she concluded that Valéry too often falls into rhetoric, didacticism, and a "frozen academicism," with artifice supplanting enthusiasm and lyric inspiration. Furthermore, by culling from his work a number of passages so reminiscent of other, well-known poets as to consti-

tute veritable pastiches, she found his writing to be "imitative" —
the ultimate stigma.[14]

Originality, the antithesis of imitation, is the prime requisite for
the artist. This is the burden of the essay "The Age of Suspicion,"
which not only summarizes the very specific innovations that Sarraute and her contemporaries were contributing to fiction in terms
of fresh forms and techniques, but in a more general way calls for
the perpetual renovation of literature. Imitation is sterile and can
result only in a dead copy of what was once alive and vibrant. The
search for something new, undiscovered, untried, is an effort
required of every true artist — of the *bona fide* writer in *Between
Life and Death,* of Nathalie Sarraute herself. In order to ensure the
aesthetic quality and vigor of the novel, it is essential that the sensations it exposes be of a kind that have never been expressed before:
"The entire value of the form depends on the spontaneous, virgin,
intact quality of the vision which is at its origin. It is the endeavor
to express something as yet unsaid, that gives and allows the form
to keep forever its initial impact, its strength and its freshness."[15]

II   *In Quest of a New Reality*

In what do freshness and originality consist? What goal, if any,
does the novel pursue? In an interview commemorating the twentieth anniversary of Virginia Woolf's death, Sarraute asserted her
credo: "Every work of literature, like every work of art, consists in
revealing an unknown reality."[16] The novel seems to have as its
mission the quest for "reality" — that "unending quest," as Harry
Levin has called it, whose object "changes its appearance in differing contexts and to different observers."[17]

In "What Birds See" (1956) — the last essay included in *The Age
of Suspicion* — Sarraute distinguishes between two kinds of
writers, the "realists" and the "formalists," who differ radically in
attitude and methods. She defines a "realist" as someone who
attempts with utmost sincerity to pin down his personal vision of
reality. To do so, he has to abandon preconceived ideas and images,
ignore the surface reality that everyone around him perceives, and
attain something still unknown that he feels he is the first to discover. The force and passion of his vision are so overriding that he
accepts the greatest sacrifice a writer is obliged to make: solitude,
and the doubt and distress that often attend it (ideas echoed fictionally in *Between Life and Death*). When the writer succeeds in

capturing this elusive "reality," it is sensed as a hard core that gives cohesiveness and power to his entire work, something that everyone recognizes but can designate only by such imprecise terms as "truth" and "life" (*Suspicion,* pp. 133–37). The "formalist," on the other hand, is less interested in "reality" than in emulating the forms that others invented before him — conventional means for imitating life which, through repeated use, have degenerated into schematic outlines of character and oversimplification of sentiments. Sarraute deplores the fascination that this kind of writer still exerts on readers and critics alike, to whom he offers a false, superficial reality that fails to reflect their own lives and to present difficulties they can recognize as their own, thus discouraging their efforts to find in literature its essential satisfaction, "a deeper, more complex, clearer, truer knowledge of what they are, of their circumstances and their lives" (p. 145).

Sarraute has frequently theorized about the nature of reality for the artist. She is fond of paraphrasing Paul Klee's remark that the function of art is to render visible what was heretofore invisible.[18] This "invisible reality" that art expresses is composed of scattered, confused, amorphous elements and possibilities, of fleeting, indefinable sensations, imprisoned beneath a solid shell of convention and familiarity. The artist disengages these inchoate elements from the matrix in which they are embedded, endows them with cohesiveness and meaning, and constructs them into a model that is the work of art itself.[19] To express this new and invisible reality, the artist must create suitable forms of expression, however novel or disconcerting they may be: "The newer the reality revealed by a literary work, the more unaccustomed will be its form and the greater the force it will have to exert to pierce the thick curtain that shields from disturbance our ingrained habits of feeling."[20] In order to vanquish the resistance opposed by conventionalized attitudes, the artist must push his search to its farthest reaches, pursuing his unknown reality with all the perseverance he can muster, abandoning hackneyed techniques and forging a new instrument of expression, a living form.[21]

Sarraute points to certain forerunners of the modern novel who succeeded in capturing and conveying an unknown reality. Among them, she hails Flaubert as having brought to literature a substance whose richness is still being explored in contemporary fiction and theater. In his masterpiece, *Madame Bovary,* he introduced a new element into the novel: the concept of "inauthenticity." Flaubert's high-flown style, trite imagery, and conventional sentiments here compose a *trompe-l'oeil* that is presented as such; all the desires, yearnings, and dreams on which Emma Bovary constructs her existence are formed of the most degraded and hackneyed clichés of Romanticism. Flaubert's innovation, says Sarraute, was to pierce the veil of illusion and to make of platitude itself the stuff of fiction. Additionally, certain of his assertions were uncanny portents of things to come. "What I should like to do," he once stated, "is to compose a book about nothing . . . a book with almost no subject or at least where the subject was almost invisible, if possible. The most beautiful works are those whose subject matter is slightest; the more closely expression approximates thought . . . the more beautiful it is. I believe that the future of art lies in this direction." This is precisely what Sarraute says the modern novel tends to be: a book about nothing, almost devoid of a subject, unencumbered by characters, plot, and all the former accessories of fiction, reduced to pure movement, approaching abstract art.[22]

One of the strongest influences Sarraute discerns on the contemporary course of the novel is that of Dostoevsky, whom she has called the precursor of nearly every European writer of our time (*Suspicion,* p. 25). It is Dostoevsky who first showed that certain "twilight" states of mind, ambivalent feelings, and "abnormal" actions, which had previously been ignored in literature, exist naturally in people and can form the subject of fictional exploration.[23] Sarraute finds in Dostoevsky's characters manifestations of inner turmoil, ambivalent states of mind, and turbulent hidden sensations, as revealed in her description of old Karamazov in the essay "From Dostoevsky to Kafka" (1947):

All of these strange contortions [. . .] all of these disordered leapings and grimacings, are the absolutely precise, outward manifestation [. . .] of those subtle, barely perceptible, fleeting, contradictory, evanescent movements, faint tremblings, ghosts of timid appeals and recoilings, pale shadows that flit by, whose unceasing play constitutes the invisible woof of all human relationships and the very substance of our lives (*Suspicion,* p. 29).

These "subterranean" movements constitute the dramatic action of Dostoevsky's novels. They correspond to a need that originates deep within the recesses of the psyche, to something Katherine Mansfield called "this terrible desire to establish contact" (p. 33), which impels Dostoevsky's characters — like Sarraute's — to reach out toward and try to penetrate the "unbearable opaqueness" of the other person. All their dissimulations, furtive maneuvers, and inconsistent actions are coquetries designed to pique the other person's curiosity; their humility is a timid, devious appeal; their abrupt bouts of pride are painful attempts, after a rebuff, to seek another path of approach. Because it is impossible for them to remain at a distance, they are willing to model themselves on the reflected image that others have of them, or to wallow in self-abasement, forestalling a rupture at any cost (pp. 33–35). The inner psychological states that Dostoevsky depicts seem to approximate or herald the tropisms in Sarraute's books. In fact, Nathalie Sarraute has said that when she rereads Dostoevsky's novels she finds "tropisms" existing among his characters, just as they exist in real people, without his having attempted to study or analyze them.[24]

The main revolution in modern fiction Sarraute adjudges to have been accomplished by Proust and Joyce, both of whom "revealed a world seen through a microscope" and taught their readers new ways of perceiving that world.[25] The essay, "Conversation and Sub-Conversation" (1956), discusses their contributions to the elaboration of a new "psychological subject matter," an "anonymous" material existing in all human beings, which is divorced from particularities of background and personality (*Suspicion*, p. 89). This essay has frequently been misunderstood, perhaps because the opening pages are so heavily laden with sarcasm that, if read hastily and out of context, they appear to say the opposite of what they mean.[26] The sentence most often misquoted is the following: "The word 'psychology' is one that no present-day writer can hear spoken with regard to himself without casting his eyes to the ground and blushing" (p. 79). Because it has been taken at face value, without regard to the irony of the entire passage in which it appears, this statement has had to be amended, explained, and restated many times.

Far from denigrating psychology, Sarraute has always considered that "psychology is the raw material of fiction, just as color is the raw material of painting. . . . There is no such thing as a novel that is not psychological, even when it is a metaphysical novel, like Kafka's."[27] Of course, she has also specified that when she speaks of "psychology" she does not refer to a traditional analysis of feelings and character, but to the revelation of "unknown psychic forces, which are the basis for all literature and which no literary form can fail to take into account."[28] The major innovations of writers like Proust, Joyce, and Woolf lay in opening the reader's eyes to the possibility of a new "psychological reality" outside the authoritative system of literary conventions that seemed to confer indisputable laws on the novel. Deprived of his accustomed landmarks, bewildered and disoriented, the reader was suddenly obliged to confront for himself the innovative substance that lay behind the words. He discovered, for instance, hidden beneath Joyce's interior monologue, "an immense profusion of sensations, images, sentiments, memories, impulses, little larval actions that no inner language can convey, that jostle one another on the threshold of consciousness, gather together in compact groups and loom up all of a sudden, then immediately fall apart, combine otherwise and reappear in new forms; while unwinding inside us, like the ribbon that comes clattering from a telescriptor slot, is an uninterrupted flow of words" (pp. 91–92).

Sarraute explains that Proust observed these same movements, but from a distance, after they had run their course and were congealed in memory. He treated them as a sequence of cause and effect, which he tried to study and explain after they occurred; almost never did he portray them in the process of taking shape, developing and unfolding like minuscule dramas. He charted these inner movements from afar, like a cartographer looking at the waves in the sea, or like an astronomer describing their respective positions, "as though they were stars in a motionless sky" (p. 92).[29] Sarraute later asserted that after reading his work she became convinced that it was impossible to write except in Proust's wake. Determined to examine the same inner states that Proust had displayed statically, in the form of memories, but to capture them dynamically at their incipient stage, Sarraute had the idea of trying to "analyze movement, to study not what was already formed but psychological states in the process of formation"[30] — which is what she attempted to do in *Tropisms,* and has been doing ever since.

III *New Directions for Fiction*

In the title essay, "The Age of Suspicion" (1950), Sarraute posits the breakdown of traditional concepts of the novel and outlines the directions in which she finds fiction to be moving. She notes basic changes in characterization, as well as an altered relationship between reader and author.

The fictional personage, enthroned between reader and writer, object of their common fervor, like the saint in a primitive painting enshrined between the painting's donors, has been deposed. The time has passed when writers like Balzac and Flaubert succeeded in creating characters so true-to-life that they assumed an autonomous existence of their own. Little by little, the fictional character has been divested of his pedigree, his home and furnishings, his property and income, his appearance, even his name and personality. There have come into existence an increasing spate of literary works in which "a being devoid of outline, indefinable, intangible and invisible, an anonymous 'I,' who is at once all and nothing, and who as often as not is but the reflection of the author himself, has usurped the role of the hero, occupying the place of honor" (p. 56).

This evolution in the conception of character is a sign of distrust on the part of both writer and reader. The character has become the meeting-ground of their mutual doubts; the "age of suspicion" has dawned. The reader has first of all become wary of what the author's imagination proposes to him. He has become surfeited with the plethora of physical matter surrounding the character, which retains only the superficial appearance of reality, the flatness and illusion of a *trompe-l'oeil* painting; he has grown skeptical of spectacular actions and plot, entwined around the character like a mummy's bands. By reading Joyce, Proust, and Freud, he has been exposed to interior monologue and to the unexplored regions of the unconscious, with the result that his curiosity and attention have become centered on the development of new states of psychological awareness. The writer, meanwhile, recognizing the reader's misgivings, is himself hesitant to pose as the omniscient arbiter of destiny (pp. 57–65). He is also mistrustful of the reader's tendency to create literary "types" that he can add to the collection of waxen figurines in his memory.

To combat this predilection, the reader must be deprived as much as possible of the specifics that enable him to fabricate characters: physical appearance, commonplace sentiments and gestures, all the external semblances of verisimilitude, including a name. By a subtle process of identification, he must learn to recognize characters from the inside, at precisely the same place as the author, where he can be "immersed ... in a substance as anonymous as blood, a magma without name or contours. If he succeeds in finding his way, it is thanks to stakes that the author has planted for purposes of his own orientation. No reminiscences of the reader's world, no conventional concern for cohesion or likelihood, distract his attention or curb his effort" (p. 71). The concentration on psychological impulses and feelings, rather than on the individual persons in whom they are housed, by logical extension leads to the anonymity and increasing abstraction of character:

As a result of an evolution similar to that in painting ... the psychological element, like the pictorial element, is beginning to free itself imperceptibly from the object of which it was an integral part. It is tending to become self-sufficient and, in so far as possible, to do without exterior support. The novelist's entire experimental effort is concentrated on this one point, as is also the reader's entire effort of attention (p. 68).

The new psychological reality for which modern writers strive necessitates a new kind of dialogue. In "Conversation and Sub-Conversation," Sarraute considers the projection of inner movements in speech. Since these delicate and minuscule dramas, arising within remote interior regions, do not manifest themselves in acts but tend to surface, if at all, in conversation, spoken discourse replaces action more and more in the modern novel. However, as the outward continuation of these subterranean movements, such dialogue adapts poorly to traditional forms. Quotation marks or devices like "he said" or "John replied" are conventional symbols of an unbreachable distance between the writer and his characters.

As an example of modern experimentation, Sarraute cites the novels of Ivy Compton-Burnett, "one of the greatest novelists that England has ever had" (p. 112), whose books are distinguishable by an absolutely new feature: they consist entirely of dialogue. These are strange dialogues, situated on the fluctuating border that separates conversation from subconversation, with interior movements attempting to obtrude into speech and surfacing in an assortment of maxims, metaphors, and clichés. Ivy Compton-Burnett's method hints at the complexity and variety of these inner dramas, but fails to plunge the reader into their midst.

Sarraute sees the need to move even further ahead. She dreams of a technique that would precipitate the reader directly into the stream of subsurface movements as they occur and would give him the illusion that he is repeating these actions "in a more clearly aware, more orderly, distinct and forceful manner than he can do in life, without losing that element of indetermination, of opacity and mystery that one's own actions always have for the one who lives them" (p. 111). Imperceptibly, through changes of form and rhythm, the reader would realize that the action had passed from inside to outside the character's consciousness; dialogue would be liberated from its former conventions and constraints.

IV *Style*

Every writer seeking to capture an original vision of reality must find his own distinctive means of communicating it. The more innovative his conception, the more unaccustomed will be its expression. This is axiomatic for Sarraute. There is an indissoluble connection between content and form, between the "unknown reality" the artist discovers and the method he chooses to convey it: "Every exploration of this reality constitutes an exploration of language."[31] Once the writer has determined which form of language most nearly approximates his innate concept of reality, he cannot express himself in any other way. It is inconceivable that an identical content be represented in a different form. It follows, therefore, that a work of literature cannot be paraphrased, summarized, or recounted in any other wise. The literary text is a self-contained and self-sustaining entity, as intrinsic to the work it constitutes as color is to a painting or sound to a musical composition. It is as impossible, Sarraute believes, to "recount" a novel or a poem as it would be to "recount" a painting or a piece of music. This is especially true with respect to her own novels: "The incessant and rapid fluctuations of states in perpetual transformation, which give my writing ... its distinctiveness, cannot be perceived except within and through the text. Separated from it, they cease to exist."[32]

Style is the hallmark of the artist's unique creative venture, the means by which he conveys his personal vision of reality. Its purpose is to express as accurately and succinctly as possible what he is trying to say. It strives neither for beauty of language nor harmony of forms for their own sake. It is not to be confused with what the French call *le beau style* — that effete elegance of language that was brought to perfection in the eighteenth century and still serves as a model of composition and rhetoric in the classroom, and whose outmoded artificiality Sarraute has never ceased to deplore. Style is beautiful in the way that an athlete's gesture is beautiful, only to the extent that it is adapted to its aim (*Suspicion,* pp. 135–36). Its sole criterion is its efficacity. Style, as Roland Barthes has put it, is "the writer's 'thing,' his splendor and his prison — and his solitude."[33]

Sarraute detects a continual process of interaction between sensation and verbalization — a process evoked fictionally in her reconstruction of the creative act in *Between Life and Death*. She is aware of a perception antecedent to verbal expression — an "unnameable" sensation that she seeks to put into words. The "unnameable" cannot exist without language, but at the same time it resists delimitation within accustomed terms and expressions. Her entire effort consists in finding language that is capable of rendering an impression without labeling it directly or pinpointing it with a crude and constraining definition. For example, if she wishes to evoke a certain kind of accent and intonation, instead of calling it "vulgar" or "coarse" — restrictive and meaningless terms — she tries to isolate and reproduce the various feelings generated inside the listener when he hears this kind of accent.[34]

The act of rendering "tropisms" is a difficult and delicate one. The unique property of tropisms is their perpetual movement and transformation. These fluctuating sensations are as elusive as quicksilver. Moreover, the mind experiencing tropisms does not verbalize them, as in the case of interior monologue or stream of consciousness; it merely senses their presence and their instantaneous passage. Sarraute's struggle is to capture in language something that flutters on the borderline of language and that threatens to congeal when put into words. The effort is both a challenge and a paradox: to express the inexpressible, to grasp the ineffable, to immobilize movement.

In order to preserve the fluidity of the sensations she is trying to convey, Sarraute avoids using a delimiting terminology. From the outset, she has always sought to undermine conventional terms and labels, to burrow beneath these appeasing classifications and to extract the mobile essences they temporarily shield. She avoids the convenient but calcifying use of trite expressions that have become sterile through repetition. Instead, she has recourse to synonyms and parallel constructions, whereby she encircles her meaning without targeting it directly and rendering it lifeless. The text proceeds in the form of circumlocutions, clusters of diverse qualifications, swarms of metaphors and near-synonymous approximations that surreptitiously close in upon the sense of what Sarraute is saying. As an example of this method, Jean Ricardou has noted the multiple images of cristalline laughter in *Do You Hear Them?* — bells, droplets, fountains, waterfalls, rivulets, etc.[35] Sarraute has a predilection for piling up words in a series, in a collaborative association of nearly identical elements.[36] It is as though one word alone could never suffice, as if every conceivable angle or facet of an impression needed to be exposed. Where another writer — a Flaubert, for example — might pick and choose among synonyms before settling on *le mot juste,* Sarraute seems to use them all, in reckless profusion, each fresh term contributing an extra nuance of meaning or altering the reader's perspective by a hair. It is only in their aggregate that the cumulative possibilities contained in a single tropism can be apprehended.

In his preface to *Portrait of a Man Unknown,* Sartre praises Sarraute's style above everything:

The best thing about Nathalie Sarraute is her stumbling, groping style, with its honesty and numerous misgivings, a style that approaches the object with reverent precautions, withdraws from it suddenly out of a sort of modesty, or through timidity before its complexity, then, when all is said and done, suddenly presents us with the drooling monster, almost without having touched it, through the magic of an image (p. xiv).

One of the most striking features of Sarraute's writing — a recognizable hallmark of her "style" — is the abundance and richness of her imagery. Sarraute eschews analysis, description, explanation; each sensation is crystallized around an image. She never introduces images gratuitously, for the sake of elegance or ornamentation. Metaphor and simile are not external appendages but integral structural devices. They have a specific, functional purpose, for they serve as a means of apprehending, with a minimum of distortion, the ever-changing tropism. It is primarily through imagery that Sarraute impresses certain sensations on the reader, forcing him to experience and relive them himself. Since tropisms develop and vanish with lightning rapidity, producing inner responses that are sometimes intense but invariably fleeting, the only way to communicate them is through images that offer a mental "equivalent" and arouse analogous sensations in the reader (*Suspicion,* p. 8). For this reason, Sarraute deliberately chooses simple images from everyday experience that will strike a vibratory chord in the reader and will at the same time coincide with the sensations that the characters experience.

The various types of metaphors that crop up regularly, especially in Sarraute's books, have been catalogued in detail.[37] A few examples may serve to indicate their tenor. There is a prevalence of animal and insect imagery — packs of dogs, chattering magpies, lions, tigers, wild bulls, clumsy elephants, monkeys, pigs, snakes and bees and butterflies, snails withdrawing inside their shells, octopuses with viscous tentacles, serpents, vipers, and worms —a Noah's ark from which Sarraute extracts every conceivable kind of creature, whose instinctive reactions are consonant with the prerational nature of tropistic responses. There are also frequent martial metaphors — ranging from the hand-to-hand combat of medieval tourneys to the shells and grenades of modern warfare — all representing interpersonal conflicts in the form of deadly battles. Abundant references to bleeding wounds, festering abscesses, suppurating sores, and gangrenous limbs correlate mental anguish with physical pain. Fairy-tale metaphors of wicked fairies and Prince Charmings, giants and ogres, the three little pigs and the big bad wolf, little Red Riding Hood and Tom Thumb, succeed in rendering the dreamlike terror of adults reduced to the helplessness of children.

Particular types of imagery, recurring from one novel to the next, seem to bear a special significance in Sarraute's universe. Symbols of hardness and softness, rigidity and fluidity, solid masses and gaseous vapors represent the dichotomy between certainty and doubtfulness, assuredness and insecurity, the opaque world of appearances and the invisible region where tropisms hold sway. Whatever is solid, concrete, well-defined, impenetrable, belongs to the domain of objective reality; in contrast, whatever is soft and spongy, blurred and nebulous — oozings and drippings, cracks and crevices, noxious odors and emanations — suggests those disquieting regions of the psyche where black holes gape, abysses yawn, and tropisms abound. A fissure appears in a solid wall, nauseating liquids seep through, efforts to sponge them away are useless. The ground gives way and the planetarium's dome starts to spin. The comforting assurance of a stable world is constantly being eroded. Nothing is immutable, dependable; human relationships are in perpetual flux, and attempts to render them permanent are forever doomed.

The passage from limited to generalized comparison is a key procedure for Nathalie Sarraute and constitutes one of the fundamental structures of her writing.[38] In her earlier books, the terms of comparison are usually stated explicitly. In *Portrait,* the daughter is compared to a hyena, the narrator to a crab in its hole, the father to a spider waiting in its web to catch a fly, etc. The narrator preparing to tell the daughter about her father is *like* a surgeon about to perform an operation. Eventually, the terms denoting comparison tend to be suppressed. In *The Planetarium,* Germaine Lemaire *is* a queen surrounded by her courtiers, Aunt Berthe *is* a sorceress presiding over secret rites. The ultimate development of these metaphors, which are increasingly prolonged in *The Planetarium* (the regal image attends Germaine Lemaire throughout the book), is the construction of entire imaginary scenes to represent tropistic responses (e.g., the courtroom scene in *Do You Hear Them?,* the funeral scene in *"fools say",* and the innumerable fragmentary dialogues — like tiny scenarios in which tropisms are enacted — that occur in every novel beginning with *The Golden Fruits*).[39]

The tropistic movements that Sarraute is trying to reproduce require colloquial language and syntax for their expression. To imitate their rapidity, she seeks a swift, fluid patter of speech which is incompatible with the formality and inflexibility of classic modes. Even traditional sentence structure is too cumbersome and slow-paced to suggest the mercurial and ephemeral nature of these inner states. As a result, Sarraute's language is simple, her syntax uncomplicated, her sentences short and staccato and — in her more recent books — often left suspended, to be completed in the reader's mind. Colloquialisms of everyday speech, hackneyed phraseology, even threadbare clichés are the instruments Sarraute applies to rupture the outer shell of usage and to analyze its hidden components. Many of her metaphors are clichés in themselves — clichés she chooses to take literally. When Berthe is obliged to "tread carefully" or "watch her step" with her brother, Sarraute pictures her stepping gingerly across a minefield. Alain's attempt to "bridge the chasm" between his audience and himself is quite literally a tightrope walk across a ravine. Sarraute does not say that someone is "as scared as a rabbit" or "fawns like a dog"; she shows him instead cowering inside his burrow or fetching delectable morsels to lay at his master's feet. Certain platitudes of imagery recur like leitmotivs in Sarraute's novels: expressions like the French *se mettre martel en tête* or *une tempête dans un verre d'eau* ("a tempest in a teapot"). Trite metaphors like these are picked apart, reduced to their basic components, and presented as if they constituted some bright and original idea.

In her efforts to capture tropistic movements, Sarraute has acknowledged that she is obliged to express them "through the rhythm of the style, as poetry does."[40] Her conception of "poetry" is both a matter of style and of vision. She does not accept the designation of "poetry" to cover conventional subjects, like nature or death or love, for example. Rather, the idea of poetry is bound up with the artist's personal exploration and innovation: "Every literary work, like every work of art, consists in revealing an unknown reality. The invisible, as Paul Klee said. The greater the share of the invisible, the more powerful the force with which the novelist pierces appearances to render the visible visible, the more poetic the work will be."[41] According to these criteria, Sarraute calls Virginia Woolf's novels "poetic," as well as the works of Dostoevsky. When asked whether she considered her own writing "poetic," her reply was almost identical. "Poetry in a work of art," she observed, "is what makes the invisible visible. The stronger the force that permits piercing appearances . . . the greater will be the portion of poetry in the work." According to her own definition, she went on to say, how could she regard her work as *not* being poetic?[42]

If poetry is a question of vision — of dedication to an ideal of originality, of unceasing striving for renewal and re-creation in art, of a tireless effort to extract an undiscovered reality out of the bedrock of objective appearances — then Sarraute is a poet. If poetry is a matter of style — of transforming tenuous and fragile states of mind into language, of approximating feelings with words — then Sarraute's work is poetic. To the extent that poetry is sensation entrapped and transmitted through the creative imagination of the poet, then Sarraute's work is a long poem in prose.

CHAPTER 7

Sarraute and the New Novel

I   Background of the New Novel

IN the early 1950s, while some critics were proclaiming that the
novel as a genre was dead, other theoreticians — mostly
Marxist-oriented critics like George Lukács, Lucien Goldmann,
and Roland Barthes — postulating a close connection between the
history of the novel and the rise of capitalism in the west, were
predicting fundamental changes in fiction corresponding to
changes in socioeconomic conditions which they considered to pre-
determine the state of literature.[1] It was at this period that a handful of innovative French novelists, writing independently of one another, began attracting critical interest. At first referred to by
various names (L'Ecole du Regard, the School of Refusal, the New
Wave, La Chapelle de Minuit, Romans de la table rase, Romans
blancs, Anti-Novels, and even Ante-Novels), their works eventually
came to be designated under the umbrella title of the "New
Novel."

What is meant by this term and to whom was it applied? The
New Novel did *not* signify an organized group or a "school" or
even a conscious literary movement. It had no leader and no mani-
festo, no deliberate program of reform, not even a journal to
express its ideas. Rather, the name was loosely applied as a common denominator for a number of different writers, following
divergent paths, who were united in their determination to discard
outmoded conventions of fiction and to search for ways of renew-
ing the novel as an art form. Primacy was placed on originality of
outlook and freedom of expression. There were no prescribed rules
or models to follow. In the words of Alain Robbe-Grillet, one of
the foremost proponents of fictional regeneration: "Every novelist,
in every novel, must invent his own form. No recipe can replace this

continual preoccupation. The book creates its own rules for itself alone."[2] Amorphous, unpredictable, undefinable, the New Novel was — and continues to be — the product of each writer's subjective vision.

A certain imprecision exists with respect to the identity of the New Novelists. Like the Pléiade poets four hundred years ago, a fixed nucleus of writers is generally agreed upon, around which gravitate a fluctuating number of other names that vary according to the assessment of individual critics. Thus, the list appearing in the 1958 issue of *Esprit* — Beckett, Butor, Jean Cayrol, Marguerite Duras, Jean Lagrolet, Robert Pinget, Robbe-Grillet, Sarraute, Claude Simon, Kateb Yacine — differs from the list compiled fourteen years later by Francoise Baqué in her book on *The New Novel*[3] — Beckett, Butor, Cayrol, Claude Ollier, Pinget, Robbe-Grillet, Sarraute, and Simon. Each writer on the subject has his own variations.[4] The names that reappear dependably, almost without exception, are Sarraute, Robbe-Grillet, and Michel Butor.

Although Nathalie Sarraute and Alain Robbe-Grillet are the acknowledged precursors of the New Novel in France, Sarraute's chronological precedence has perhaps been insufficiently recognized. A reminder of certain dates will confirm her position as *avant-coureur* of the New Novel. The first edition of *Tropisms* (written between 1932 and 1937) appeared in 1939; Sarraute's first critical articles came out in *Les Temps modernes* in 1947 and 1950; *Portrait* was published in 1948 and *Martereau* in 1953 — the same year that Robbe-Grillet published his first novel and critical essays. Although Sarraute had begun writing "a new kind of novel" long before the others, it was Robbe-Grillet's *Les Gommes* (*Erasers*), accorded the Prix Fénelon in 1953, that first drew critical attention to their experimentations in fiction. Sarraute's *Age of Suspicion* (1956) and Robbe-Grillet's theoretical writings (composed over a ten-year period, 1953–63) confirmed the group's reputation as iconoclasts and innovators. Enthusiastic articles by Roland Barthes,[5] who soon became the spokesman for the New Criticism (allied hand-in-glove with the New Novel),[6] and a special issue of the literary review *Esprit* in the summer of 1958, helped establish and circularize the phenomenon. Sarraute's earlier novels, which had received little attention, gained prominence with the publication and popularity of *The Age of Suspicion* and the notice accorded the New Novel in general.

Despite the tenuousness of their association and the heterogeneity of their writing, the so-called New Novelists exhibit certain characteristics in common. For one thing, their works were first published by small, secondary houses: Sarraute by Robert Denoël and Robert Marin, Butor and Robbe-Grillet by the Editions de Minuit, Claude Simon by Sagittaire; eventually, two companies became the primary distributors of the New Novel: the Editions de Minuit and Gallimard.[7] The writers themselves are united by a common admiration for certain precursors, among them Flaubert, Dostoevsky, Proust, Joyce, Kafka, and Faulkner.[8]

"Creators have always been preoccupied by technical questions," says Claude Mauriac,[9] whose own dual function as literary critic and New Novelist is representative of the modern writer's involvement in the problems of his craft. There is scarcely a New Novelist who has not turned his attention to the question of literary creativity, whether it be in the technical area of linguistics and the structure of language, or in the more abstract and subjective realm of aesthetics. In addition to Sarraute and Robbe-Grillet, writers like Butor, Jacques Borel, Claude Mauriac, Maurice Blanchot, Philippe Sollers, Jean Ricardou, Bernard Pingaud, Robert Pinget, Robert Sabatier, Marc Saporta, and Philippe Boyer — the list could be extended indefinitely — have all crossed the line between criticism and creative expression. For this reason, the New Novel is as much a reflection of its own essence as it is the presentation of a fictional substance.

If there is any single characteristic that distinguishes the New Novel, it is "self-consciousness." That is to say, the New Novel is at all times "conscious" of being exactly what it is — a novel. Traditional works of fiction often went to extraordinary lengths to establish credentials of veracity — purporting to be an exchange of letters the writer has merely sorted and edited, or the revised oral narrative of an infamous lady, or the translation of a book by an ancient Persian sage, or a sheaf of papers found in a prison cell, or a centuries-old document discovered by chance in the customhouse where the writer was employed, or — perhaps most farfetched of all — a ms. received in a cemetery from the hands of a young man who died at once of despair after dotting the final "i."[10] The New Novel unreservedly rejects all pretenses of this kind. It never masquerades as "fact," but deliberately exposes itself as "fiction." It refrains from claiming to imitate "reality"; neither does it permit the reader to settle snugly into the illusion that it is "true to life." To the contrary, so that there may be no possibility of confusing "art" with "life," it continually reminds the reader of its inauthenticity by exploring and emphasizing its own fictional nature.

II   *Affinities with the New Novel: Aims*

Many of the ideas Sarraute propounded in *The Age of Suspicion* and exemplified in her novels have become identified with the New Novel as a whole — a robust confidence in the evolutionary process of literature, an insistence on the primacy of art as distinct from social or political commitment, a belief that form and content are inseparable components of a work of art, an appeal to the reader's contributory participation, and the adoption of specific methods and procedures for achieving the goal of reinvigorating fiction.

Sarraute has repeated many times, in many ways, her concept of literature as a "search" for new ways of perceiving reality, as outmoded conventions are rejected and new methods are explored. She is not alone in predicating the natural evolution of literature and in stressing the need for new approaches to fiction. Michel Butor and Alain Robbe-Grillet are foremost among the many writers who second this sentiment. For Butor, the novel is an instrument of knowledge, a means of apprehending reality. He emphasizes the need for a perpetual invention of new narrative forms to correspond to new ways of perceiving reality. In the transformation of fictional concepts, he envisions new subjects as well as fresh techniques of language, style, composition, and structure. In fact, he foresees a metamorphosis in the very notion of the novel, which he finds evolving slowly but inevitably toward "a new kind of poetry."[11] Robbe-Grillet, who has written even more extensively on the evolutionary course of fiction, notes that every great writer has contributed to this ongoing process. Flaubert wrote the "new novel" of 1860; Proust, the "new novel" of 1910. Forms live and die in all branches of art and must continually be renewed; in this respect, the New Novel merely follows the natural evolution of literature. Like Sarraute, Robbe-Grillet insists that he and his contemporaries are not rejecting the past; their aim is to continue the work of their predecessors (not to improve on them, which would be a non-sense, but to follow in their lead).[12]

In the elaboration of the New Novel, form and content are closely connected. A "new" view of reality implies a "new" mode of expression; these must be absolutely suited to one another. As Maurice Blanchot has remarked, "the nature of the novel is such that its content determines its form."[13] Robbe-Grillet is equally emphatic about the impossibility of separating content from form:

To speak of the content of a novel as of something independent of its form is to remove the entire genre from the domain of art. For strictly speaking, a work of art contains nothing (that is, in the sense that a box may or may not contain some object whose nature is foreign to it). Art is not an envelope of more or less brilliant hue, designed to ornament the author's "message." ... Art obeys no servitude of this order, nor for that matter any other predetermined function.... [Art] expresses nothing other than itself.[14]

This view is staunchly upheld by Sarraute, who has often noted the existence of an indissoluble link between the unknown reality the writer is seeking to express and the new form in which he gives it substance. She is convinced that form and content are "one and the same thing" and that a work of art is an entity that suffices unto itself; nothing can be added to or subtracted from its total expression.

The concept of art as an end in itself, unencumbered by didactic aims, is a tenet that almost all the New Novelists share. Robbe-Grillet is one of the chief spokesmen for separating artistic expression from social or political dogma. Like Sarraute, he believes that art cannot be subjected to the service of a cause, however worthwhile, because the slightest external compulsion paralyzes creativity, and the most infinitesimal concern with a moral or instructive purpose becomes an unbearable constraint on the writer. The artist's sole commitment is to his art: "Let us restore to the notion of *engagement* ["commitment"] the only meaning it can have for us. Instead of being political in nature, *engagement* for the writer signifies complete awareness of the immediate problems of language, a conviction of their extreme importance, and the will to resolve them from within."[15] During his participation in the Leningrad conference of writers in August 1963, Robbe-Grillet negated the concept of any social or moral value in the novel, and rejected the idea of the writer's "function" or "responsibility." Literature is not a tool, intended to serve a utilitarian purpose, he said; the novel is a form of search, which does not even know in advance what it is seeking.[16] Bernard Pingaud, the third member (with Nathalie Sarraute) of the French delegation to the Leningrad meeting, echoed their common sentiment that art is divorced from a moralistic purpose. Literature is not an "action" but an "appeal," he noted. A writer's morality has nothing to do with his "commitment" to a cause; his responsibility lies instead in conveying the impalpable relationship between his experience and the reality surrounding him.[17]

It is this position of withdrawal from contemporary problems and immersion instead in questions of aesthetics that has stimulated some of the most heated objections to the New Novel.[18] Writers like Jean-Paul Sartre and Simone de Beauvoir, whose own works are commentaries on the sociopolitical causes to which they have devoted their lives, are among those most intensely opposed to what they conceive to be an attitude of disinvolvement and unconcern. Simone de Beauvoir, in particular, attacks the New Novelists for establishing an artificial distinction between the person and the writer (the one embracing causes, signing proclamations, participating in demonstrations, and the other shutting himself up in his ivory tower to write); in fact, she goes so far as to attribute the "degradation" of French society to the "mutilation" of the writer and his utilitarian role.[19]

Sarraute maintains a totally different point of view. She deplores the didactic use of literature, even for the most idealistic goals. She feels that art degenerates into stereotype and sterility when it becomes an instrument of propaganda, however "revolutionary" the cause it claims to serve; paradoxically, what is intended to be a radical force in fiction is usually couched in reactionary forms, with lifeless characters, old-fashioned intrigue, a hackneyed "style" — all of which are supposed to render the novel accessible to a mass audience. Thus, in the name of a moral imperative, "revolutionary" literature attains what Sarraute calls an eminently "immoral" state for a work of art — that is to say, "a negligent, conformist, insincere or disloyal attitude with respect to reality" (*Suspicion,* p. 144).

To the contention by some critics that the New Novel is impersonal and "objective," aiming at the "reification" of the external world, Robbe-Grillet has countered by insisting that the New Novel is not only centered on a human presence but strives for total subjectivity:

The New Novel is interested only in man and his situation in the world. . . . Man is present on every page, on every line, in every word. Even if there are many objects, described in minute detail, there is always the eye that sees them, the thought that considers them, the passion that deforms them. The objects in our novels never have any existence outside of human perception, real or imaginary. . . .[20]

In Sarraute's case, where external description is minimal and objects are virtually nonexistent except insofar as they set tropisms in motion, everything depends on the vision of the perceiving and recording consciousness. Her work is focused solely on human sensations and interrelationships. Although she disclaims any moral message as such, Sarraute delineates experience at so fundamental a level that she transcends the limitations of political or social boundaries and attains that deeper degree of "morality" that consists in attesting to the bonds of a common humanity. But no lessons are taught, no behavioral guidelines offered. It is up to the reader to comprehend the moral overtones of the work, just as it is up to him to pursue through his own mental exertions the enigmatic indications that the New Novel offers him.

A basic premise Sarraute shares with the other New Novelists is an insistence on the reader's participatory role. Reading is no longer a passive experience; it has become a demanding, sometimes strenuous, activity. No more the idle spectator of a prefabricated world, the reader is now a partner in the process of creation. He is solicited to make his own contribution of sensitivity, intellect, and imagination to the elaboration of the literary text. By withholding information that the reader must supply, by fragmenting chronology which the reader must rearrange, by presenting anonymous characters whom the reader must recognize by his own wits, the modern novelist proves that fiction is a cooperative venture. Into that special one-on-one relationship that has always existed between writer and reader, a new element of collaboration has entered. Discussions of Sarraute's individual novels have emphasized the extent to which she obliges the reader to enter the consciousness of the "characters" and to perceive reality through their eyes. The shifting optic which is so integral a part of Sarraute's presentation necessitates the reader's alert participation. Even so simple a stylistic device as Sarraute's frequent utilization of three dots, in lieu of complete sentences, is a deliberate appeal to the reader's supplementary effort. The key word of a phrase often remains unexpressed, or the tail end of a sentence is left dangling in suspense. The reader is expected to supply the missing words or thoughts — and hence to contribute his portion of creativity to the finished work.[21]

Robbe-Grillet also calls for a complementary effort on the part of the reader to complete the work begun by the writer, in a joint literary endeavor: "Far from neglecting [the reader], today's writer proclaims his absolute need of the reader's assistance, of his active, conscious, *creative* cooperation. What he asks of him is no longer to receive a world already finished, closed in upon itself, but on the contrary to participate in its creation, to invent the work — and the world — and thus learn to invent his own life."[22] Northrop Frye has put it somewhat differently: "It is the reader who is responsible for the way literature functions, both socially and individually.... One's reading ... becomes an essential part of a process of self-creation and self-identity."[23] There are no preestablished verities or values, any more than there are definite characters, a traceable plot, or a linear time sequence. The reader must supply them all.

The New Novel brings out the latent sleuth in every reader. The need to resolve ambiguities and furnish missing elements provides an intellectual stimulus — like the challenge of solving a puzzle, for which there is never any single correct answer. Perhaps this is why the New Novel has often been compared to a detective story, whether the "investigation" in progress has to do with a real crime (as in Robbe-Grillet's *Erasers* and *Voyeur*) or is merely a quest that leads nowhere (like his *In the Labyrinth*). While this atmosphere of suspense and mystery is pronounced in the overt subject matter of novels by Robbe-Grillet, Claude Simon, Claude Mauriac, and Michel Butor, it is more subtle, but equally pervasive, in the works of Sarraute. It has been suggested that the "suspicion" obtaining among Sarraute's characters, their relentless scrutiny of one another's actions, their probing and interpretation of motives, convey all the tension and drama of a police investigation.[24] Moreover, the narrator of *Portrait* has been compared to a detective in the best tradition of Poe's Auguste Dupin, Simenon's Inspector Maigret, and, at a further remove, Conan Doyle's Sherlock Holmes — a man who is fascinated by the intellectual puzzle of piecing together human relationships, searching out secret vices, and examining evidences of disorder beneath the smooth façade of family life.[25] However one may wish to characterize the phenomenon, there is an undercurrent of mystery, a confusion of identities, a repetition of scenes from diverse points of view, an ambiguity between "real" and imagined incidents, even an indeterminate quality of language itself, which is disorienting to the reader and requires patient unraveling to be understood. Bernard Pinguad is not far off the mark when he calls the New Novel "enigmatic as a matter of principle."[26]

III   *Affinities with the New Novel: Methods*

To implement their common aim of injecting new vitality into literature, the New Novelists utilize certain of the same methods and techniques. Despite the fact that they have continued to work independently, their writings exhibit a number of shared characteristics, many of which are to be found in Sarraute's earliest works. This is less a case of specific influence than a confluence of responses to a single and immediate problem perceived equally by all — the need to disengage fiction from the quagmire of convention.

A principal innovation is the elimination or suppression of plot. There is scarcely any traceable storyline in the New Novel, and consequently — or incidentally — no linear chronology. Everything takes place *now,* at some impalpable moment in the present, usually divorced from external historical time. The preferred use of the present tense is an attempt to achieve a form of narration that is contemporaneous with what is being experienced or enacted in the novel.[27] Past events are integrated into the present in the form of recollections that visit the mind with the same immediacy as thoughts, emotions, and perceptions. Like all other manifestations of the external world, time is subjectified. It exists only insofar as it is perceived by the mind, which shortens or lengthens its span, jumbles its sequence, equates present with past or future according to its whim. The distance between an event and the memory of it — a distinction still present in Proust — is obliterated, as reality and imagination fuse. There is no chronological order in the workings of the mind; one idea or image conjures up another, according to some internal and indefinable sequence of its own, beyond the laws of temporality. Emotional responses, imaginings and suppositions, future projects and past remembrances may present themselves repeatedly and in infinite (and infinitesimal) variations; hence the repetition of scenes, thoughts, visions, in a cyclical continuum. The modern novel, following these convolutions of thought as they occur, is thus governed by none of the external controls that regimented traditional approaches to fiction.

The suppression of plot and chronology entails a corresponding disappearance of narrative discourse as a means of recounting past events. The predominance of dialogue in Sarraute's novels — either spoken discourse or the subconversation that prepares and accompanies speech — signifies the immediacy of the sensation Sarraute strives to communicate. Her rapid-fire dialogue, with its semi-formed sentence structure, incomplete syntax, fragmented bursts of speech, and breathless interruptions, expresses the spontaneity and urgency of the present moment. The impression is of a narrative so immediate and instantaneous that it appears to be in the process of formation at the moment it is read.

When narration gives way to dialogue in this manner, the form of expression is that of everyday speech, in all its banal simplicity. Colloquial language, hackneyed phrases, clichés of conversation — these are the *lingua franca* of contemporary fiction. Banality is both the form and the substance of the new writing. It is an envelope that must be pierced to yield its portion of poetry. Germaine Lemaire was convinced that banality was no fit subject for literature; Sarraute proves the contrary. She cracks open the commonplace and extracts the deeper meaning hidden underneath. She invests banal language with poetic meaning, like Butor, who said: "The poet, in order to effect his marvelous crystallizations, makes use of everyday words; the object of poetry, its very act, is the preservation of ordinary language.... The poet restores their meaning to everyday words and endows them with a new significance...."[28]

Another characteristic shared by Sarraute and other exponents of the New Novel is the disintegration of the traditional *personae* of fiction. Characters are no longer presented objectively by the author, with complete physical description and biographical detail; their motivations are not explained and interpreted for the reader, as in the past. Not only are they divested of distinguishing traits of personality and background, but their identity is further clouded by their anonymity. If a character does bear a name, it is almost as an afterthought, a useless appendage that obscures his presence to the reader — as if a name were a misleading label that falsifies a character's identity by inhibiting the reader's identification with him. The confusion, ambiguity, and interchangeability of characters — often denoted by the imperceptible passage from the pronoun "he" or "she" to "I" or "we" — further contributes to the effacement of the individual.[29] At the same time, the reader is internalized within the consciousness of the character, situated at the same point as the author, presumably knowing no more and no less. The reader's experience tends to coincide with the experience of both author and character, in a convergence of sensation.

"Reality" itself acquires a new meaning. It can no longer be confused with "realism" or — more accurately — "verism." Reality is a way of perceiving the world; it differs from person to person, from one artist to the next. As Sarraute has repeated on many occasions, each writer pursues his unique vision of "reality," which he strives to express in his work. The subjective approach to reality, reflecting the artist's personal view, elicits a subjective response on the part of the reader. The artist's reality ceases to be a common, neutral, anonymous ground that is recognizable to everyone; instead, it is a private space, rearranged in conformity with the artist's inner vision, into which he invites the reader to step.

Verisimilitude ceases to be an aim of fiction. Art no longer mirrors life. Hypothesis and the products of the imagination weigh equally with objective facts. The line of demarcation between truth and falsehood, reality and fiction, is smudged beyond recognition. The possible and impossible exist side by side. There is no certainty in the New Novel, only a perpetual "perhaps."

CHAPTER 8

Conclusion

ALTHOUGH Nathalie Sarrute may have been a precursor of the New Novel in many of its aims and methods, she has always held herself aloof from identification with any literary movement or school. She refuses the application of any labels to her work, just as she rejects all delimiting classifications. The terms on which she accepts designation as a New Novelist are problematical. In an interview in *Tel Quel* (1962), to explain her affiliation with the New Novel, she first outlined her own innovations — a radical negation of the forms of the traditional novel; the absence of characters with definable personalities and proper names; a mixture of imaginary and "real" scenes, together with the repetition of identical scenes perceived from different points of view; a certain manner or treating time and utilizing dialogue in the novel — then summed up with a quip: "If all this has nothing to do with what is today called the New Novel, then I have nothing to do with it."[1]

Ten years later, she was equally adamant in upholding her independence. When Robbe-Grillet asked her, in 1972, if she belonged to the group of writers (loosely comprised of himself, Pinget, Ricardou, and Simon) who were then being designated as exponents of a "New New Novel," she firmly disclaimed her adherence. Most of these novelists, she pointed out, had experienced an abrupt rupture in their work about 1960, after which their fiction assumed a new orientation; instead of continuing to "represent" the world, either subjectively or objectively, they tended now to concentrate on questions of language and textuality *per se,* with a consequent subversion of literary and social structures.[2] In her own case, she acknowledges no rupture of this kind:

I have never deviated from my line, and were I to do so it would assuredly

169

not be in order to submit to theoretical presuppositions. It does not matter to me in the slightest if what I do is still called the "New Novel," the "New New Novel," or even the "New New New Novel." As far as I am concerned, labels have no importance.[3]

Even at an early period in her writing, Sarraute recognized a distinction between her own position and the tendency of other New Novelists, particularly with respect to objective description. The New Novelists are acutely attuned to the presence of physical objects, endlessly catalogued and recorded in their minute manifestations. While Robbe-Grillet may depict in microscopic detail the movements of a fly on a ceiling (in *Jealousy*) or the flotsam clinging to the bow of a ferryboat (in *The Voyeur*), Sarraute keeps external description to a minimum. Where she indulges in descriptive passages (more prevalent in her earlier books, like *Portrait* and *Martereau*), these are not related to the outside world, but serve to externalize the inner sensations of tropisms. Sarraute clearly distinguishes between the divergent aspects of reality that she and Robbe-Grillet present. Whereas he shows the exterior of things, objects, places, and people, she concentrates on interior movements and psychological states. His universe is static, immobile, transfixed; hers is in a process of perpetual movement and transformation. They are almost opposite in temperament and vision.[4]

In his review of *The Age of Suspicion,* Robbe-Grillet confirms the antithetical orientation of their writings. Sarraute's work, he says, is focused on a "psychology of the depths," while he prefers exploring the visible surface; Sarraute's dialogue of conversation and subconversation plunges deep into distant, inaccessible regions where all that can be attained are "shadows, reflections, and shreds of mist"; he chooses instead the solid exterior of things, a tangible, definitive, and dependable presence.[5]

Sarraute has always been a loner, plying her craft on the sidelines of popularity. When her writing happened to coincide with the tendencies of her contemporaries, she was willing to accept a modicum of kinship. When her former colleagues veered off in other directions, she was satisfied to continue along the track she had outlined for herself. Because she has allowed others to assume the role of spokesmen for the New Novel and has restricted herself to discussing her own work and intentions, her pioneering position in the vanguard of modern literature has often been overlooked. The breath of vitality she has infused into the concept of fiction, the strength of her conviction in the restorative powers of the novel, have yet to be adequately acknowledged, even by those who, wittingly or unwittingly, follow the directions and recommendations she was the first to call for.

In the construction of her private universe of tropisms, Sarraute can lay claim to a devout readership. Critics as diverse in outlook as Maurice Nadeau, Lucien Goldmann, Ludovic Janvier, Victor Brombert, Gaëtan Picon, Jean Blot, André Dalmas, Mary McCarthy, René Micha, and Bernard Pingaud have admired and praised her accomplishments, but perhaps no one more enthusiastically than Claude Mauriac. Again and again, he has extolled Sarraute's originality and cited her example to prove the possibility of fictional renewal. He considers her major contribution to be the "subconversation" with which all modern literature is enriched. What Sarraute has achieved is so novel, in Mauriac's opinion, that she can be compared to no other writer. Coming after Dostoevsky, Proust, and Joyce, she undoubtedly owes much to them, as do all contemporary writers; however, in the area that she has discovered and that belongs to her alone — the realm of tropisms — she advances by herself, explorer of the unknown. These zones of sensitivity had existed prior to Sarraute — in fact, they constitute an element of experience that all of us have known — but they had never been brought to notice before: "What has not yet been named exists only as a potential reality. That is why it can be said that Nathalie Sarraute, of all living writers, is the one who has most profoundly and fundamentally renewed our knowledge of mankind."[6]

Once having appropriated to herself the tiny domain of tropisms, Sarraute has persevered in exploring it inch by inch, in all her works, novels and plays alike. By exposing these hidden, unbidden fragments of feeling that underlie human discourse and behavior, she has isolated a timeless quality common to all human beings, of whatever background, nationality, or social stratum. The critics who accuse her of depicting a "bourgeois" milieu or a middle-class mentality[7] have failed — like many of her own characters — to transcend appearances, to discover the kernel of eternal truth concealed beneath a semblance of momentary circumstance.

From the initial observation of tropisms as they *exist* and as they precondition behavior in the restricted arena of the family, Nathalie Sarraute has expanded the terrain in which tropisms flourish to include every conceivable area of human relationships. But if she were merely repeating the evidence of the earlier books in a broader field, her works would be repetitious and, eventually, stagnant. It is because she has used the medium of tropisms as a lens through which to view fundamental issues of human concern that Sarraute's work has attained a panoramic dimension. Never deviating from the very particularized tropistic response, Sarraute manages to call into question problems of both individual and universal scope. From the dilemma of "knowing" another person, she progresses to the concept of "knowledge" about literature, art, and ideas; from everyday clichés of speech, she proceeds to the totalitarian possibilities inherent in the misuse of language generally; from a concern with standards of aesthetic judgment, she advances to the broader consideration of ethical values and conduct. Her earliest novels unmasked the dangers and conflicts menacing members of the same family; her latest works hint at the far more dangerous threat that collective ignorance, fearfulness, and intolerance pose to individual members of society. It is the recapitulation of certain universal themes — their unifying resonance from book to book — that welds the self-contained entities of the individual novels and plays into a cohesive *oeuvre*. It is the unlimited human implications of these evanescent impulses that turn the minuscule domain of tropisms into a microcosm of the world.

Notes and References

Chapter One

1. Personal interview (April 22, 1976).
2. Most of the factual information in these pages and in the Chronology has been culled from the introductory chapter of *Nathalie Sarraute,* by Mimica Cranaki and Yvon Belaval (Paris: Gallimard, 1965), to which Madame Sarraute referred me for biographical data.

Chapter Two

1. Interview by Pierre Schneider, "The Novelist as Transmuter: Nathalie Sarraute Talks about Her Art," *New York Times Book Review* (February 9, 1964), p. 5.
2. Interview by Germaine Brée, "Nathalie Sarraute," *Contemporary Literature,* 14, No. 2 (Spring 1973), 138.
3. "New Movements in French Literature: Nathalie Sarraute Explains Tropisms," *The Listener* (BBC Third Programme), 65, No. 1667 (March 9, 1961), 428 and 429. Sarraute has variously described the meaning of "tropisms" over the years, in interviews with Anne Villelaur (1959), Pierre Demeron (1959), Pierre Schneider (1964), Bettina Knapp (1969), and Germaine Brée (1973); in the Preface to *The Age of Suspicion* (1956), the Foreword to the English-language edition of *Tropisms* (1963), and in a lecture at Columbia University (1964). It must be borne in mind that these explanations were promulgated long after the book first appeared, and are an attempt not only to trace the genesis of the original idea in her mind — which Sarraute has admitted is extremely difficult to do — but also to define "tropisms" as they developed in her subsequent writing.
4. *Ibid.,* p. 428.
5. Foreword to *Tropisms,* tr. Maria Jolas (New York: George Braziller, 1963), p. vi.
6. Brée interview, p. 138.
7. Micheline Tison Braun, *Nathalie Sarraute ou la Recherche de l'authenticité* (Paris: Gallimard, 1971), p. 47.
8. Ruby Cohn, "Nathalie Sarraute's Sub-Conversations," *Modern Language Notes,* 79, No. 3 (May 1963), 262.
9. Foreword to *Tropisms,* pp. viii–ix.

Chapter Three

1. Preface to *Portrait of a Man Unknown,* tr. Maria Jolas (New York: George Braziller, 1958), p. viii.

2. Interview by Jean-Louis Ezine, "Nathalie Sarraute: 'Sartre s'est trompé à mon sujet,' " *Nouvelles Littéraires,* No. 2552 (September 30–October 6, 1976), p. 5.

3. Personal interview (April 22, 1976).

4. "New Movements in French Literature," p. 429.

5. *The Age of Suspicion,* tr. Maria Jolas (New York: George Braziller, 1963), pp. 70–71.

6. John H. Matthews, "Nathalie Sarraute: An Approach to the Novel," *Modern Fiction Studies,* 6, No. 4 (Winter 1960–61), 338–39.

7. This is Micheline Tison Braun's contention when she notes a "sociological crevice" separating the world of *Tropisms* and *Portrait,* written or conceived before World War II, and *Martereau (op. cit.,* pp. 92 *et seq.).*

8. Lecture at the French Institute, New York City (April 26, 1977).

9. Interview by Geneviève Serreau, "Nathalie Sarraute nous parle du 'Planétarium,' " *Lettres Nouvelles,* No. 9 (April 29, 1959), p. 29. This is a "technique" that has led Claude Mauriac to expand into a full-length book, *La Marquise sortit à cinq heures,* the account of events occurring within the space of a single hour, and then to write a second novel, *L'Agrandissement,* which is like the photographic enlargement of two minutes lifted out of the earlier book.

10. Foreword to *Tropisms,* p. vii.

11. Bernard Pingaud, "Le Personnage dans l'oeuvre de Nathalie Sarraute," *Preuves,* No. 154 (December 1963), p. 25.

12. *A la Recherche du temps perdu,* Pléiade ed. (Paris: Gallimard, 1954), II, 269.

13. Quotation from *Justine,* appearing as epigraph to Lawrence Durrell's *Balthazar* (London: Faber & Faber, 1958).

14. Cranaki and Belaval, p. 46.

15. *"Le Planétarium*: le jeu compliqué des paroles et des silences," *Arts* (June 3–9, 1959), p. 2.

16. Cf. Ruth Temple's interpretation of the scene as the "confrontation (real or imaginary) of a New Novelist by a traditionalist novelist or critic," in *Nathalie Sarraute,* Columbia Essays on Modern Writers, No. 33 (New York: Columbia Univ. Press, 1968), p. 19.

17. Gerda Zeltner, "Nathalie Sarraute et l'impossible réalisme," *Mercure de France,* No. 1188 (August 1962), p. 602.

18. "New Movements in French Literature," p. 429.

19. *Martereau,* tr. Maria Jolas (New York: George Braziller, 1959), p. 77.

20. Tison Braun explains the narrator's attachment to Martereau as

"the touching need for security" of an "orphan seeking a father, protec-
tor, and guide" [though nowhere is it explicitly stated that his parents are
dead]; later, when the narrator suspects he has been betrayed, everything
crumbles (*op. cit.,* p. 107). It should be pointed out, however, that it is not
Martereau who betrays the narrator, but vice versa. In his need to get close
to his uncle, he offers up Martereau as a sacrificial victim.

21. Innumerable examples of this technique of "mixed motives" can be
found overtly expressed in the early novels. Cf. this passage from *Portrait*:

Perhaps, as a result of a vague feeling that his strength had diminished, he no longer
dared to attack it directly [...] *or perhaps* his sensitivity had become such that
almost anything, as on a delicate skin, resulted in irritation; *or again,* if you prefer,
his distress may by now have attained such consistency that [...] the tiniest particle
produced crystallization; *or perhaps* [...] he could only fix his attention on minute
details; *or was it all these together?* (p. 122; italics are mine).

As this technique evolves, Sarraute will suppress the terms denoting sup-
position and will express alternate "possibilities" as a series of coexistent
declarations, as in the following passage from *Between Life and Death,* tr.
Maria Jolas (New York: George Braziller, 1969):

Poor dear, she's so frightened [...] she doesn't know what happened to her.... *It's*
the sacrilegious impulse, [*it's*] the headlines of scandal, [*it's*] the daring of shy people,
[*it's*] the attraction toward suicide, [*it's*] an outburst of concealed rage, [*it's*] the
need children feel for destruction.... *No, it's* hyperingenuousness, the innocence of
a very pure spirit... (p. 2; I have restored the repetition of the French *"c'est"* and
italicized it, to underscore my point).

22. This is a somewhat archaic rendition, in the English translation, of
the French expression *homme de paille,* or "straw man."

23. Jean Ricardou has written a detailed analysis of the *four* "floating"
variations of this scene (by my count, there are five). He concludes that
none of these variants is definitive; none represents, or purports to represent, reality. They are fantasies of the narrator as he attempts to reconstruct a crucial scene (*Le Nouveau Roman* [Paris: Editions du Seuil, 1973],
pp. 93–95).

24. See pp. 108, 112, 210, 220, 222, 225. Ruth Temple suggests another
expression whose punning approximation to the name "Martereau" is
apparent only in French: "se mettre martel en tête," which means to be
preoccupied or obsessed with something — an apposite characterization of
the narrator's fixation with Martereau (*op. cit.,* p. 22).

25. "New Movements in French Literature," p. 429.

26. At this point in the book, there is no indication of names or relationships; I have provided these labels for the sake of convenience, with
the caveat that none of this information is provided by the author but must
be derived experientially from hidden clues in the text.

27. *The Planetarium,* tr. Maria Jolas (New York: George Braziller, 1960), p. 50.

28. "Le Personnage dans l'oeuvre de Nathalie Sarraute," p. 30.

29. For a discussion of the theme of the "double" in *Portrait,* see Temple, p. 16.

30. Serreau interview (1959), p. 30.

31. For a discussion of the planetarium symbolism, see Ruby Cohn (p. 268), Temple (p. 28), Tison Braun (pp. 132–33), Helen Watson-Williams, "Etude du *Planétarium,*" *Essays in French Literature,* No. 1 (November 1964), p. 97, and Maurice Cagnon, *"Le Planétarium*: quelques aspects stylistiques," *French Review,* 40, No. 2 (February 1967), p. 621. Alone among them, Cagnon sees Berthe — mistakenly, in my opinion — as the novel's center of gravity.

32. Even Aunt Berthe exhibits what Sarraute calls a "degraded form of the creative effort" (Serreau interview [1959], p. 28).

33. Interview by Geneviève Serreau, "Nathalie Sarraute et les Secrets de la création," *Quinzaine Littéraire,* No. 50 (May 1-15, 1968), p. 4.

34. The concept of art as a religious symbol becomes a dominating theme in *Fruits* and *Do You Hear Them?.*

Chapter Four

1. Brée interview, p. 143.

2. "Nathalie Sarraute: *Tropismes,*" *Nouvelle N.R.F.,* No. 62 (February 1958), p. 337.

3. *Arts,* p. 2.

4. Serreau interview (1968), p. 4.

5. In this respect, I must disagree on two scores with Gaëtan Picon's otherwise laudable article, "Sur *Les Fruits d'or" (Mercure de France* [July 1963], pp. 485–93). Picon assesses the tropisms in this work as intellectual rather than "affective"; although tropisms may be activated by an intellectual object, I would maintain that they are invariably of an emotional nature. He also states that the tropisms here are conventionalized and inauthentic, rather than being natural and spontaneous; I consider that tropisms are always spontaneous and "authentic," because they arise at a preconscious point that escapes the control valve of rationalization, and often they are the only "authentic" manifestations of attitudes and feelings which, on a conscious level, are indeed disguised by stereotypes and convention.

6. *The Golden Fruits,* tr. Maria Jolas (New York: George Braziller, 1964), p. 21.

7. Tison Braun, pp. 166–67.

8. "Il existe dans tout critique un auteur impuissant" ("Monographie de la presse parisienne," *Oeuvres complètes* [Paris: Conard, 1912–40], XL, 577).

9. The same criteria, expressed in the same imagery, are applied by the creative writer in judging his own work:

[The words] are vibrating ... he listens as their *resonance* reverberates. [...] He is delighted with their *movements,* he places and displaces them, to make them form more *skillfully*-shaped *arabesques.* Their *vibration* increases, it has now become music, song, an accentuated march. The rhythms create one another, as though by attraction words arrive from all sides. [...] Now the words have more brilliance, other rarer, more exquisite ones keep coming, the play of their *nuances,* of their *shimmerings,* is more subtle... (*Between Life and Death,* p. 65; italics are mine).

10. See discussion of *Isma,* below, p. 127.

11. Ruth Temple insists it cannot be a book by Sarraute because of the absence of tropistic elements (*op. cit.,* pp. 33-34), but this is a dubious claim.

12. Serreau interview (1968), p. 4.

13. The critic and novelist Jean Ricardou has remarked: "You don't become a writer because you have something to say, strong and unusual feelings to express, but because words strike sparks inside you" (*Les Critiques de notre temps et le Nouveau roman,* ed. Réal Ouellet [Paris: Garnier, 1972], p. 170).

14. Cf. Gretchen R. Besser, *Balzac's Concept of Genius* (Geneva: Droz, 1969), ch. 1: "The Romantic Concept of Genius."

15. Cf. Brée interview, p. 144.

16. This scene will be repeated almost word for word in *"fools say"* (cf. discussion below, p. 137). To preserve the reverberatory effect the author intended and to stress the Writer's arrogance in pretending to resurrect the dead, I have maintained the literal reference to *morts* and Moors in both places, instead of interjecting "deadlines" and "journalism," as Maria Jolas has done.

17. Germaine Lemaire was also called a "predestined child," who had been a repository of sense impressions from girlhood: faces, gestures, words, shades of feeling, cloud formations, the color of the sky, trees, birds, sandy beaches, dusty roads — she had treasured them all, with fervor and reverence (*Planetarium,* pp. 181-82).

18. *The Writing on the Wall and Other Literary Essays* (New York: Harcourt Brace, 1970), p. 184.

19. Brée interview, p. 145.

20. *Ibid.,* pp. 144-45.

21. The alternate titles that Sarraute considered, "Le Cercle" and "Le Geste," also lend themselves to symbolic interpretation. A "Circle" — in harmony with the novel's repetitive movement — represents the necessity of returning with each new work to the source of inspiration. "Geste" has several possible meanings, all allied étymologically. It is the "gesture" with which the book opens and which is later repeated — crumpling up and discarding a sheet of paper — outward sign of the inward need for

continual revaluation and revitalization in art; "geste" also has the medieval connotation of a quest, the epic narrative of a hero's adventures in pursuit of a transcendent goal, including his victory over the dangers of worldly temptation; "geste" can also imply the "gestation" process that Sarraute imaginatively transcribes as she evokes the genesis of a literary work.

22. Interview by Bernard Pivot, "Nathalie Sarraute a réponse à tous," *Figaro Littéraire,* No. 1342 (February 4, 1972), p. 3.

23. Serreau interview (1968), p. 3.

24. Colloquium held at Cerisy-la-Salle (July 1971), reported in *Nouveau roman: hier, aujourd'hui,* ed. Jean Ricardou and Françoise van Rossum-Guyon (Paris: Union Générale d'Editions, 1972), II, 47.

25. Maurice Nadeau, "Nouvelles formules pour le roman," *Critique,* 13, No. 123-24 (August-September 1957), 716.

26. *Physiologie du mariage, O.C.,* XXXII, 4.

27. Brée interview, p. 139.

28. In the same way, the frequent references to sweet peas and chintz represent a sensation of serenity and simulated well-being often associated with England in Sarraute's imagery: cf. pp. 37, 69, 90, 94, 99, 110, 127 of *Do You Hear Them?,* tr. Maria Jolas (New York: George Braziller, 1973).

29. As is often the case, the repercussive effect of the French is lost in translation. *"C'est* tout de même rudement *beau,"* says the father (my italics), enunciating the same formula that another father tries to foist on his son in the play, appropriately titled *C'est beau.*

30. Pivot interview, p. 3.

31. Lecture at French Institute (March 25, 1974).

32. Brée interview, pp. 138–39.

33. This is the same attitude that the Writer's father decried when he claimed that anyone at all who strings words together is called a poet or a "genius" these days (*Life and Death,* p. 122).

34. A spate of reviews in American newspapers and periodicals all expressed this opinion: *New York Times Book Review* (February 4, 1973), *Pittsburgh Press* (February 25, 1973), *Christian Science Monitor* (February 28, 1973), *Atlantic Monthly* (March 1973), *New Yorker* (March 17, 1973), *Hartford Courant* (March 25, 1973), and *New York Review of Books* (April 19, 1973).

35. Lecture at French Institute (March 25, 1974).

36. "Rebels in a World of Platitudes," *Times Literary Supplement* (June 10, 1960), p. 371.

Chapter Five

1. "Le Gant retourné," *Cahiers Renaud Barrault,* Vol. 83 (Paris: Gallimard, 1973), p. 72.

2. *Ibid.,* p. 73.

3. Bettina Knapp, "Nathalie Sarraute: A Theatre of Tropisms," *Performing Arts Journal* (Winter 1976), p. 16.

4. Interview by Gretchen R. Besser, "Colloque avec Nathalie Sarraute: 22 avril 1976," *French Review,* 50, No. 2 (December 1976), p. 288.

5. "Gant retourné," p. 79.

6. Besser interview, p. 288.

7. Interview by Nicole Zand, "Entretien avec Nathalie Sarraute à propos du 'Mensonge' et du 'Silence,' " *Le Monde* (January 18, 1967), p. 18.

8. "Gant retourné," p. 74.

9. *Isma, Le Silence* et *Le Mensonge* (Paris: Gallimard, 1970), p. 53. Since none of the plays has been published in English, page references will be to the French edition. The translations are my own.

10. I have cited the characters' names for purposes of convenient discussion, not identification.

11. "Gant retourné," p. 79.

12. In a moment of frustrated helplessness, the father in *Do You Hear Them?* contemplates a similar recourse to authority, to stifle his children's merriment with handcuffs and paddywagons and the third degree (p. 59).

13. *C'est beau, Cahiers Renaud Barrault,* Vol. 83 (Paris: Gallimard, 1973), p. 16.

14. Claude Régy, "Nathalie Sarraute: un théâtre d'action," *Cahiers Renaud Barrault,* Vol. 83 (Paris: Gallimard, 1973), p. 85.

15. Sarraute has said that this scene was inspired by Sartre's account of the way Mme Flaubert treated her infant son (French Institute lecture on March 17, 1975).

16. Richard N. Coe, *Eugene Ionesco,* 2nd ed. (New York: Grove Press, 1968), p. 19.

17. Ezine interview, p. 5.

18. Viviane Forrester, "Nathalie Sarraute dénonce le but meurtrier de la bêtise langagière," *Quinzaine Littéraire* (October 1-15, 1976), p. 5.

19. *"fools say",* tr. Maria Jolas (New York: George Braziller, 1977), p. 70.

20. The same phrase is translated in *"fools say"* as "Up, the dead" and in *Between Life and Death* as "The dead shall rise." These discrepancies in the official English translation result in a failure to preserve the echoing effect from one book to the other.

21. French Institute lecture (April 26, 1977).

22. *Ibid.*

23. Herbert Mitgang, "Publishing: A Visit from Four Writers," *New York Times* (May 13, 1977), p. C23.

24. Ezine interview, p. 5.

25. Sarraute's latest play, *Elle est là* (1978), represents a recapitulation and variation on a theme from *"fools say"* — the impossibility of countenancing some idea that is antagonistic to one's own. Although this

attitude may be considered "intolerant," it is an obsessive reaction which, in its extreme consequences, can lead to acts of suppression and even murder. The tyranny of ideas is in actuality a tyranny of the emotions.

Chapter Six

1. Cf. Harry Levin discussion of this subject in *The Gates of Horn* (New York: Oxford Press, 1963), pp. 446 *et seq.* Among the many writers who have abandoned hope for the future of fiction are Alberto Moravia and the Spanish novelist Ortega y Gasset. A special issue of the journal *Confluences* was devoted to "Problems of the Novel" (1943), and the *Evergreen Review* (in 1957) contained an article by Alain Robbe-Grillet predicting that the novel could not survive without radical changes.

2. "La Littérature, Aujourd'hui — II," *Tel Quel,* 9 (Spring 1962), p. 51.

3. Pivot interview, p. 3.

4. "Speaking of Books: The Novel for Its Own Sake," *New York Times Book Review* (April 24, 1966), p. 2.

5. Interview by R.-M. Albérès, "Le Procès du nouveau roman," *Nouvelles Littéraires,* No. 2023 (June 9, 1966), p. 11.

6. "Ce que je cherche à faire," in *Nouveau Roman: hier, aujourd'hui,* II, 34.

7. "Littérature, Aujourd'hui," p. 50.

8. Interview by Guy Le Clec'h, "Entretien avec Nathalie Sarraute: Drames microscopiques," *Nouvelles Littéraires,* No. 2318 (February 28–March 5, 1972), p. 4.

9. *Nouveau Roman: hier, aujourd'hui,* II, 51, 57–58.

10. "Rebels in a World of Platitudes," p. 371.

11. Pivot interview, p. 3.

12. Schneider interview, p. 37.

13. "Les Deux réalités," *Esprit,* No. 329 (July 1964), p. 74.

14. *Temps Modernes,* 2, No. 16 (January 1947), pp. 624–25.

15. "Speaking of Books," p. 2.

16. "Virginia Woolf ou la Visionnaire du 'Main Tenant,' " *Lettres Françaises,* No. 882 (June 26–July 5, 1961), p. 3.

17. *Gates of Horn,* p. 446.

18. Cf. "Virginia Woolf," p. 3; "Littérature, Aujourd'hui," p. 49; "Deux réalités," p. 72.

19. "Littérature, Aujourd'hui," p. 49; Deux réalités," p. 72.

20. "Nouveau Roman et Réalité," *Revue de l'Institut de Sociologie,* No. 2 (1963), p. 433.

21. *Ibid.,* p. 434.

22. "Flaubert le précurseur," *Preuves,* No. 168 (February 1965), pp. 8–11.

23. Interview by François Bondy (Cranaki and Belaval, p. 214).

24. Interview by Pierre Demeron, "Nathalie Sarraute ou Littérature sans cabotinage," *Arts, Lettres, Spectacles* (June 3–9, 1959), p. 2.

25. Bondy interview, p. 214.

26. To erase any misconceptions about her intentions, Sarraute wrote a letter that appeared on March 13, 1959, in the *Times Literary Supplement* (p. 145), reiterating that her essays had all been written in defense of "psychology" and that the writers she was accused of disparaging were in effect pioneers of modern fiction.

27. "Virginia Woolf," p. 3.

28. "Flaubert le précurseur," p. 7.

29. It is hardly coincidental that this "planetarium" metaphor describing Proust's method was written simultaneously with the novel bearing that title, in which Sarraute envisaged a more immediate means of grasping subterranean dramas.

30. Demeron interview, p. 2.

31. "Littérature, Aujourd'hui," p. 49.

32. "Ce que je cherche à faire," p. 38. It is precisely this concept that renders the task of "paraphrasing" and "summarizing" Sarraute's works so difficult and so antithetical to the spirit in which they were written.

33. *Le Degré zéro de l'écriture* (Paris: Editions du Seuil, 1972), p. 12.

34. *Nouveau Roman: hier, aujourd'hui,* II, 44–45.

35. *Nouveau roman,* p. 131.

36. A few heterogeneous examples will suffice:

With my eyes glued to him, I watch, I obey [. . .] like a well-trained dog, off I go, I hunt, I dig, I unearth, with infallible flair I find, I retrieve. I am both skillful and prompt. Remarkably disciplined (*Martereau,* p. 61).

The atmosphere, which was saturated with the vapors of boredom, of being at loose ends, of irritation, of disappointment, of a feeling of emptiness, of inanity, of a complete mess (*Planetarium,* p. 203).

Nothing mushy, sprawling, fleshy, hanging, nothing that swells, thickens. . . (*"fools say",* p. 33).

He wanted to keep others from touching it, from being infected by it. [. . .] He wanted to surround with electrified wire, threaten, seize, bully, pillory, designate for opprobrium, expose to jeers all those who appropriate and propagate it. . . (*Ibid.,* p. 52).

37. See Cranaki and Belaval, pp. 103 *et seq.;* John A. Fleming, "The Imagery of Tropism in the Novels of Nathalie Sarraute," in *Image and Theme: Studies in Modern French Fiction,* ed. W. M. Frohock (Cambridge: Harvard Univ. Press, 1969), pp. 74–98; Léon Roudiez, "A Glance at the Vocabulary of Nathalie Sarraute," *Yale French Studies,* No. 27

(Spring-Summer 1961), pp. 90–98.

38. A. S. Newman, *Une Poésie des discours* (Geneva: Droz, 1976), p. 43. This technique has also been noted by Cranaki and Belaval (pp. 109–11).

39. Newman has suggested that the scenes and dialogues composing *Fruits, Life and Death,* and *Do You Hear Them?* are actually metaphoric representations of the tropisms that Sarraute formerly expressed in visual images (p. 182).

40. "New Movements in French Literature," p. 428.

41. "Virginia Woolf," p. 3.

42. "Littérature, Aujourd'hui," p. 53.

Chapter Seven

1. Cf. George Lukács, *La Théorie du roman* (Paris: Gonthier, 1963); Lucien Goldmann, *Pour une sociologie du roman* (Paris: Gallimard, 1964); Roland Barthes, *Le Degré zéro de l'écriture* (Paris: Editions du Seuil, 1972).

2. *Pour un nouveau roman* (Paris: Editions de Minuit, 1963), p. 11.

3. Paris: Bordas, 1972.

4. For an interesting pattern of alternatives, consult the names cited in the following studies: Maurice Nadeau, "Nouvelles formules pour le roman," pp. 707–22; Laurent Lesage, *The French New Novel: An Introduction and a Sampler* (University Park: Pennsylvania State Univ. Press, 1962); Bruce Morrissette, "The New Novel in France" (*Chicago Review,* 15, No. 3 [Winter-Spring 1962], 1–19); Ludovic Janvier, *Une Parole exigeante: le nouveau roman* (Paris: Editions de Minuit, 1964); Claude Mauriac, part III of *L'Alittérature contemporaine* (Paris: Albin Michel, 1969); Vivian Mercier, *The New Novel from Queneau to Pinget* (New York: Farrar, Straus, and Giroux, 1971); Léon Roudiez, *French Fiction Today: A New Direction* (New Brunswick: Rutgers Univ. Press, 1972); Stephen Heath, *The Nouveau Roman: A Study in the Practice of Writing* (Philadelphia: Temple Univ. Press, 1972). The writers cited as New Novelists include all of the following, some more frequently than others: Samuel Beckett, Hélène Bessette, Maurice Blanchot, Michel Butor, Jean Cayrol, Jacques Cousseau, Marguerite Duras, Jean Pierre Faye, Jean Lagrolet, Claude Mauriac, Claude Ollier, Robert Pinget, Raymond Queneau, Jean Reverzy, Jean Ricardou, Alain Robbe-Grillet, Raymond Roussel, Nathalie Sarraute, Marc Saporta, Claude Simon, Philippe Sollers, and Kateb Yacine. Jean Ricardou, who is himself both a theoretician and exponent of the New Novel, has suggested applying the criterion of self-definition, according to which the New Novelists would be those authors who voluntarily attended the colloquium on the New Novel held at Cerisy-la-Salle in July 1971: Butor, Ollier, Pinget, Robbe-Grillet, Sarraute, Simon, and himself (*Nouveau Roman,* p. 13).

5. Cf. "Littérature objective," *Critique,* No. 86–87 (July-August 1954), pp. 581–91, and "Littérature littérale," *Critique,* No. 100–101 (September-October 1955), pp. 820–26.

6. For a list of these critics and a sampling of their writings, see Laurent Lesage, *The French New Criticism: An Introduction and a Sampler* (University Park: Pennsylvania State Univ. Press, 1967).

7. Ricardou, p. 17.

8. These names, which Robbe-Grillet cites in his essay "Nouveau Roman, homme nouveau" (*Pour un nouveau roman,* p. 115), are identical with the ones acknowledged by Sarraute.

9. *L'Alitérature contemporaine,* p. 342.

10. Choderlos de Laclos, *Les Liaisons dangereuses*; Daniel Defoe, *Moll Flanders*; Voltaire, *Zadig*; Victor Hugo, *Les Derniers jours d'un condamné*; Nathaniel Hawthorne, *The Scarlet Letter*; Balzac's youthful novel, *Le Vicaire des Ardennes.*

11. "Le Roman comme recherche," *Cahiers du Sud,* No. 334 (April 1956), pp. 353–54.

12. *Pour un nouveau roman,* pp. 10, 114–16.

13. Quoted by Gaëtan Picon in "L'Oeuvre critique de Blanchot," *Critique,* No. 111–112 (August-September 1946), p. 687.

14. *Pour un nouveau roman,* p. 42.

15. *Ibid.,* p. 39.

16. "L'écrivain, par définition, ne sait où il va, et il écrit pour chercher à comprendre pourquoi il écrit," *Esprit,* No. 329 (July 1964), pp. 63, 64.

17. "L'Année dernière à Léningrad," *Esprit,* No. 329 (July 1964), p. 19.

18. For a diatribe against the "a-morality" of the New Novel, see R.S.M. Albérès interview, "Le Procès du nouveau roman," pp. 1, 11.

19. *La Force des choses* (Paris: Gallimard, 1963), p. 650.

20. *Pour un nouveau roman,* p. 116.

21. There are additional reasons for this incomplete effect. Sarraute has explained that by this method she transcribes the *movement* of tropisms, which are themselves constantly interrupted and suspended, intermingling with great rapidity. This half-finished quality also contributes a trembling feeling to the form, which she deems essential (Ezine interview, p. 5).

22. *Op. cit.,* p. 134.

23. *The Secular Scripture: A Study of the Structure of Romance* (Cambridge: Harvard Univ. Press, 1976), p. 186.

24. Janvier, pp. 40, 65–68.

25. H. A. Bouraoui, "Sarraute's Narrative Portraiture: The Artist in Search of a Voice," *Critique,* 14, No. 1 (1972), 79.

26. "The School of Refusal," *Yale French Studies,* No. 24 (Summer 1959), p. 20.

27. For a discussion of the problems of "temporal distance" and chronology in the modern novel, see Michel Butor's essays on "L'Usage

des pronoms personnels dans le roman" and "Recherches sur la technique du roman," in *Répertoire II* (Paris: Editions de Minuit, 1964), especially pp. 64 and 90–94, as well as Robbe-Grillet's "Temps et Description dans le récit d'aujourd'hui" (*Pour un nouveau roman,* pp. 128 *et seq.*).

    28. *Répertoire II,* p. 23.

    29. Cf. Janvier, pp. 20–21.

Chapter Eight

    1. "Littérature, Aujourd'hui," p. 48.

    2. Pivot interview, p. 3.

    3. Quoted by Camille Bourniquel, "Nathalie Sarraute: *Vous les entendez?,*" *Esprit* (April-May 1972), p. 890. When interviewed by Jean-Louis Ezine in 1976, Sarraute again rejected the "New New Novel" appellation (*op. cit.,* p. 5).

    4. Interview by Bettina L. Knapp, *Kentucky Romance Quarterly,* 14, No. 3 (1969), 286.

    5. "Le Réalisme, la Psychologie et l'Avenir du roman," *Critique,* No. 111–112 (August-September 1956), pp. 700–701.

    6. *L'Alittérature contemporaine,* pp. 319–21, 324.

    7. Cf. Jean-Paul Sartre interview, in *Critiques de notre temps,* pp. 23–24.

Selected Bibliography

PRIMARY SOURCES

1. Novels, collected essays, plays

Tropisms. Paris: Robert Denoël, 1939. *Tropisms*. Tr. Maria Jolas. New York: George Braziller, 1963.

Portrait d'un inconnu. Paris: Robert Marin, 1948. *Portrait of a Man Unknown*. Tr. Maria Jolas. New York: George Braziller, 1958.

Martereau. Paris: Gallimard, 1953. *Martereau*. Tr. Maria Jolas. New York: George Braziller, 1959.

L'Ere du soupçon. Paris: Gallimard, 1956. *The Age of Suspicion*. Tr. Maria Jolas. New York: George Braziller, 1963.

Le Planétarium. Paris: Gallimard, 1959. *The Planetarium*. Tr. Maria Jolas. New York: George Braziller, 1960.

Les Fruits d'or. Paris: Gallimard, 1963. *The Golden Fruits*. Tr. Maria Jolas. New York: George Braziller, 1964.

Entre la vie et la mort. Paris: Gallimard, 1968. *Between Life and Death*. Tr. Maria Jolas. New York: George Braziller, 1969.

Isma, Le Silence, et Le Mensonge. Paris: Gallimard, 1970.

Vous les entendez?. Paris: Gallimard, 1972. *Do You Hear Them?*. Tr. Maria Jolas. New York: George Braziller, 1973.

C'est beau. Cahiers Renaud Barrault, Vol. 83. Paris: Gallimard, 1973.

"disent les imbéciles". Paris: Gallimard, 1976. *"fools say"*. Tr. Maria Jolas. New York: George Braziller, 1977.

Théâtre: Elle est là. C'est beau. Isma. Le Mensonge. Le Silence. Paris: Gallimard, 1978.

2. Articles and interviews

"Paul Valéry et l'Enfant d'éléphant." *Temps Modernes*, 2, No. 16 (janvier 1947), 610–37.

Interview by Anne Villelaur. "Le Roman est en train de réfléchir sur lui-même." *Lettres Françaises*, No. 764 (12–18 mars 1959), pp. 1, 4.

Interview by Geneviève Serreau. "Nathalie Sarraute nous parle du 'Planétarium.' " *Lettres Nouvelles*, No. 9 (29 avril 1959), pp. 28–30.

Interview by Pierre Demeron. "Nathalie Sarraute ou Littérature sans cabotinage." *Arts, Lettres, Spectacles* (3–9 juin 1959), p. 2.

"Rebels in a World of Platitudes." *Times Literary Supplement* (June 10, 1960), p. 371.

"New Movements in French Literature: Nathalie Sarraute Explains

Tropisms." BBC Third Programme. *The Listener,* 65, No. 1667 (March 9, 1961), 428–29.

"Virginia Woolf ou la Visionnaire du 'Main Tenant.' " Interview. *Lettres Françaises,* No. 882 (26 juin–5 juillet 1961), pp. 1, 3.

"La Littérature, Aujourd'hui — II." Interview. *Tel Quel,* No. 9 (printemps 1962), pp. 48–53.

"Nouveau Roman et Réalité." Lecture at Tribune Libre Universitaire, Brussels. *Revue de l'Institut de Sociologie,* No. 2 (1963), pp. 431–41.

"Les Deux réalités." Participation in Leningrad conference of East-West writers (August 5–8, 1963), *Esprit,* No. 329 (juillet 1964), pp. 72–75.

Interview by Pierre Schneider. "The Novelist as Transmuter: Nathalie Sarraute Talks about her Art." *New York Times Book Review* (February 9, 1964), pp. 4, 5, 36, 37.

"Flaubert le précurseur." *Preuves,* No. 168 (février 1965), pp. 3–11.

"Speaking of Books: The Novel for Its Own Sake." *New York Times Book Review* (April 24, 1966), pp. 2, 43.

Interview by R.-M. Albérès. "Le Procès du nouveau roman." *Nouvelles Littéraire,* No. 1342 (4 février 1972), pp. 1, 3.

Interview by Nicole Zand. "Entretien avec Nathalie Sarraute à propos du 'Mensonge' et du 'Silence.' " *Le Monde* (18 janvier 1967), p. 18.

Interview by Geneviève Serreau. "Nathalie Sarraute et les Secrets de la création." *Quinzaine Littéraire,* No. 50 (1–15 mai 1968), pp. 3–4.

Interview by Bettina L. Knapp. *Kentucky Romance Quarterly,* 14, No. 3 (1969), 283–95.

"Ce que je cherche à faire." Participation in Colloquium at Cerisy-la-Salle (July 20–30, 1971). In *Nouveau Roman: hier, aujourd'hui.* Ed. Jean Ricardou and Françoise van Rossum-Guyon. Paris: Union Générale d'Editions, 1972, II, 25–58.

Interview by Bernard Pivot. "Nathalie Sarraute a réponse à tous." *Figaro Littéraire,* No. 1342 (4 fevrier 1972), pp. 1, 3.

Interview by Guy Le Clec'h. "Entretien avec Nathalie Sarraute: Drames microscopiques." *Nouvelles Littéraires,* No. 2318 (28 février–5 mars 1972), pp. 4–5.

Interview by Germaine Brée. "Nathalie Sarraute." *Contemporary Literature,* 14, No. 2 (Spring 1973), 137–46.

"Le Gant retourné." Lecture at University of Wisconsin (1974). *Cahiers Renaud Barrault,* Vol. 83. Paris: Gallimard, 1973, pp. 70–79.

Interview by Jean-Louis Ezine. "Nathalie Sarraute: 'Sartre s'est trompé à mon sujet.' " *Nouvelles Littéraires,* No. 2552 (30 septembre–6 octobre 1976), p. 5.

Interview by Gretchen R. Besser. "Colloque avec Nathalie Sarraute: 22 avril 1976." *French Review,* 50, No. 2 (December 1976), 284–89.

SECONDARY SOURCES

BELAVAL, YVON. "Nathalie Sarraute: *Tropismes." Nouvelle N.R.F.,* No. 62 (février 1958), pp. 335–37. Early, perceptive assessment of Sarraute's first book.

BOURAOUI, H. A. "Sarraute's Narrative Portraiture: The Artist in Search of a Voice." *Critique,* 14, No. 1 (1972), 77–89. Interesting sidelights on the narrator's creative role.

BUTOR, MICHEL. *"Le Planétarium*: le jeu compliqué des paroles et des silences." *Arts* (3–9 juin 1959), p. 2. Brief glance by a fellow novelist at complexities of meaning and structure in *The Planetarium.*

――――. *Répertoire II: Etudes et Conférences, 1959–63.* Paris: Editions de Minuit, 1964. Musings on problems of fiction, composition, structural techniques, and related questions, by one of the foremost proponents of the New Novel.

CAGNON, MAURICE. *"Le Planétarium*: quelques aspects stylistiques." *French Review,* 40, No. 2 (February 1967), 620–26.

CALIN, FRANÇOISE. *La Vie retrouvée: Etude de l'oeuvre romanesque de Nathalie Sarraute.* Paris: Minard, 1976. Thematic approach to novels. Some fine, pertinent observations, especially in "stylistic" discussion, but validity of study as a whole is marred by numerous errors of fact and interpretation.

COHN, RUBY. "Nathalie Sarraute's Sub-Conversations." *Modern Language Notes,* 79, No. 3 (May 1963), 261–70.

CRANAKI, MIMICA, and YVON BELAVAL. *Nathalie Sarraute.* "Bibliothèque idéale." Paris: Gallimard, 1965. Good introduction to author's innovative aims and methods. Abundance of quotations from her writings. Sole biographic source.

Les Critiques de notre temps et le nouveau roman. Ed. Réal Ouellet. Paris: Garnier, 1972. Collection of critical texts relating to New Novel, pro and con.

FLEMING, JOHN A. "The Imagery of Tropism in the Novels of Nathalie Sarraute." In *Image and Theme: Studies in Modern French Fiction.* Ed. W. M. Frohock. Cambridge: Harvard Univ. Press, 1969, pp. 74–98. Analyzes imagery as a complex structural device, and catalogues basic types of images in early works.

GOLDMANN, LUCIEN. *Pour une sociologie du roman.* Paris: Gallimard, 1964. Establishes correlation between contemporary novel and social reality. Analyzes and compares work of Sarraute and Robbe-Grillet.

HEATH, STEPHEN. *The Nouveau Roman: A Study in the Practice of Writing.* Philadelphia: Temple Univ. Press, 1972. A somewhat turgid attempt to apply structuralist criticism to the New Novel.

JANVIER, LUDOVIC. *Une Parole exigeante: le nouveau roman.* Paris: Editions de Minuit, 1964. Excellent study of New Novel, with emphasis on the works of Sarraute, Butor, Robbe-Grillet, and Claude Simon.

KNAPP, BETTINA. "Nathalie Sarraute: A Theatre of Tropisms." *Performing Arts Journal* (Winter 1976), pp. 15-27. Comprehensive analysis of tropistic elements in Sarraute's plays.

LESAGE, LAURENT. *The French New Novel: An Introduction and a Sampler.* University Park: Pennsylvania State Univ. Press, 1962. Global presentation of New Novel, with sample texts from a variety of authors, Sarraute included.

MAGNY, CLAUDE-EDMONDE. "Retour au paganisme." Chapter about Sarraute in *Littérature et Critique.* Paris: Payot, 1971. Perceptive view of interrelationships among Sarrautian "characters."

MAURIAC, CLAUDE. "Nathalie Sarraute." Chapter in *L'Alittérature contemporaine.* Paris: Albin Michel, 1969. Enthusiastic encomium, extolling Sarraute's originality.

MCCARTHY, MARY. "Hanging by a Thread." Chapter in *The Writing on the Wall and Other Literary Essays.* New York: Harcourt, Brace, 1970. Admiring analysis of *Between Life and Death.*

MERCIER, VIVIAN. *The New Novel from Queneau to Pinget.* New York: Farrar, Straus, and Giroux, 1971. Traces development of New Novel and examines individual writers. Chronological treatment of Sarraute's works provides no new insights.

MICHA, RENE. *Nathalie Sarraute.* Paris: Classiques du XXe siècle, 1966. Fundamental analysis of "tropisms" as Sarraute's contribution, but meager discussion of individual works. Situates Sarraute with respect to predecessors and contemporaries.

MORRISSETTE, BRUCE. "The New Novel in France." *Chicago Review,* 15, No. 3 (Winter-Spring 1962), 1-19. Clear, cogent, informative discussion of current trends in French novel.

NADEAU, MAURICE. "Nouvelles formules pour le roman." *Critique,* 13, No. 123-24 (août-septembre 1957), 707-22. In context of review of *Tropisms* and works by two other authors, discerns new trends in fiction.

NEWMAN, A. S. *Une Poésie des discours.* Geneva: Droz, 1976. First "structuralist" critique of Sarraute's novels. Best in its detailed analysis of dialogue and point of view.

PICON, GAËTAN. "Le Planétarium." *Mercure de France,* No. 1151 (juillet 1959), pp. 491-94. Admires *Planetarium* as successful blend of aims and techniques.

PINGAUD, BERNARD. "Le Personnage dans l'oeuvre de Nathalie Sarraute." *Preuves,* No. 154 (décembre 1963), pp. 19-34. One of most perspicacious outlooks on Sarraute's work. Full of fascinating and provocative ideas.

_____. "The School of Refusal." *Yale French Studies,* No. 24 (Summer 1959), pp. 18-21. Astute and lucid appraisal of "antenovel" as form of literary commitment, divorced from psychological and ideological preoccupations.

Régy, Claude. "Nathalie Sarraute: un théâtre d'action." *Cahiers Renaud Barrault,* Vol. 83. Paris: Gallimard, 1973, pp. 80–89. Subjective impressions of *C'est beau* by the man who directed its stage presentation.

Ricardou, Jean. *Le Nouveau roman.* Paris: Editions du Seuil, 1973. Through precise textual analyses, shows the various methods by which New Novelists abolish, transform, or fragment the narrative process. Seminal study.

Robbe-Grillet, Alain. *Pour un nouveau roman.* Paris: Editions de Minuit, 1963. Collection of essays, written 1953–63, presenting Robbe-Grillet's conceptions about novel.

————. "Le Réalisme, la Psychologie et l'Avenir du roman." *Critique,* No. 111–112 (août-septembre 1956), pp. 695–701. While sympathetically reviewing *The Age of Suspicion,* he postulates similar intentions but divergent methods.

Roudiez, Leon. *French Fiction Today: A New Direction.* New Brunswick: Rutgers Univ. Press, 1972. A wide-angled view of fifteen contemporary French writers.

————. "A Glance at the Vocabulary of Nathalie Sarraute." *Yale French Studies,* No. 27 (Spring-Summer 1961), pp. 90–98. Emphasizes frequency of recurring words and images.

Temple, Ruth Z. *Nathalie Sarraute.* Columbia Essays on Modern Writers, No. 33. New York: Columbia Univ. Press, 1968. Within its extremely limited format, a succinct and informative glance at Sarraute's novels and plays to date, with a number of original interpretations.

Tison Braun, Micheline. *Nathalie Sarraute ou la Recherche de l'authenticité.* Paris: Gallimard, 1971. Thoroughgoing analysis of individual novels examined in the light of a unifying theme: the search for "authenticity." Presupposes a prior acquaintance with Sarraute's works.

Watson-Williams, Helen. "Etude du *Planétarium.*" *Essays in French Literature,* No. 1 (November 1964), pp. 89–104. One of the best short studies of an individual work, chock full of ideas.

————. "Nathalie Sarraute's Golden Apples." *Essays in French Literature,* No. 3 (November 1966), pp. 78–93. Fine exploration of aesthetic experience, but debatable interpretation about presence of a discernible hero.

Wunderli-Müller, Christine. *Le Thème du masque et les Banalités dans l'oeuvre de Nathalie Sarraute.* Zurich: Juris Druck Verlag, 1970. Superficial, unscholarly, and irritatingly repetitious. Composed largely of strings of quotations, linked by paraphrases.

Zeltner, Gerda. "Nathalie Sarraute et l'impossible realisme." *Mercure de France,* No. 1188 (août 1962), pp. 593–608. Laudable attempt to come to grips with problems of internalized vision and language.

Index